DATE D'

Managing
Organizational
Behavior

Managing Organizational Behavior

David A. Nadler
Graduate School of Business
Columbia University

J. Richard Hackman
School of Organization and Management
Yale University

Edward E. Lawler III
Institute for Social Research
University of Michigan
and
School of Business Administration
University of Southern California

LITTLE, BROWN AND COMPANY
Boston Toronto

Library of Congress Catalog Card No. 78-70453

9 8 7 6 5 4 3   ISBN 0-316-59679-5

Published simultaneously in Canada
by Little, Brown & Company (Canada) Limited

Printed in the United States of America

ACKNOWLEDGMENTS

Figure 3.1. Adapted from L. W. Porter, E. E. Lawler, and J. R. Hackman, *Behavior in Organizations,* p. 332. Copyright © 1975 by McGraw-Hill, Inc. Reprinted by permission of McGraw-Hill Book Company.

Table 4.1. Adapted from L. W. Porter, E. E. Lawler, and J. R. Hackman, *Behavior in Organizations.* Copyright © by McGraw-Hill, Inc. Reprinted by permission of McGraw-Hill Book Company.

Tables 4.3 and 4.4. Adapted from Edward E. Lawler, *Pay and Organizational Effectiveness: A Psychological View,* pp. 164, 165. Copyright © 1971 by McGraw-Hill, Inc. Reprinted by permission of McGraw-Hill Book Company.

Figures 5.1 and 5.3. From J. R. Hackman, G. R. Oldham, R. Janson, and K. Purdy, "A New Strategy for Job Enrichment." © 1975 by the Regents of the University of California. Reprinted from *California Management Review,* volume XVII, number 4, pp. 58, 62, by permission of the Regents.

Table 5.2. Reprinted from J. P. Wanous, "Who Wants Job Enrichment?" (New York: AMACOM, a division of American Management Associations, 1976), p. 258.

Pages 135–136. Adapted with permission from the *World of Work Report,* published by Work in America Institute, Inc., November 1977, pp. 124–126.

Figure 9.3. Reprinted from *Leadership and Decision-Making* by Victor H. Vroom and Philip W. Yetton by permission of the University of Pittsburgh Press. © 1973 by the University of Pittsburgh Press.

Figures 10.5, 10.8, 10.9, and 11.9. Adapted by permission from M. L. Tushman and D. A. Nadler, "Information Processing as an Integrating Framework in Management Design," *Academy of Management Review,* 1978, 3.

Pages 220–221. Adapted from Household Products Inc., in W. H. Newman and E. K. Warren, *The Process of Management: Concepts, Behavior, and Practice,* 4th ed., pp. 627–631. Adapted by permission of Prentice-Hall, Inc., Englewood Cliffs, New Jersey.

Figure 12.4. Adapted by permission from Stuart M. Schmidt and Thomas A. Kochan, "Conflict: Toward Conceptual Clarity," *Administrative Science Quarterly,* Volume 17, No. 3 (September 1972), p. 363.

Table 13.1. Adapted from Robert L. Katz, *Cases and Concepts in Corporate Strategy,* © 1970, pp. 197–203. Reprinted by permission of Prentice-Hall, Inc., Englewood Cliffs, New Jersey.

To our daughters

Amy, Beth, Cara, Cindy, Eve, Laura, and Leslie

Preface

THIS BOOK is an attempt to communicate ideas and concepts about organizational behavior in a clear, readable, and usable form. We have written the book for students, managers, and others who seek to learn why people in organizations behave as they do and why organizations function as they do. Our goal is to convey an understanding of organizational phenomena so that the reader can recognize patterns of behavior, make some sense of that behavior, and determine courses of action to influence it.

We made a number of important choices about this book to achieve our goals:

1. We decided to build the book around a basic framework or organizing model. Organizations are seen as being made up of individuals and groups doing tasks within both formal and informal organizational structures. We chose this framework to integrate the book and to give our discussion some logic and order. The framework will provide a sense of how material in one part of the book relates to material in other parts.

2. We decided to be broad in our definition of organizational behavior. We have included discussions of individual and group behavior as well as organizational design. Topics such as strategy and political processes have also been considered because we feel these issues are crucial to understand how and why behavior occurs in organizations.

3. We chose to select specific theories and concepts to aid in understanding organization rather than to review, compare, and contrast theories. This is a book about organizational behavior; it is *not* a book about different theories of organizational behavior. Therefore, we used certain concepts and theories that we found helpful for our own thinking and teaching, such as expectancy theory (for individual motivation), and information processing concepts (for organizational design). There are risks in this choice, since everyone's favorite theory is not going to be represented in the book. We feel, however, that the value of having a single and consistent approach far outweighs the risks.

4. We attempted to make the concepts, theories, and ideas real and comprehensible by illustrating them with concrete examples. Most chapters of the book begin with a short case, drawn from an actual situation, to introduce the concepts and to illustrate the application of the theories to actual managerial problems.

5. We attempted to make the concepts, theories, and ideas as usable and applicable as possible by identifying their implications for understanding and changing organizational behavior.

6. We have at times been speculative. Where the existing theory and research has not been definitive (such as in the area of group effectiveness, for example), we chose to put forward our "best shot" at analyzing the phenomena rather than to beg off with a statement about the need for more research. We have tried to base our suppositions in the existing theory and research, but we faced the possibility that, over time, some of our speculation might not be borne out. Again, we decided to take the risk in the service of offering usable concepts to the reader.

The organization of this book also reflects our goal of teaching basic organizational behavior. The first section introduces the general subject area and presents a *conceptual framework* for thinking about organizations. This framework is then used to integrate the rest of the book. Section II focuses on *individuals in organizations:* why individuals behave as they do and how their behavior is affected by decisions about staffing, rewarding performance, and designing work. In Section III we move to a more complex level of analysis and consider the nature of *groups in organizations*. The emphasis is on how groups influence individuals, how groups perform tasks, and how groups can be effectively designed and managed. Section IV examines questions of *organization design*, which provides the context for individual and group behavior. An approach to design is presented, methods of coordination and control are discussed, and the areas of conflict management and strategy are covered. In the final section, the *manager's role* in human systems is discussed, with an emphasis on the concepts and skills needed to diagnose and change patterns of organizational behavior.

The book is intended for undergraduate and beginning graduate level courses in organizational behavior, management, administration, and related areas. In lower level courses, we see the book as a core text, with readings, cases, and exercises as possible supplementary material. In upper level courses, we envision the book as one of a number of texts that might be used in a term-long course. In some specialized courses, the book may be a required first reading to give students a common orientation and background before moving on to specific issues such as organization design, change, and interpersonal behavior.

The book was also written with practicing managers very much in mind. Our intention is to expose managers to recent thinking and approaches in the behavioral sciences, with an eye toward providing usable, practical tools for managerial action.

Finally, we hope that the book will provide a stimulus for our colleagues in the field of organizational behavior. In our speculation we have suggested what we feel are productive directions for inquiry. In addition, we hope that our efforts to communicate concepts of organizational behavior to an audience of practitioners will stimulate others to do the same. When we provide those who work and live in organizations with useful theories, we make a contribution to the quality of life around us. The test of our theories, we believe, is their ultimate usefulness in practice. We have had the audacity to try to summarize our field in a short book. We hope that others will have a similar audacity, tempered with a respect for scientific values.

The ideas and concepts presented in this book reflect the contact that we have had with our own teachers, colleagues, and students. Our ideas also reflect our experiences with organizations that agreed to tolerate organizational psychologists in their midst. We have also benefited from some special assistance on this volume. Three reviewers, Hans Pennings, Arthur Brief, and James Lau, provided us with thoughtful criticism of our first draft. Professor Michael Tushman of Columbia University also helped us greatly through his comments, criticisms, and suggestions. To all of these people we owe much, and we thank them. Ultimately, of course, we bear the responsibility for what we have written here.

The process of writing a book from three different geographical locations is a noteworthy organizational behavior case in itself. The experience has been a confirming one for us, underscoring the real value of collegial enterprise. In the course of this enterprise, we were aided greatly by talented individuals on our staffs; in particular, Allyn Ostrow, Naomi Buchanan, Susan Campbell, and Carole Stone worked hard and long on the preparation and integration of this manuscript. To them we express our appreciation.

D.A.N.
J.R.H.
E.E.L.

Contents

Section I

CHAPTER 1
ORGANIZATIONS
AND BEHAVIOR

3

A Perspective on Organizational Behavior   1

Organizational Effectiveness   4
  The W. T. Grant bankruptcy / General Electric grows while
  Westinghouse shrinks / The manager's job
The Role of Models and Frameworks   8
  Examining our models and building new ones / The nature of
  knowledge about organizational behavior / Building
  pragmatic models
A General Framework for Understanding Organizations   14
  A perspective / Basic elements of organizational behavior /
  The organization / The environment / The framework
Using the General Framework — A Plan   20
Summary   21

Section II

CHAPTER 2
UNDERSTANDING
INDIVIDUAL
BEHAVIOR IN
ORGANIZATIONS

25

Individual Behavior in Organizations   23

Understanding the Nature of Individuals   28
  People differ in their behavior capabilities / People have
  different needs that they try to satisfy / People think about
  the future and make choices about how to behave / People
  perceive their environment in terms of their past experiences
  and needs / Individuals have affective reactions / Behaviors
  and attitudes are caused by multiple factors
Summary: Nature of Individuals   37

CHAPTER 3
STAFFING
ORGANIZATIONS

39

The Staffing Problem in Organizations   41
Managing the Attraction and Selection Process   42
  Perspective of individuals / Perspective of the manager /
  Individual–organization conflicts / Attracting individuals /
  How organizations select individuals / Summary: attraction
  and selection
Entry and Initial Socialization   48
  Methods of promoting socialization / Summary: entry and
  socialization
Careers in Organizations   51
  Training individuals / Career planning / Summary: careers
  in organizations
Summary: Managing Staffing   54

**CHAPTER 4
MEASURING AND
REWARDING
PERFORMANCE**

56

Measuring Performance 58
    Problems in performance appraisal / Making performance
    appraisal effective / Performance appraisal and feedback —
    a continuous process / Summary: performance appraisal
    effectiveness

Extrinsic Rewards 66
    Reward systems and organizational membership / Extrinsic
    reward and absenteeism / Reward systems and performance
    motivation / Summary: extrinsic rewards

**CHAPTER 5
JOB DESIGN**

75

Approaches to the Design of Work 78
    Scientific management / Individual job enrichment /
    Principles for designing enriched jobs / Designing work for
    groups — the autonomous work group approach / Summary:
    design choices

Issues in Choosing Work Designs 88
    Individual differences / Technology and cost factors /
    Organizational structure and climate / Making a choice of
    job designs / Diagnosis of potential design-based problems /
    The process of making the choice

Summary: Job Design as a Management Process 93

Section III

Group Behavior in Organizations   **95**

**CHAPTER 6
GROUPS IN
ORGANIZATIONS**

97

The Diversity of Groups in Organizations 99

Functions Served by Groups in Organizations 101
    Functions for the organization / Functions for the
    individual / Individual vs. organizational goals

The Social Intensity of Groups 106
    Traditional groups / Coacting groups / Reference groups

Consequences of Social Intensity 108
    Group control of members / Assembly effects

A Summary Framework for Describing Groups in
Organizations 109

**CHAPTER 7
GROUP
INFLUENCES ON
ORGANIZATION
MEMBERS**

112

Group Influences on Member Beliefs and Attitudes 114
    Discretionary stimuli / Effects on member beliefs / Effects on
    member attitudes / Summary: direct and indirect influences
    on behavior

Group Norms 120
    A model of norms / How do norms develop? / When do
    members comply with group norms?

Fostering Healthy Group–Individual Relationships 129

Summary 133

CHAPTER 8
DESIGNING
EFFECTIVE
WORK TEAMS

134

What Are the Ingredients of Work Team Effectiveness?   136

Intermediate Criteria of Team Effectiveness   137

Key Features in the Design of Work Teams   139
   Design of the group task / Composition of the group / Group
   norms about performance processes / Summary

Fostering and Supporting Work Group Effectiveness   145
   Creating a supportive environment / Interpersonal processes

Summary: The Role of the Manager   152

CHAPTER 9
MANAGING
INDIVIDUALS AND
GROUPS

156

Leadership as a Social Influence   160
   Leader power bases / Influence processes / The power
   balance

Leader Behavior and the Work Performance of
Individuals   164
   Using power / Path-goal theory / Organizational systems and
   leadership

Leadership of Coacting Groups   167
   Guidelines for managing groups / A decision-making model

Leadership of Intact Work Teams   171

The Many Faces of Leadership in Organizations   172

Summary   174

Section IV

The Design and Management of Organizations   177

CHAPTER 10
ORGANIZATION
DESIGN

179

The Nature of Organizational Structure   182

How Does Organization Structure Affect Behavior?   182

Organization Design Leverage Points   185

A Model for Choosing Organization Designs   186
   Different tasks require different information processing /
   Different organizational structures provide different
   information processing capacities / Organizational
   effectiveness and information processing fit

Using the Model to Design Organizations   195
   Steps in using the model

Summary   198

CHAPTER 11
DESIGN
MECHANISMS FOR
COORDINATION
AND CONTROL

200

Coordination and Control Mechanisms   203
   Hierarchy of authority / Rules and procedures / Planning and
   goal setting / Vertical information systems / Lateral
   relations / Matrix organizations

Designing to Reduce Information Processing Needs   212
   Environmental management / Slack resources / Self-
   contained units

Additional Design Mechanisms   214

Choosing Appropriate Coordination and Control
Mechanisms   215
   Choice from a range / The design model revisited

Summary   218

**CHAPTER 12
MANAGING
CONFLICT IN
ORGANIZATIONS**

219

What Is Conflict?   222

The Political Context of Conflict   223
   A different perspective / Organizations as networks /
   Dynamics of networks / Politics and conflict

How Conflict Comes About — A Model   227

The Conflict Episode   230

Conflict Outcomes   231
   Constructive outcomes of conflict / Destructive effects of
   conflict

Approaches to Conflict Management   233
   Methods of conflict resolution / Structural approaches /
   Process approaches / Mixed approaches

The Manager and Conflict   237
   Choice of resolution strategies / The manager as actor in the
   conflict

Summary   238

**CHAPTER 13
ORGANIZATIONAL
STRATEGY AND
BEHAVIOR**

239

What is Organizational Strategy?   242
   Relating to the environment / Using a set of resources /
   Strategy as the environment-resources match

Methods of Strategy Formulation   246
   Rational planning approach / Political processes approach /
   Adaptive processes approach

An Expanded View of Strategy Formulation   249

The Components of Strategy   250

Implications for Organizational Behavior   252

Summary   254

Section V

Effective Management of Organizational Behavior   257

**CHAPTER 14
MANAGING
HUMAN SYSTEMS:
DIAGNOSIS
AND ACTION**

259

Perspectives on the Manager's Job   260
   Classical perspectives / Empirical perspectives / A diagnosis-
   action perspective

The Diagnosis of Organizational Behavior   264
   Types of organizational diagnosis / Symptom-based
   diagnosis / Comprehensive diagnosis

Managerial Action: Bringing About Organizational Change   269
    The content of managerial action / The process of making changes
Limitations on Managerial Action   274
    Individual skills / Limits on managerial rationality / The managerial role / Values and the multiple constituents of organizations
Summary   279

References   281

Author Index   287

Subject Index   291

Section I

A Perspective on Organizational Behavior

OVERVIEW / This section provides a general introduction to the issues of organizational behavior and the management of organizations. First, we will address the question of why organizational behavior is important. Examples of effective and ineffective organizations will be considered to illustrate how management behavior relates to organizational goal accomplishment, performance, and effectiveness. Then we will identify the elements of a manager's job and review the impact of these on organizational effectiveness.

Second, we will describe a particular perspective on organizations. If people are to understand how organizations function and how they can be managed effectively, they need conceptual tools or road maps to guide their thinking. In this section, we will present a model or conceptual framework that can help untangle the complexities of organizational life and guide managerial behavior. The framework or model that is presented here views organizations as social systems that have to deal with an external environment, are made up of individuals and groups who perform tasks, and have formal and informal organizational arrangements to facilitate task performance. This model is used as a basic organizing framework for the rest of the book, and as a result, a thorough understanding is essential.

Chapter **1**

Organizations and Behavior

WHY ARE SOME ORGANIZATIONS more effective than others? This question has been studied and debated — mostly debated — for centuries, as has a second question: How can organizational effectiveness be defined and measured? Recently, the attention given these questions has increased severalfold. The simple reason for this is that we are more and more dependent on organizations. We depend on organizations for most of the goods and services that are necessary for survival and for most of those goods, services, and activities that make life more than simply a struggle to survive. In addition, more and more people are working, and although people are spending fewer of their waking hours at work, most people still spend over one-third of their waking hours there. The result is that for many people in our society, the quality of life at work has an important influence on the quality of life in general.

Organizational Effectiveness

It is precisely because life at work plays such an important part in peoples' lives that we do not believe organizational effectiveness can be or should be defined solely in terms of economic or productivity measures. It needs to be defined both in terms of the degree to which the economic and productivity goals of the organization are met and also in terms of the degree to which the organization provides a quality of work life that meets the needs of its employees.

No simple, straightforward answer has been found to the question of what makes an organization effective. Organizational effectiveness seems to result from a complex interaction of a number of factors; there are very few absolute rights or wrongs. What is right for an organization seems to depend, at least partially, on factors such as the business it is in, the people it employs, and the environment it must operate in.

The fact that there are few simple answers to the question of organizational effectiveness should not be taken to mean that there are no answers at all or that organizational effectiveness is completely a matter of luck or good fortune and that, as a result, it cannot be managed. Quite the opposite seems to be true. The way organizations are designed and managed seems to have a strong impact on their effectiveness. Admittedly, some things largely beyond the control of organizations and their management influence their effectiveness (for example, the market for their goods, government regulations, political events in other countries), but organizations and the people who manage them are, in part, masters of their own fate. The importance of effective management has been clearly illustrated by some of the more spectacular business failures that have occurred and by the dramatically different economic results that organizations in the same business often report. The bankruptcy of W. T. Grant provides a clear example of an organizational failure brought on by poor management, while the vastly different fortunes of General Electric and Westinghouse provide a good example of how management practices can lead to organizations that are similar in many ways and yet have very different performance results. These examples are discussed in detail below.

THE W. T. GRANT BANKRUPTCY

The stunning collapse of the W. T. Grant Company in October 1975 is a classic example of a company that failed because of management problems. At the time of its collapse, W. T. Grant operated 1,070 retail stores and was one of the largest retail merchandising firms in the United States. It collapsed at a time when many of its competitors, most notably the S. S. Kresge Company (now K Mart) and Sears, were setting new sales and profit records. Thus, the failure of Grant cannot be explained by market conditions. An explanation for its failure can, however, be found in many of its management practices.

According to the sworn testimony that emerged from the bankruptcy hearings on W. T. Grant:

▫ The information and control system in the organization was in total chaos. Management lacked information on inventories, accounts receivable, and consumer credit ratings.

▫ Managers in many stores reported false information and manipulated inventories and selling margins in order to increase their own pay.

▫ Management development at W. T. Grant was virtually non-existent and, as a result, when the crisis struck, the existing management had to go outside the company for a new chief executive officer. This proved to be expensive and was not adequate to stop the impending bankruptcy.

▫ Managers for the W. T. Grant stores were hit in the face with custard pies, had their ties cut in half, were forced to run around their stores backwards, and were not promoted if they didn't meet their credit quotas. Soon, delinquent customer accounts became an overwhelming problem at Grant.

▫ Major banks, including Morgan Guaranty which had $35 million in bad loans to Grant, continued to make loans even as the company headed for bankruptcy. According to them, they never knew how bad the internal information system was.

The numbers that Grant continually produced for their external auditors were wrong and, as one banker said, "The deeper we got in, the more bad apples we found."

Overall, W. T. Grant Company emerges as a very poorly managed company. They failed to deal effectively with many of the crucial areas that an organization must deal with if it is to perform adequately. Management development, staffing, motivation, information, control, and training were all poorly handled. As we shall see throughout this book, these areas are not ones that lend themselves to easy or universal solutions, but a great deal is known about how they can be managed effectively. W. T. Grant failed to capitalize on this knowledge, and the result was organizational suicide.

The contrast between Grant and Sears is particularly informative and dramatic. Sears, the country's largest retailer, is known as an innovator in many areas of management. In the 1950s, Sears became known for its innovative organization structure. Sears has also invested heavily in management development and is one of the largest users of employees' attitude surveys to improve communication. It has been rewarded with an exceptionally good growth rate.

GENERAL ELECTRIC GROWS WHILE WESTINGHOUSE SHRINKS

In 1977, Westinghouse Electric Corporation was beset by the backfiring of a huge gamble on uranium contracts. At the same time, Westinghouse was further bled by the high cost of a hodgepodge of questionable programs and acquisitions. In order to protect its existence, Westinghouse had to cut back dramatically on its overseas operations. Meanwhile, the General Electric Company, which competes head-to-head with Westinghouse in such major markets as consumer goods, utility power equipment, and industrial electric products, was growing and setting new profit records. Why has GE been so much more effective than Westinghouse?

Part of the answer seems to lie in the management philosophies and practices of the two organizations. Westinghouse's management has been described as "laissez faire." It has had an absence of planning and lacks adequate information and control systems. Westinghouse is a company that has been very weak in management training and in dealing with the problems of organizational structure that large organizations typically have.

GE has a very different kind of management style. It is acknowledged to have a very sophisticated management training and development program and brings executives up through succeeding levels of responsibility while acclimating them to corporate methods and goals. For a long time, GE has been a leader in research on management. It has also been an innovator in creating an organizational structure that emphasizes decentralized businesses with a centralized financial information system. GE has done this by creating a large number of strategic business units, each of which has known goals and operates somewhat like an independent company. General Electric has also developed a sophisticated decision process on new investments that involves a wide search for information and a careful consideration of alternatives. Its long-range planning system is the envy of most of its competitors.

THE MANAGER'S JOB   The W. T. Grant and General Electric/Westinghouse cases highlight some of the generic issues that must be dealt with in managing an organization. It is not accidental that in our report of both cases, we so strongly stressed information gathering, decision making, problem solving, and dealing with people. These activities are the very essence of a manager's job. The effective management of an organization depends on the availability of accurate, complete data about how the organization is functioning. These data must then be used in a decision-making process that allows them to be brought to bear in a way that leads to high quality, broadly accepted decisions that improve the future decision-making capability of the organization. The mention of future in this statement is not accidental; decision processes that deal with short-term needs in ways that damage the long-term, decision-making ability of the organization are unacceptable since they inevitably lead to decreased organizational effectiveness.

The mention of broadly accepted decisions is also not accidental. In order for a decision-making process to be effective in an organization, it must operate in a way that will lead to implementation. Without implementation, the highest quality decision is of little use. One of the things that separates the manager's job from most others in an organization is that the manager is responsible for more work than he or she can perform personally. In most situations, therefore, successful decision implementation by a manager requires that a number of people change their behavior. Thus, the effective manager must manage the decision process in such a way that others will change their behavior as a result of the decisions that are made.

What can a manager do to ensure that the decision-making process in his or her organization will be effective? A short answer to this question is that a manager can understand, predict, and influence organization behavior. In other words, the manager must manage the behavior of the members of his or her organization. How can this be done? The research on organizational behavior suggests a number of ways. The behavior of the members of an organization and of the organization as a whole is influenced by a number of processes and practices, each of which can be influenced by managers. These include such things as staffing decisions, training programs, reward systems, job and organization design, and leadership style. When these are handled well, decisions can be made and implemented effectively; when they are not, the result is poor decision making and organizational ineffectiveness. If they are going to manage organization behavior, managers need to know what effective practice is in each of these areas.

The Role of Models and Frameworks

How can managers know the best way to deal with staffing, motivation and leadership issues? There are a number of possible ways, but our view is that one approach is superior — using models and frameworks based on scientific research. Models and frameworks are ways of organizing our perceptions of the world around us. A *framework* is a device that provides categories or labels which help us to collect and organize data, in this case, data about organizations. It is a map that can help to interpret the nature of the terrain around us. As used here, a *model* goes one step further, by providing a representation of the real world and how it functions. Models not only tell us what to pay attention to and what not to pay attention to; they help us to understand why events occur as they do. For example, consider the simple model below.

Performance = f(Motivation × Ability)

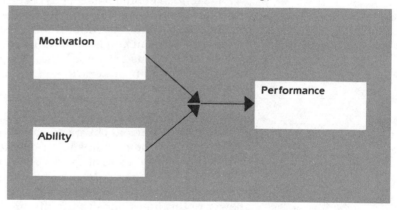

In words, this model means that an individual's performance is a function of the motivation to do the task multiplied by the ability to do the task. It implies that if we want to know what causes different people to work at different levels of performance, we should look at their respective levels of motivation and ability. It also implies that if we want to increase performance, we should do something to either increase ability (by selecting different workers, by training the ones we have, and so on), or we should do something to increase levels of motivation (through changes in the way people are paid, through the behavior of supervisors, and such). Thus, this model not only tells us what to look at, it gives us a picture of what causes certain events (levels of performance) and provides guidance about how to bring about change.

As is apparent from this example, the kinds of conceptual tools that managers use can be important aids in understanding and managing organizational behavior because they can influence the action that is taken. This can occur in three ways (see Figure 1.1):

1. *Conceptual tools can guide data collection.* At the core of most effective approaches to action is the collection of information or data. The kind of conceptual tools one uses determines the type of information that is collected. There are more data in any situation than can possibly be collected. Therefore, anyone in an organization must make critical choices about what data to collect and what data to ignore. The choice is important because organizational effectiveness depends on the ability to ignore data that are not critical as well as the ability to pay attention to what is important. Having a conceptual road map helps one to make that choice more systematically and effectively.

2. *Conceptual tools can help in interpreting data.* Once data are collected, the manager is faced with the question, What does it all mean? Here again, frameworks and models can help the manager to classify the information that is at hand and to make some sense out of it. For example, using the simple perfor-

Figure 1.1 *How Models Influence Managerial Action*

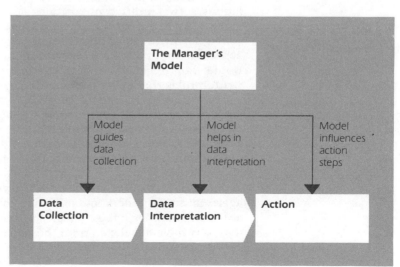

mance model discussed before, we are able to take data about training, skill levels, aptitudes, and such and classify these as information about an individual's level of ability. Similarly, we are able to take information about individual needs, perceptions of rewards, and intentions to work hard and classify these under the general heading of motivation. Both of these general classes, when combined, tell us something about performance.

3. *Conceptual tools can guide action steps.* The third step is to take action based on the diagnosis or interpretation of the data. Here again, conceptual tools can be useful. They can guide the manager toward action steps. To illustrate this, let's return to the performance model, which states that work performance is a function of motivation multiplied by ability. One of the implications of this model is that if either of the two causal factors (motivation or ability) is at zero (no motivation or no relevant ability), then performance will not occur. If ability is high but there is absolutely no motivation on the part of the worker to make use of that ability, then no performance will result. The important implication here for managerial action is that if motivation is zero, then any efforts to increase ability (through training, for instance) will be wasted. The manager must deal with the motivation problem before any changes in performance will occur.

EXAMINING OUR MODELS AND BUILDING NEW ONES

When thinking about organizations, most people already have models that they use automatically or intuitively. One way to establish this is to ask someone to draw a picture of an organization. Many different types of pictures will result, but most people faced with this task will produce a picture like that in Figure 1.2. This way of thinking about organizations basically says that we can understand them by looking at the formal authority relations between different positions or jobs within a specific organization, along with the formal grouping of jobs into subunits called departments or divisions. If a manager were to use this approach to understand organizational behavior, he or she would want to get copies of the formal table of organization, the written rules that govern conduct, the job descriptions and goal statements of each individual position and work group, and so forth. Unfortunately, the model depicted in Figure 1.2 ignores many facets of organizational life, including informal relationships, the actual distribution of power, the nature of the individuals, and a host of other facets that will be dealt with in later chapters.

The use of incomplete or poorly developed models by managers is quite understandable and common. When thinking about organizations, most people draw on models or frameworks that they have developed from their own experiences. These *experiential* models reflect what an individual has learned about

Figure 1.2 *One Way of Thinking about Organizations*

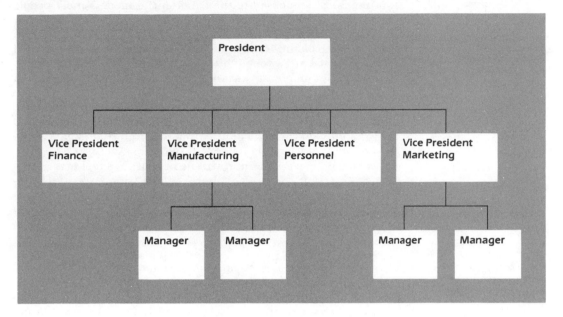

organizations as a result of his or her experience. These models are usually intuitive and implicit, rather than explicitly stated or written. Being experiential models, they are inherently limited to the background of the particular individual. Because they are intuitive and implicit, experiential models do not tend to be systematically examined and modified over time. They do tend to be simplistic in that they are universal — they assume that one set of rules and principles is applicable in all situations. On the other hand, experiential models do have some redeeming features. People learn from their experiences and thus experiential models are rarely all wrong, naive, or simplistic. In addition, because they are intuitive and developed from the individual's own experience, they make sense, fit in with a general perspective of the world, and are easily usable.

In this book, our intent is to move beyond the experiential model and to introduce new models that reflect systematic thinking about how organizations work and how individuals behave in organizational settings. Until the 1950s, much of what was written about organizations was based on knowledge that had not been subjected to scientific study. At the present time, however, the situation has changed noticeably. A number of models exist that have been tested and proven to be accurate or valid by scientific research methods. Many of these models have the advantage of being developed and systematically tested over a range of organizations and situations. We will label these *scientific* models, as opposed to the experiential models most people carry around with them. Scientific models tend to be explicit; they draw their validity from the fact that they have been tested in a number of different organizational situations and exceed the experience of any one individual. They also reflect the unfortunate reality of life in that they are much more complex than many straightforward experiential models.

Throughout this book as we discuss what is known about such things as leadership, motivation, and group functioning, we will draw heavily on the body of scientific research that is part of the field of organizational behavior. In those instances in which we do go beyond the research, it will be because we feel it is important to deal with a subject that has not been extensively researched or because a generally validated theory suggests an as yet untested conclusion. It is our belief that the methods of science and the evidence they produce are the best keys we have to the understanding and management of organizational behavior.

THE NATURE OF KNOWLEDGE ABOUT ORGANIZATIONAL BEHAVIOR

Most early researchers seemed to look for a single universally correct way to manage most aspects of organizational behavior. They tried to identify the best leadership style, the correct way to design jobs, and the best selection programs. In most cases, they were disappointed; few universally best or correct solutions emerged. Instead, the research suggested that the impact of a particular practice or design was dependent on a number of other factors. The result of this is that most researchers today do not look for absolute rights and wrongs; instead, they try to determine which conditions lead to specific practices or policies having a positive impact and which ones lead to their having a negative impact. It is not that there are no absolutes; it is more that the absolutes are fewer than many people expected and are fairly general in nature (for example, reward the behavior you want people to demonstrate).

Basically, the research shows that what is effective management practice in a given area depends on factors in the environment of the organization as well as on practices and policies in other areas. Organizations are complex systems that interact with their environments. To be effective, they must deal with that environment. It is not surprising, then, that what is effective management practice depends somewhat on what the environment of an organization is like. Dealing with a rapidly changing, resource-rich environment is clearly different from dealing with a stable, resource-poor environment. It is predictable that different management practices are required to deal with each.

Organizations are systemic in nature. Therefore, it follows that what is effective practice in one management area depends on what is done in others. Because of this, what is done in one area impacts on what is done in another. Thus, if one area of management practice is going in one way (such as toward an authoritarian approach to decision making) and the other is going in another way (such as toward a democratic practice), conflict and organizational ineffectiveness are likely. For example, it does not make sense to design a selection system that will identify and recruit ambitious, upwardly mobile college graduates if there is no management development system to help them develop or no jobs available that are challenging enough to use their skills.

Because many of the findings in organization behavior do show that there are few absolutes in management, much of our discussion in this book will stress when we would expect certain practices to be effective. In some cases, this may be frustrating to the reader; unfortunately, little can be done about this because the problem is inherent in the nature of organizations. The one thing that can be done is to present scientific models which try to summarize and clearly capture what has been found through research.

BUILDING PRAGMATIC MODELS

While our view is that scientific models offer the greatest promise for understanding complex organizations, we are not proposing that experiential models be totally abandoned in favor of scientific ones. Many experiential models are useful tools, while many scientific models are cumbersome and nearly impossible to use. What we are proposing is a melding of the two in what has been referred to as a process of building a pragmatic model of organization (Tichy, Hornstein, and Nisberg, 1976).

As you proceed through this text, we hope that you will dig out and "dust off" your experiential models and take a good look at them. At the same time, we will be suggesting and asking you to think about some scientific models of organizational behavior. Our hope is that out of this process, you will draw on both sets of models to put together tools that have some basis in scientific findings, but also are consistent with your own experience (see Figure 1.3). The output should be models that are both valid and usable, or, in other words, pragmatic models of organizational behavior.

In subsequent chapters, therefore, we will be presenting and discussing a host of different models. Some will be relatively simple and straightforward, such as the motivation-ability-performance model, while others will be more elaborate and complicated. Some of these will deal with how individuals behave in organizational settings, others will help to explain the functioning of groups within organizations, and others will address questions of how large organizations are structured and function within complex environments. Thus, different models with both different levels of complexity and different points of focus will be presented.

Figure 1.3 *The Sources of Pragmatic Models of Organizational Behavior*

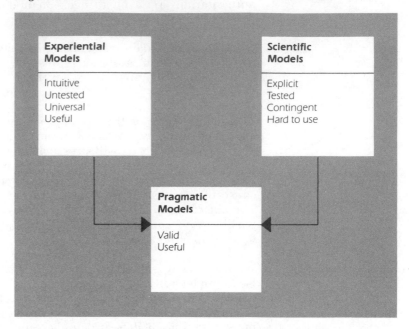

When thinking about all the specific elements of organizations and the models that help us to explain how and why they work the way they do, we run the risk of having many pieces of a puzzle but no way to put them together. To deal with this, we need an organizing framework that provides us with a common way to think about organizations at the most general level. With such a framework in hand, we can then begin to examine different issues, always keeping in mind how they fit into the larger picture. We will present such a model next. The reader should study it carefully and become aware of the various relationships specified in it before going on to the rest of the book. It was designed to help you fit into context the various elements that go together to make up an organization. Only if you keep these relationships in mind can you hope to understand the various factors which must be considered when a practice, policy, or decision is being evaluated.

A General Framework for Understanding Organizations

A PERSPECTIVE

There are many different ways of thinking about or looking at organizations. The basic perspective taken here is that organizations are social systems operating within larger environments

(Katz and Kahn, 1966, 1978). In its simplest form, a *system* is a set of interrelated elements or components. Systems can also be thought of as mechanisms that receive inputs from the environment (such as raw materials, capital, the efforts of individuals, and so on) and subject those inputs to a transformation process (such as cutting, painting, or editing) to produce outputs (such as products or services).

The systems perspective is important for a number of reasons. First, open systems organizations exchange input and output with a larger environment. Therefore, a key to understanding an organization is to identify its role within the larger environment in which it functions. We must be aware of the organization's strategy for coping with the environment, its contribution to the environment, and its objectives with respect to the environment.

Second, once we know the organization's strategy for coping with the environment, we need to focus on the transformation process. In other words, the starting point for understanding organizations is the work that the organization performs. Organizations exist to do goal-oriented work. More specifically, organizations exist so that work can be done collectively to meet some joint goal. They bring people together, form groups, and link together sets of groups to do tasks more effectively than could be done by individuals alone.

Third, if organizations are systems made up of interrelated elements, then it is important to keep in mind the relationships that exist among the different elements or parts. In systems, it is the relationship between elements that is of critical importance, not just the elements themselves.

BASIC ELEMENTS OF ORGANIZATIONAL BEHAVIOR

Given the perspective of organizations as open, goal-oriented social systems, three critical elements which form the core of organizational behavior can be identified (see Figure 1.4).

Tasks. The most obvious and perhaps most central element of an organization is the set of tasks that need to be performed. Tasks refer to the work that needs to be done by the organization in order for it to meet its goals effectively. Tasks can be considered at two different levels. First there is the organizational task. This is the work that directly stems from the organization's strategy and that must be performed by the total organization if it is to meet its goals. Organizational tasks vary in their complexity, the kinds of competence required, the degree of uncertainty, and the degree to which different portions of the task need to be coordinated with each other. Organizations, however, do not ultimately perform tasks; people do. Thus, the second level of tasks includes the subtasks that individuals and groups need to perform to accomplish the larger organizational task. Subtasks vary

Figure 1.4 *Basic Elements of Organizational Behavior*

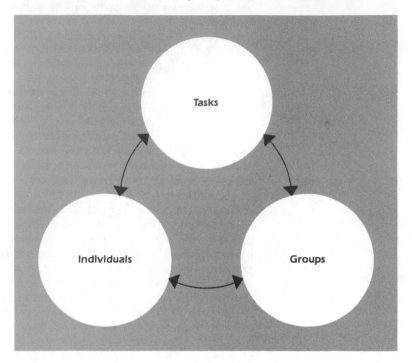

in the demands that they make on the individuals and groups that perform them and the types of rewards they provide to those who perform them.

Individuals. A second basic element of organizations is the individuals who perform tasks. Three characteristics of individuals are particularly important. First, individuals vary in skills, aptitudes, and abilities. They therefore enter the organization with different capacities to perform tasks. Second, individuals vary in such important psychological characteristics as needs, beliefs, and past history. Third, the attitudes and behaviors of individuals are influenced by the kinds of tasks they are asked to perform as well as by a host of social factors that are present in the work place.

Groups. A third basic element is that of groups. While individuals perform tasks, much organizational work is performed by collections of people working in a coordinated manner. These collections of two or more people who interact with each other and think of themselves as a unit are called *groups*. Three aspects of groups are particularly important. The first aspect is composition; that is, who is a member of the group. As a result of composition, different combinations of both capabilities and needs are present in groups. A second aspect is the nature and characteristics of the tasks assigned to the group. The final aspect is how the group goes about doing its work, and what kinds of patterns exist in the social relationships among the group members.

Thus, there are three basic elements of organization: tasks, individuals, and groups. What is important in looking at organizations is not these elements per se but rather the relationships that exist among them. Indeed, what we are ultimately interested in is how individuals and groups perform tasks and the consequences of individual and group behavior, not the simple fact that individuals, tasks, and groups exist.

We can label the crucial relationships among individuals, tasks, and groups for the purpose of clarification. The key relationship between the individual and the task is *individual work effectiveness,* or how well individuals perform their tasks and what consequences result from that performance (satisfaction, stress, and such). Similarly, the key to the relationship between the group and the task is *work group* effectiveness, or how well the group performs tasks and the consequences of such performance. Finally, there is the relationship between the individual and the group. The key here is *social influence,* or how groups are influenced by individuals and how individuals are influenced by the groups of which they are members.

THE ORGANIZATION   Tasks, individuals, and groups do not exist in a vacuum, unconnected and free floating; they exist within the context of organizations. *Organizations* are collections of individuals and groups performing tasks linked together so that, ideally, these different groups and individuals will perform their tasks in a coordinated manner. To achieve this coordination, *organizational arrangements* are created. These arrangements have two major features. First, individuals are grouped together into work units, departments, divisions, and so on, based on their needs to relate to and work with one another. This creation of *subunits* is an essential feature of organizational arrangements, but by itself creates another need, that of linking the subunits together. Thus, various *coordinating mechanisms* also are created to link together subunits so that they will perform their work in a coordinated and controlled manner. This process of identifying and creating subunits and developing linking mechanisms among them is what is frequently called *organizational design.*

Almost all organizations have formal prescribed arrangements or designs that can be drawn on charts and laid out through descriptions of the jobs in the organization. At the same time, there is another set of organizational arrangements which is impossible to identify through formal written procedures or charts. This other set of organizational arrangements emerges over time as a product of the informal relationships that exist among individuals and groups and is frequently called the *informal organization*. It includes the emergent or informal patterns of communication, networks, and political coalitions which exist in all organizations.

THE ENVIRONMENT

As we mentioned earlier, organizations exist in environments. In order to be effective, any organization must be able to maintain favorable transactions with the environment in which it functions. Therefore, the study of organizations must consider the nature of the environment and the different aspects of that environment. The environment includes the various institutions or groups with which the organization interacts. It includes competitors, suppliers, customers or clients, financial institutions, the government, the larger systems of which some organizations are a part (such as a parent company), and so on.

The environment is important in several ways. First, the environment provides a set of *opportunities* for the organization to provide a distinctive product or service. Indeed, the whole process of identifying a strategy for an organization (and implicitly a set of tasks and goals) is that of identifying the opportunities the environment presents for a particular organization with a particular set of resources and a particular distinctive competence. At the same time, the environment provides a set of *demands* on the organization. For example, in an industry where the technology is changing rapidly and new products are almost constantly being developed, the organization must respond and change course quickly if it is to survive. Third, the environment provides certain *constraints* on organizational action. The actions of most organizations are limited by governmental regulation, by the limited amount of resources in capital markets, by the limitations of existing technology, and by a host of other constraints. Thus, organizational effectiveness requires sets of organizational arrangements that coordinate the work of individuals and groups doing tasks in a way that enables the total system to work within constraints, respond to demands, and take advantage of opportunities in the environment.

THE FRAMEWORK

If we put together all the elements we have discussed so far, we have a general framework for studying, thinking about, and understanding organizations (see Figure 1.5). At the core of the framework are the basic components of tasks, individuals, and groups. We are concerned about the relationships among these elements and, in particular, the issues of individual work effectiveness, work group effectiveness, and social influence. These components are embedded within a configuration of subunits and coordinating mechanisms called *organizational arrange-*

Figure 1.5 *A General Framework for Understanding Organizational Behavior*

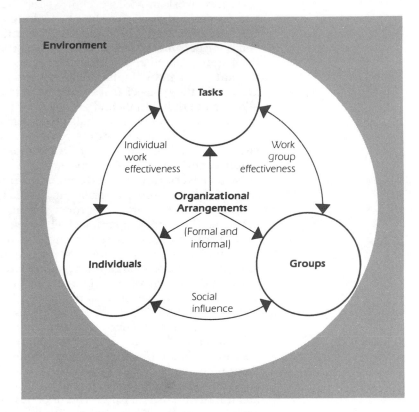

ments, which include both formal organizational arrangements and the emergent or informal arrangements. As indicated by the arrows in Figure 1.5, the organizational arrangements are important because they impact on individual and group effectiveness and on social influence processes in a variety of ways. For instance, individual work effectiveness may be influenced directly by changes in an aspect of organizational arrangements (such as how people are paid). On the other hand, individual work effectiveness might be influenced through changes in the nature of individuals working (through selection or training) or in the nature of tasks to be performed (through the design or redesign of jobs). Finally, this total system of tasks, individuals, groups, and organizational arrangements exists within and interacts with a larger environment, which includes many different and changing elements.

Using the General Framework — A Plan

Our framework provides a context for the examination of specific issues and problems. Just by looking at the framework, the types of tools that a manager has to influence organizational behavior become apparent. If a manager is interested in effecting organizational performance, he or she may make changes in the nature of individuals, in the composition or functioning of groups, in the types of tasks that are performed or how they are allocated to individuals and groups, and in the formal organizational arrangements. The kinds of changes that can and should be made are the subject of the remainder of the book. Our purpose so far has been to lay out, in the most sketchy form, a road map to show you where we are going. In subsequent chapters, we will be working our way through this framework, considering each of the components, terms, and issues in greater depth and in more concrete form. As we move through the various chapters in this text, we will keep track of where we are in the framework.

In a framework such as this one, it is difficult to pick a starting point. If all the pieces are in some way related to one another, it is hard to think about starting at any one point, since one has to think about everything at once. For discussion and learning, however, we have to pick someplace to begin and have·chosen to start with individuals for several reasons. First, our ultimate goal is to understand organizational behavior — the patterns of individual behavior as well as the behavior of groups and organizations. To do this, it is necessary to understand some fundamental concepts of why people behave as they do and what determines behavior in organizational settings. Some thought about individuals and the causes of behavior seems useful before moving on to the discussion of collections of individuals, either in groups or organizations. Second, for those who have not systematically thought about organizations before and for those who may not have extensive work experience in organizations, concepts such as organizational strategy, organizational structure, and environmental demands may be abstract and have little meaning in and of themselves. On the other hand, almost everyone has had a job of some sort or has been an individual member of an organization (such as a school, retail store, manufacturing firm, and so forth). Thus, concepts about individuals entering organizations and working on jobs are concepts that people can relate to easily as a starting point for thinking about organizations.

Once we have completed our consideration of individual behavior in organizations, we will then consider groups and group behavior. This discussion logically precedes our discussion of organizational issues because group behavior, like individual behavior, is a major element that must be dealt with in the design and management of the total organization.

Summary

Organizations are complex systems that are not easy to understand. The task of the manager, however, is to understand how organizations function and work so that he or she can manage organizational behavior effectively. Given the complexity of organizational life, tools are needed to help understand, predict, and manage behavior in organizations. One type of tool is the conceptual model or framework, and a number of such models and frameworks will be presented as we talk about aspects of organizational behavior. On a larger scale, however, a general framework is needed as a road map. The general framework presented here provides a perspective on organizations and will be used through the remaining chapters as a road map for our explorations into organizational behavior.

Suggested Readings

Katz, D., and Kahn, R. L. *The Social Psychology of Organizations*. 2nd ed. New York: Wiley, 1978.

Porter, L. W., Lawler, E. E., and Hackman, J. R. *Behavior in Organizations*. New York: McGraw-Hill, 1975.

Schein, E. *Organizational Psychology*. 2nd ed. Englewood Cliffs, N.J.: Prentice-Hall, 1965.

Section II

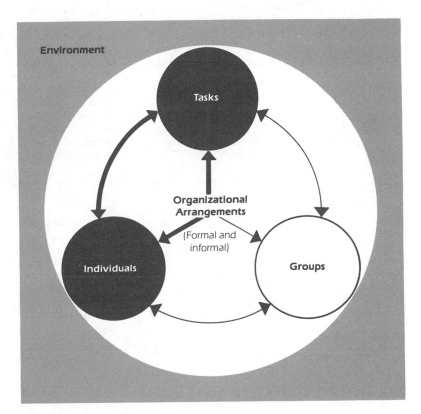

Individual
Behavior in
Organizations

OVERVIEW / *The basic building block of work organizations is the individual organization member. This section is aimed at providing an understanding of how and why individuals behave as they do within organizations.*

As a starting point, in Chapter 2 we will present some basic material about individuals themselves. People come into organizations with different capabilities and needs, and they respond to the environment around them in varying ways. An examination of the causes of behavior, therefore, is the starting point in exploring the framework for understanding organizational behavior, which was presented in Chapter 1 (see Figure 1.5 on p. 19).

The organization itself can do a number of things to influence how individuals behave. First, the systems that the organization develops for attracting and selecting people to work for it, helping them to enter the organization, and developing their skills over time are important. Questions concerning how organizations perform these functions will be considered in Chapter 3, where staffing organizations is discussed. Second, the systems that organizations develop to measure and reward the performance of individuals are important determinants of motivation. We will consider how approaches to measuring and rewarding performance

influence motivation and performance in Chapter 4.

The behavior of individuals in organizations is also greatly influenced by the nature of the work that they perform. Over time, it has become clear that there are alternative methods of allocating tasks to individuals and designing individual jobs. Depending on the nature of the individual performing the job, some types of job designs lead to a high level of motivation and performance, while other job designs result in low motivation, performance, and satisfaction. In Chapter 5 we will consider the whole question of job design, including the relationship between the characteristics of individuals and the characteristics of tasks. We will also examine the approaches that can be taken by organizations to designing the tasks to be performed.

In total, Section II provides an understanding of individual performance in organizations. It starts with an understanding of the individual and then examines how three different factors — organizational staffing, measurement and rewards systems, and the nature of the work to be performed — influence how individuals behave. This is summarized in the figure at the beginning of this section which shows the parts of our framework of organizational behavior that will be considered.

Chapter 2

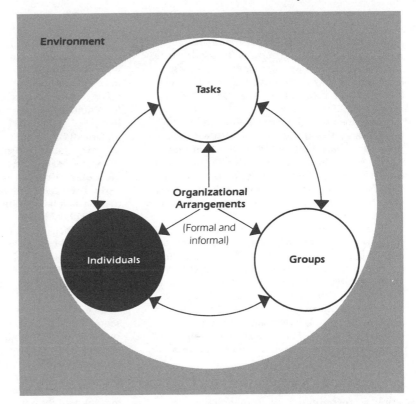

Understanding
Individual Behavior
in Organizations

Mrs. Ellen Johnson has a routine repetitive job. She works in a garment factory where she sits over a Singer sewing machine from eight each morning until four each afternoon, and by the end of a week she has guided 1,500 linings into 1,500 coats.

How does Mrs. Johnson feel about her job? She likes it. Mrs. Johnson has been with her present employer since the death of her husband twenty-nine years ago. Her day begins at 6:40 A.M. when she leaves her home in Brooklyn. Two subway trains and fifty minutes later, she changes into a work smock in a makeshift dressing room.

She can do any job on the assembly-line in the garment factory where she works. Most of the time, by her own preference, she sews linings into coats. She moves with astonishing speed and deftness and her productivity rate is far above the engineered standard for the job. After over a quarter of a century of practice, she can carry on a lively conversation with co-workers and still keep the coats flowing through her sewing machine with faultless precision.

Mrs. Johnson earns about $125 a week. She has more than made her peace with the job. "I wouldn't recommend it to someone with an education," she says, "but for someone like me, it's good. You learn to take it in stride. You make up your mind it's your livelihood and then you don't get bored."

Mrs. Johnson cannot imagine any other way of spending a day. To her, going to the garment factory is almost an involuntary function of the body and mind. It is, she says, "like everything else — you gotta eat, you gotta sleep, you gotta work." Indeed, to her, the run-down garment factory is almost like a home. "I'd come in here with a fever," she says. "Even if there's a blizzard, I come."

Mrs. Johnson is fiercely proud of her good record as a worker and is scornful of younger workers who are not willing to devote as much to the job as she is. "They want easy jobs, like office jobs. I like this place here, but I do sweat for a dollar. We know what a dollar is worth here."

One of the women Mrs. Johnson is scornful of is Mrs. Janet Henson. Mrs. Henson works in the same garment factory as Mrs. Johnson. Most of the time her job consists of cutting loose threads off finished coats and packing the coats in boxes. She is twenty years old and a high school graduate. Mrs. Henson failed to find an office job when she graduated from high school two years ago. As she says, "This was the cleanest factory job I could find at the time."

Although she used to try hard, Mrs. Henson has never mastered her job and her performance is constantly below standard. She seems to lack the finger dexterity and hand speed required to do her job.

How does she feel about her job? "I dread coming to work. The pay is too low and the boredom is driving me crazy. I am starting to have nightmares about it. If I could get a better job, I would take it in a minute. My biggest fear is that I am trapped in this job and that I will never be able to get an office job."

Mrs. Henson may not find an office job, but there is a good chance she will be leaving her present one before long. Her supervisor, Miss Abelson, has just about given up on her. According to Miss Abelson, "Janet is a nice girl, but she just doesn't fit here. She doesn't seem to be able to learn the job and she is more interested in her appearance than in the work. I just cannot tolerate this any longer. I am afraid I am going to have to let her go."

CLEARLY THE REACTIONS of Mrs. Johnson and Mrs. Henson to their jobs are quite different. They differ in how they feel about their jobs as well as in how effectively they are able to perform them, despite the fact that their jobs are similar in many important respects.

Can the differences between these two women be explained, or should they simply be dismissed as due to unexplainable differences in people? Although it is not easy to explain differences like these, they usually can be dealt with by models that are available to analyze individual behavior. Basic to all these models and to understanding the work behavior of individuals is the principle that human behavior is jointly determined by characteristics of individuals and characteristics of the work environment.

As is shown in Figure 2.1, human behavior is a function of

Figure 2.1 *A General Model of Behavior in Organizations*

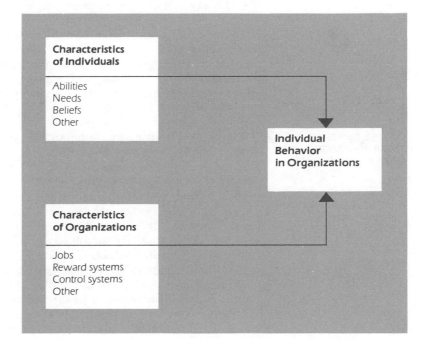

characteristics of both the *person* and the *environment*. Individuals bring things to the organizational setting including abilities, personal beliefs, expectations, and past experience. The environment provided by the organization has a number of features: jobs, relationships among people, work that needs to be done, rewards that are available to individuals, and so on. Neither the nature of the individual nor the nature of the organization completely determine behavior. Rather, behavior is the result of the interaction between individual and organizational characteristics. As the field of organizational behavior has matured, researchers and theorists have developed more complex views of what the key attributes of individuals are, and similarly they have developed more complex views of what the salient characteristics of organizations are. At the same time, the concept of behavior being a joint function of the person and environment has persisted as the underlying model of behavior.

The remainder of this chapter and Chapters 3–5 will be organized around this model. In the rest of this chapter, we will discuss some of the characteristics of individuals that can help us understand individual behavior in organizational settings. The next three chapters will focus on the most important characteristics of the organizational environment.

Understanding the Nature of Individuals

Psychology has developed many ways of viewing the nature of people. Although the concept of people accepted by most researchers in organizational behavior draws on some of these approaches, it is different and has its own character. It is performance oriented, and views most job behavior as the result of conscious thought processes within the individual. The best way of understanding this view is to review the basic principles that are part of it.

PEOPLE DIFFER IN THEIR BEHAVIOR CAPABILITIES

An important limiting factor on an individual's behavior is capability. People cannot respond in all the ways that might seem desirable. People can only lift so much weight, think so fast, run so far. Further, and of great significance, individuals differ widely in their response capabilities. Some people can lift many times what others can, think much faster, run much farther. Mrs. Johnson, for example, was able to master the complex manual skills that are involved in garment manufacturing, while Mrs. Henson was not.

Traditionally, psychologists have divided behaviors into those that are innate and therefore not subject to improvement by training, and those that can be altered and learned. This way of thinking about human characteristics is outmoded. Even measures like intelligence (IQ), once thought to be innately determined and fixed, can be influenced by training and experience. It remains true, however, that IQ can only be influenced within a limited range because physiological limitations exist. The same is true of the kinds of manual dexterity skills that are important in performing the jobs of Mrs. Johnson and Mrs. Henson. Consequently, it now seems reasonable to think of describing human response capabilities by placing them on a continuum. At one end are those behaviors that are difficult to influence by training and experience (for example, reaction time), and at the other end are those behaviors that are relatively open to change and not significantly constrained by genetic or physiological factors (for example, reading speed).

A large number of psychological tests have been developed that are valid measures of behavior capability and, as will be discussed in Chapter 3, research has shown that some of them can predict job performance. Tests have been developed to measure those behavior capabilities that are relatively fixed and those that are more susceptible to change as a result of experience and training. The latter tests are often called *skill tests,* while the former are called *aptitude tests.* Both kinds of tests can, and often do, play an important role in a variety of staffing decisions, including hiring, firing, promotion, and training. The significance of the fact that individuals have different behavior capabilities is not limited to decisions concerning staffing. It is also important to keep this point in mind when training decisions are being made and when jobs are designed. For an organization to be effective, individuals must hold jobs that they are capable of performing. As we shall see, a number of strategies exist for creating good fits between the capabilities of an individual and the demands of the job.

PEOPLE HAVE DIFFERENT NEEDS THAT THEY TRY TO SATISFY

Psychologists generally talk about human behavior as being motivated by a set of needs. By a need is meant some internal state in a person which causes clusters or groups of objects or outcomes to be sought by individuals. For example, various food objects are sought by individuals and are clustered together, so that when people desire one food object, they usually desire others as well; when they get enough of one, they often lose interest in the others. Thus, we say people have a need for food rather than saying that people have a need for roast beef or potatoes. Similarly, performing well in certain kinds of competitive activities seems to be attractive to individuals, and as a result, we speak of a need for achievement even though we cannot tie this need to any physiological basis.

Human beings are motivated toward a great diversity of ends. Mrs. Johnson, for instance, seems to be attracted to work because it satisfies her social needs as well as her need for security. Furthermore, needs are constantly changing. What motivates people today may or may not be potent in determining their behavior tomorrow. This, however, does not mean that the concept of need is not a useful one in dealing with human behavior in organizations. It is necessary if we are to explain and predict the goal-oriented behavior that occurs in organizations. It can also help us to understand why outcomes are important to individuals, and it can help us predict which outcomes will be important to specific individuals.

What needs do individuals have? The following list, or one like it, enjoys broad acceptance:

1. A number of existence needs, including sex, hunger, thirst, and oxygen
2. A security need
3. A social need
4. A need for esteem and reputation
5. An autonomy, self-control, and independence need
6. A need for competence, achievement and self-realization

One of the things which distinguishes the first four needs from the fifth and the sixth is that they can only be satisfied by outcomes which are external (extrinsic) to the person and which have a concrete reality (food, money, praise from another). The need for self-realization and competence, and to some extent the need for autonomy and self-control, seem to be satisfied only by outcomes which are given intrinsically by persons to themselves (for instance, the feeling of accomplishment). It is true that certain environmental conditions need to be present before the internal outcomes can be obtained, but the outcomes themselves are not observable to others nor are they controlled by others. Behavior in organizations is motivated by individuals seeking *both* intrinsic and extrinsic rewards.

Maslow's (1954) well-known need theory specifies that needs are arranged in a hierarchy. According to his theory, people move successively up a need hierarchy (like the list above). As their lower-order needs are satisfied, their higher-order needs, like self-realization, become more important. In essence, Maslow talks as if needs are arranged like a ladder that must be climbed one rung at a time. Thus, people will only be concerned with self-realization if their existence needs, their security needs, and so on are satisfied. Further, if the satisfaction of a lower-order need is threatened, that need immediately becomes predominant, and all higher-order needs will be forgotten.

Maslow also points out that a satisfied need is not motivating. Once a person has obtained a satisfying amount of food, the opportunity to obtain more food will not be motivating. The one exception to this conclusion is the need for self-actualization or growth. This need seems to be insatiable in the sense that the more individuals obtain outcomes that satisfy it, the more important it becomes and the more of it they desire. Because of this, self-realization, unlike other needs, continues to be important, and people are continually motivated by the desire to experience more of it. One important implication of this last point is that no matter how much satisfaction someone has, that person will always want more.

Research supports the view that unless existence and security needs are satisfied, people will not be concerned with the needs above them. However, very little evidence exists to support the view that a hierarchy exists once one moves above the security level. For example, studies do not indicate that social needs must be satisfied before people will be concerned with the need for self-realization. Thus, based on the research evidence, it seems best to assume a two-step hierarchy with existence and security needs at the lowest level and the remaining needs at the top level. This means that unless the lower-order needs are satisfied, the others will not come into play. It also means that when the satisfaction of lower-order needs is threatened, these needs will become predominant. Thus, attempts to influence behaviors that threaten lower-order needs will always have an impact because they dominate all others.

The existence of a two-step hierarchy also means that if the basic needs are satisfied, no one need is likely to be the "best" or "only" motivator. In fact, the evidence suggests that more than one need may simultaneously be important. For example, a person can be motivated by both social and autonomy needs. It also suggests that people differ widely in which need or needs will come into play once existence and security needs are satisfied. As a result, it is to be expected that at any point in time most organizations will employ individuals who are motivated by different needs, as exemplified by the differences between Mrs. Johnson and Mrs. Henson.

PEOPLE THINK ABOUT THE FUTURE AND MAKE CHOICES ABOUT HOW TO BEHAVE

People's needs can only be satisfied by their engaging in behaviors. In many situations, individuals are faced with a number of potentially need-satisfying behaviors from which to choose. The most widely accepted current approach to explaining how individuals make choices among the large set of alternative behaviors open to them is called *expectancy theory*. Expectancy theory is based on the relatively simple proposition that individuals choose to attempt those behaviors that they see as leading to outcomes (rewards such as pay, recognition from the boss) that are attractive to them (that meet their particular needs). The theory, based on this proposition, shows how to analyze and predict what courses of action individuals will follow when they have the opportunity to make choices about their behavior.

Figure 2.2 presents expectancy theory graphically. It shows that as individuals contemplate the performance of an act, they consider several factors. First, the probability that if they put forth effort, they will be able to attain the required level of performance (the effort to performance, or $E \rightarrow P$ expectancy); sec-

Figure 2.2 *Major Expectancy Theory Terms*

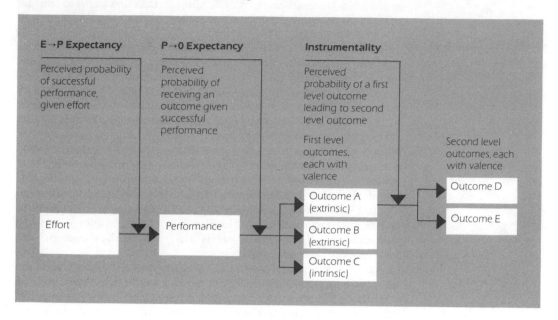

ond, if the level of performance is obtained, the probability that it will lead to acquiring outcomes (the performance to outcome or P → O expectancy); third, the attractiveness of the outcomes, seen as accruing from performance; and fourth, the degree to which some outcomes may have additional attractiveness because their acquisition in turn leads to the obtaining of other desired outcomes (such as money, which is attractive because of what it can buy). Given this model, the motivational force to behave in a certain way is greatest when the individual:

1. believes that performance at the desired level is possible (high E → P expectancy);
2. believes that the behavior will lead to outcomes (has a high P → O expectancy); and when
3. those outcomes have positive value (have high attractiveness).

Given a number of alternative behaviors (10, 15, 20 units of production per hour, or going to work vs. taking the day off, for example), the model predicts that individuals will choose the behavior that has the greatest motivational force associated with it. In other words, when faced with choices about behavior, the individual goes through a process of asking questions such as, Can I perform at that level if I try? If I perform at that level, what will happen? and How do I feel about those things that will happen? The individual then decides to behave in that way which appears to have the best chance of producing positive outcomes.

Applying this model for the moment to the performances of Mrs. Johnson and Mrs. Henson, we can see why Mrs. Henson has a low motivation to perform her job effectively. To begin with, she does not believe that she can perform at a high level because she lacks the necessary capabilities. Furthermore, she does not believe that good performance on the job will lead to rewards she values. The situation for Mrs. Johnson is just the reverse. She knows she can do well if she puts forth the effort, and good performance on the job leads to feelings of self-esteem and competence.

It is important to note that the expectancy model does not predict that people will always behave in the best way in order to obtain what they desire. It makes the assumption that individuals make rational decisions based on their perception of the situation, but it does not assume that people have accurate or complete information when they make those decisions. People often stop considering alternative behaviors when they find one that is at least moderately satisfying, even though more rewarding behaviors remain to be examined (Simon, 1957). Search behavior is time consuming and itself takes effort; thus, it is not surprising that people limit their explorations. People are also limited in the amount of information they can handle at one time, and the outcomes associated with many behaviors are multitudinous; therefore, people often do not consider all the outcomes that might result from a certain behavior. Finally, as we will discuss below, people see the world in terms of their past experience. This leads them to misperceive the world on many occasions.

PEOPLE PERCEIVE THEIR ENVIRONMENT IN TERMS OF THEIR PAST EXPERIENCES AND NEEDS

The expectancy model, like most approaches to understanding behavior, assumes that people behave according to their perceptions of the world. It indicates that perceptions lead to beliefs about what performance is possible and what outcomes will follow performance.

Perceiving the environment is an *active* process in which people try to make sense out of their environment. This active process involves individuals selectively noticing different aspects of the environment, appraising what they see in terms of their past experience, and evaluating what they are experiencing in light of their needs and values. Since people's needs and experiences often differ markedly, their perceptions of the environment do likewise. For example, people in the same organization often develop very different expectancies of what kinds of behavior lead to rewards like pay increases and promotions.

Environments provide their members with many more objects and events than an individual is cognitively able to handle. Therefore, in perceiving an organization at any given time, individuals do not notice many aspects of the environment. What aspects of the environment are noticed and processed depends in part on the nature of the objects and events themselves and in part on the previous experience of the individual. Highly distinctive objects within the usual organizational context are more likely to be noticed than are those that do not stick out in some unusual way. The written memo on the bulletin board may not serve as a very distinctive input to organization members, but a meeting in the cafeteria with the company president which is an extremely rare occurrence may have high distinctiveness and will be attended by most employees. In addition to distinctiveness, the previous learning of organization members plays an important part in determining what is noticed. Organization members learn to discriminate between those things that they need to pay attention to in order to satisfy their needs and those that they may safely overlook.

Even when an event or object is noticed or attended to, there is no guarantee that it will be perceived accurately. The meaning that any given object or event has for an individual organization member is influenced by the needs of the member. Events and objects are often distorted so that they are more congruent with needs and values. The specific nature of the distortion of a particular event or object is difficult to predict; simply too many idiosyncratic factors are involved, both in the nature of the event or object and in the psychological and emotional makeup of the individual. However, the amount of distortion likely to occur is predictable; it is a function of the degree to which the situation involves important needs. Thus, organizational events around such things as pay and promotion are particularly likely to be misperceived.

It is precisely because people misperceive the world that their behavior sometimes appears to be irrational. In fact, they often have erroneous performance outcome beliefs and behave in what they think is a rational manner. Because of this phenomenon, many things that organizations do to motivate and control behavior fail, and indeed often lead to counterproductive behavior.

INDIVIDUALS HAVE AFFECTIVE REACTIONS

People are rarely neutral about things they perceive or experience. Instead, they tend to evaluate most things they experience by whether they like or dislike them. Moreover, this evaluative response is one of the most crucial factors in influencing future behavior because it establishes the importance and attractiveness of actions and outcomes. For instance, Mrs. Johnson's relatively positive experiences at work have led her to stay at the same job for twenty-nine years, while Mrs. Henson's unpleasant experience appears to be leading to her dismissal. Literally thousands of studies have been done on job satisfaction. Studies have focused on overall job satisfaction as well as on people's satisfaction with such specific aspects of the work environment as pay, promotion opportunities, the task to be performed, fringe benefits, personal relationships, security, and the leadership style of the supervisor.

Part of the reason for the original interest in job satisfaction was the widely held belief that job satisfaction was a major determinant of job performance. Research has not supported the view that job satisfaction causes job performance. Quite the contrary, recent research shows that when a relationship exists between satisfaction and performance, it is usually because performance influences the level of satisfaction (Lawler, 1973). This has by no means signaled an end to interest in studying job satisfaction for two quite different reasons. First, satisfaction has become an important topic of study in its own right because it is an indication of the quality of work life. Second, satisfaction has turned out to be a reasonably strong determinant of absenteeism, tardiness, and turnover. The more satisfied an employee, the less likely he or she is to be absent, late to work, and to resign from the organization (Porter and Steers, 1973). This seems to come about because satisfaction influences people's expectancies about the consequences of coming to work. Satisfied employees see more positive outcomes associated with going to work and, hence, are more likely to show up for work and to remain members of their organization (as in the case of Mrs. Johnson).

In general, it appears that satisfaction is determined by the difference between what a person receives and the amount that he or she feels *should* be received. The larger the discrepancy, the greater the dissatisfaction. Moreover, the amount a person feels *should* be received has been found to be strongly influenced by what others are perceived to be receiving. People seem to compare what they are putting into a work situation and what they feel they are getting out of it with what others receive in return for what they put into their work situation. If this comparison reveals that their outcomes are unfair when compared to those of others, then dissatisfaction will result. As would be expected, since this is an important area, individuals often misperceive the inputs and outcomes of other people as well as those of themselves, and end up being dissatisfied when perhaps they would not be if they perceived the situation accurately. In some instances, however, they misperceive in ways that make them satisfied when, in fact, they might not be if they correctly perceived the situation. Precisely because misperception is so common in important areas, it is difficult for organizations to distribute rewards such as pay and promotion in a way that satisfies the majority of people.

BEHAVIORS AND ATTITUDES ARE CAUSED BY MULTIPLE FACTORS

At the beginning of this chapter, we pointed out that behavior is a function of both the person and the environment. Now we are in a position to elaborate more fully on what characteristics need to be considered in order to understand and manage organizational behavior.

We have identified a number of factors that influence how motivated an individual is, and we have stressed that the capability to perform is an important influence on performance. Organizations can influence individual behavior by changing one or more of the crucial determinants of individual behavior. None of them is easy to change, but all are open to influence. Needs and certain capabilities are particularly hard to influence because they are often limited by physiological characteristics of individuals as well as by background and nonwork experiences that are beyond the capability of the organization to influence. Expectancies and certain learned capabilities, on the other hand, are often open to influence, since they emanate from the work environment. In fact, it is through its influence on these factors that the work environment can have a direct impact on individual behavior. Based on expectancy theory, we know that those parts of the environment that involve desirable outcomes are especially important, since they can directly affect motivation. Thus, it seems only logical that every manager should determine what these desirable outcomes are and then develop a plan that relates them to performance.

The environment can also influence behavior by placing constraints on the behavioral options an individual has available. For example, a broken machine could prevent Mrs. Johnson from achieving her production quota no matter how motivated she is. Similarly, walls may prevent employees from talking and forming groups, even though employees might enjoy the social companionship. One implication of this is that organizations need to pay a great deal of attention to the working environments they create, to be sure they do not block desirable employee behavior.

Because behavior is determined by many factors, it is often difficult for organizations to establish the conditions that lead to effective individual performance. The manager who is concerned about creating the right conditions for effective performance is in a position not unlike the football coach who is designing an offensive play. For the play to work, a great deal has to go right, and some luck is also required. Nevertheless, it is usually better to have a game plan that recognizes what the key factors are and tries to deal with them. The same can be said for the manager who wants effective performance.

Summary: Nature of Individuals

In this chapter, we have presented a view of individual behavior that can be described by the following statements:

1. People have only limited behavior capabilities; individuals differ greatly in their capabilities.
2. Individuals differ in what outcomes are attractive to them; the internal conditions that make outcomes important are called needs; it is possible to list them in a two-step hierarchy of higher- and lower-order needs.
3. People make conscious choices of how to behave, based on their needs and their perceptions of the environment, particularly on their perceptions of what kinds of behavior will lead to what kinds of outcomes. One way of predicting those choices is through the use of models like expectancy theory.
4. Given the perceptual basis of behavior, it is important to note that perceptions are susceptible to distortion by individuals.
5. Once people enact a piece of behavior and experience consequences of behavior, they have affective reactions to the event, the most common being satisfaction/dissatisfaction. These affective reactions have implications for subsequent sequences of behavior, since they affect both perceptions and needs.
6. Capabilities, expectancies, needs, past experience, and en-

Figure 2.3 *The Basic Motivation–Behavior Sequence*

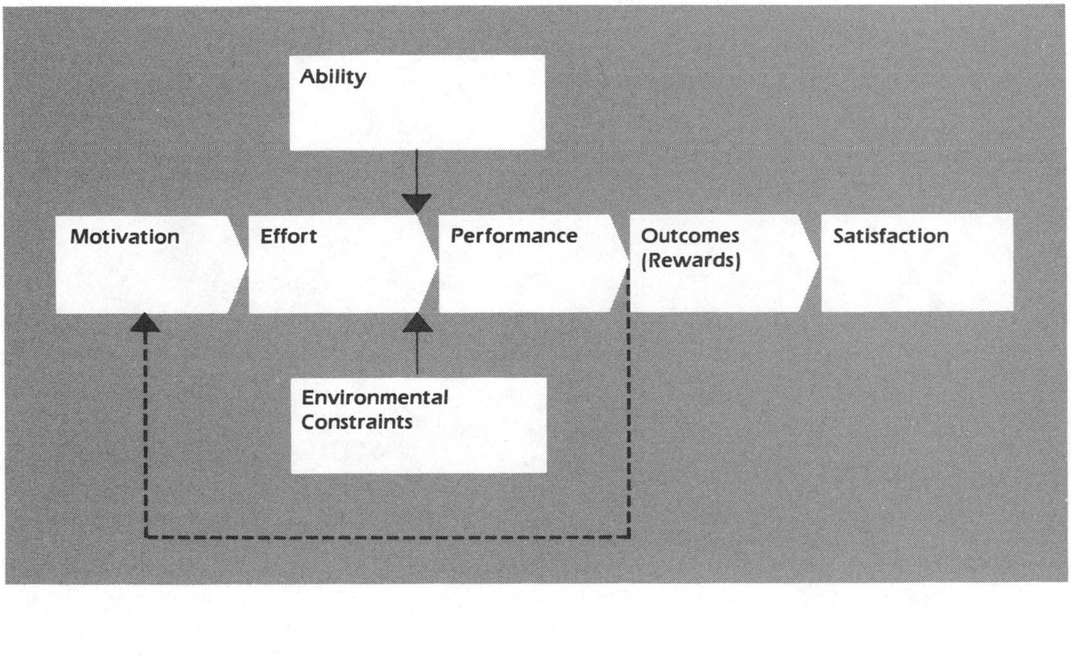

vironmental contraints are all important influences on behavior.

Figure 2.3 presents a general model of behavior in organizational settings that follows the concepts presented so far. Working from left to right in the model, motivation can be seen as the force on the individual that encourages that person to perform in a certain manner. Thus, motivation leads to a level of effort by the individual. Effort alone, however, is not enough. Performance results from a combination of the effort that an individual puts forth, the level of capability of the individual (reflecting skills and training), and constraints in the situation (broken machinery, behavior of others, and so on). As a result of performance, the individual attains certain outcomes that lead to satisfaction. As this process of performance-reward occurs, time after time, the actual events serve to provide information that influences the individual's perceptions and thus influences motivation in the future. This is particularly true in the case of the individual's expectancies; they are strongly influenced by the past relationships individuals have encountered between their performance and outcomes (see the dashed line in Figure 2.3).

Suggested Readings

Korman, A. K. *The Psychology of Motivation.* Englewood Cliffs, N.J.: Prentice-Hall, 1974.

Lawler, E. E. *Motivation in Work Organizations.* Monterey, Cal.: Brooks/Cole, 1973.

Steers, R., and Porter, L. W. *Motivation and Work Behavior.* 2nd ed. New York: McGraw-Hill, 1979.

Terkel, S. *Working.* New York: Pantheon, 1974.

Chapter **3**

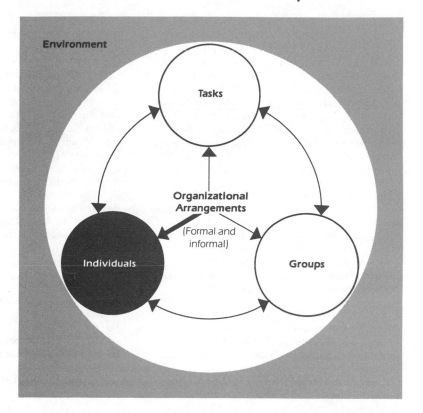

Staffing
Organizations

In 1972, when John D. deButts became the chief executive officer of the American Telephone and Telegraph Company, he took a job that by most standards is considered to be the largest managerial job in the world of business. The work force of AT&T numbers almost one million employees (it is larger than the U.S. Army), and it has $80 billion in assets. How does someone come to head a corporation the size of AT&T? Although it often looks like a haphazard process, in many cases it is the result of careful planning on the part of the individual and the organization. It took Mr. deButts thirty-six years and twenty-two jobs to reach the top. He joined AT&T straight out of college and quickly began to move up. He was transferred from one functional area to another so that he would become broadly familiar with the business. He eagerly sought out such transfers, realizing that the "only" way to get to the top was to have a broad range of knowledge. For its part, AT&T, which is committed to promotion from within, constantly assessed the performance of Mr. deButts and asked his bosses to report on his promotability.

Like many successful executives, deButts gained a considerable amount of visibility in his corporation, when he played a key role in helping AT&T successfully respond to a corporate crisis. In 1949, he wrote a carefully reasoned statement which argued that AT&T should remain highly integrated. The arguments in this paper were used by AT&T as the basis for a successful defense in a Justice Department antitrust suit.

During most of his career at AT&T, the desire of Mr. deButts for an executive position and the needs of AT&T for well-trained top managers seemed to mesh well. Although no formal joint career planning took place between deButts and the members of top management, he developed several sponsors in top management who saw to it that he made the appropriate moves. However, one day in 1958, deButts got what he described as "the shock of my life." He was offered the position of general manager of New York Telephone's Westchester office. This represented a demotion, and he could not understand why he was being punished. He called a number of friends in top mangement to find out what was going on. He was told to take the job even though he did not want to. He did so, and years later learned that the move was brought about by the president of AT&T who wanted to test deButts's suitability for the top job. He passed this test with flying colors and years later the experience paid off with the presidency of the company.[1]

[1] Based on an article by A. M. Louis, *Fortune*, 94:6 (December 1976), pp. 122–136.

FEW INDIVIDUALS aspire to careers like that of John deButts, and even fewer achieve them, but most individuals have career aspirations of some kind. In this chapter, we will be concerned with the fit or misfit between these career aspirations and the wide variety of jobs and tasks that exists in organizations.

Staffing Decisions in Organizations

Staffing decisions are one of the most important types of decisions managers make. Some managers consider them the most important decisions because they so directly impact on how effectively work is done and often they represent an extremely large investment of organization resources that continues for years. It has been estimated that it often costs organizations the equivalent of one year's salary just to replace a middle-level manager.

As we stressed in Chapter 2, effective performance depends on finding and hiring individuals who have the capability and the motivation to perform effectively. The desired situation for most managers is easy to identify. Every job they supervise would be filled by an individual who has the skills to perform the job and who is motivated to perform it. In addition, capable replacements would be available should they lose anyone.

Organizations spend a great deal of effort on such things as training and selection programs in order to insure that jobs will be filled by people who are willing and able to perform them. Despite this, managers often find themselves having relatively untrained, poorly motivated individuals reporting to them, and as would be predicted by our model of individual performance, the result is poor performance.

Filling jobs with the right individuals is a dynamic process, extremely complex and difficult to manage. Although the individual manager can affect this process, his or her influence is limited because the process is also influenced by the personnel department, other managers, and labor market conditions, to mention just a few. Adequate staffing requires finding a good fit between two changing factors — the characteristics of jobs and the characteristics of employees. It would be hard enough to correctly staff organizations if people and jobs would just hold still; however, this is not the case. People's career aspirations and capabilities change as a result of things that happen to them at work and as a result of nonwork related events (for example, aging and family changes). The kinds of jobs that organizations need to have performed are also constantly changing as a result of a number of factors (such as the changing environment). Effective staffing, therefore, must deal with changes that create misfits in the way an organization is staffed. Some of these misfits are predictable because they result from planned events such as retirement, but many others are not, since they result from such unplanned events as accidents, sickness, and employee resignations.

The staffing problem can be brought into focus for the reader if he or she thinks of a football team or a symphony orchestra, since these are relatively small organizations with clearly identifiable roles. From the manager's point of view, our performance model indicates that the perfect situation would be one in which motivation was high and every position was filled by the best qualified player in the world. Somehow this never quite happens.

First, there is the problem of attracting the best players. Not all of them want to work for the same organization and, as a result, the pool of individuals applying for work in the organization is likely to be less than ideal. Secondly, there is the problem of selecting the applicants who will develop into the best players. Sometimes, the wrong decisions are made despite a careful analysis of the applicants. In football, for example, players who are not drafted or who are released by teams occasionally end up as stars (such as Johnny Unitas of the Baltimore Colts). Finally, there is the problem of developing the individual players so that when a job opening appears (either because of personnel changes or because a new job has been created), someone will be available to fill it (such as John deButts at AT&T). All too often organizations simply do not have the individuals available to fill jobs when they open up. The reasons for this include their failure to develop individuals as well as the fact that individuals cannot be put on the shelf and stored until they are needed by the organization. People have their own personal goals and objectives, as the example of Mr. deButts illustrates.

Despite the fact that staffing is a difficult and complex area, clearly some things can be done to see that it is managed well. Three stages of the staffing task have been identified: attraction and selection, initial entry, and long-term career development. Each of these stages require different behavior on the part of managers if staffing is to be managed effectively. In the remainder of this chapter, we will consider each of these stages separately. Although the three stages of an individual's involvement will be looked at separately, it is important for the reader to remember that they are not independent stages. The early stages, which will be considered first, impact on what happens later in very important ways, because both people and organizations are affected by their past experiences.

Managing the Attraction and Selection Process

How the attraction-selection process is handled by a manager can have a large impact on whether the right people are hired. The key to making it go well is the open exchange of accurate information between the job candidate and the manager. Without accurate information, neither the individual nor the manager can make a good selection decision.

In many ways, the manager has the most options during the

attraction-selection process, since he or she does not yet have commitments to the individuals involved. Most managers are aware of this and, as a result, spend a considerable amount of effort trying to attract good job applicants and to determine who should be hired. Unfortunately, the research evidence suggests that frequently managers do a poor job and end up with people who do not fit the jobs they are in (Schneider, 1976). The reasons for this are many and complex, but they stem from the stance that applicants and managers assume in such a situation. A brief review of these reasons is needed to clarify how the process should be managed and to explain why the open exchange of accurate information is difficult during this process.

PERSPECTIVE OF INDIVIDUALS

As we stressed in Chapter 2, individuals seek a work setting where they can fulfill their needs and find satisfaction. They do this by gathering information about a number of organizations and then, as would be predicted by expectancy theory, attempting to join those that they perceive as offering the most desirable balance of outcomes. They gather information about organizations from a number of sources (such as advertisements and through friends) and usually end up with an incomplete and partially inaccurate picture of what particular organizations and jobs are like. As a consequence, they may or may not end up deciding to apply for the job that best fits them. Once they have decided which job or jobs to apply for, individuals then try to make themselves attractive to those organizations and, in most cases, they continue to try to gather information about the organization. In order to appear attractive, they may behave and dress in a certain way during an interview, prepare a resumé in a certain way, or engage in any number of other activities that prevent the organization from getting accurate information.

The two goals that the individual is trying to accomplish in the selection situation — attracting the organization and evaluating the organization as a place to work — may at times come into conflict. The job applicant could do a number of things that might make him or her more attractive to the organization, but that would make it difficult to find out about what it would be like to work for the organization (for example, presenting his or her values as in line with those of the organization). Similarly, there are many things the individual might do that would provide valuable information about the organization but would decrease his or her attractiveness to it (for example, asking in an interview detailed questions concerning how much various managers are paid). Thus, the individual often finds the selection process a conflicting one.

PERSPECTIVE OF THE MANAGER

From the manager's point of view, the attraction and selection process is a matter of both gathering the information that is needed for making selection decisions and attracting the kind of applicants who can and will do the job. Selection can never be very effective unless a relatively large pool of good applicants tries to obtain a job and those people who are offered jobs actually accept them. This often leads to the managerial strategy of presenting the job in the most favorable way. Many managers have their organizations spend large amounts of money on recruitment to attract the kind of people they want to hire. This attraction process is, of course, not independent of the selection process, since what goes on during selection influences the attractiveness of the organization. For example, there is evidence that the way in which the selection interview is conducted directly influences the probability that a person will take a job.

Because the selection process does influence the attractiveness of working for organizations, managers are faced with a difficult dilemma when considering which selection procedures to use. They need to design a system that attracts the right applicants and provides all the information that the organization needs to make intelligent selection decisions. Many approaches that are helpful in attracting people have questionable validity from a selection point of view, since they fail to distinguish the applicants who will perform the job effectively from those who will not (for example, wide-ranging, informal interviews). Further, some devices that produce good selection information can negatively affect the applicant's view of the organization. Certain kinds of psychological tests are good examples here. Sometimes they are valid, yet they often make the organization less attractive to the applicant.

INDIVIDUAL–ORGANIZATION CONFLICTS

Because of the different objectives applicants and managers have in the attraction-selection situation, four separate processes are taking place: applicants attracting, applicants selecting, managers attracting, and managers selecting. The conflict arrow in Figure 3.1, between applicants attracting and applicants selecting, illustrates that the two objectives individuals often try to accomplish (that is, selection and attraction) are in conflict. The arrow between organizations selecting and attracting illustrates that the same is true for the objectives of managers. These are not the only conflicts that occur in the selection-attraction situation, however. In fact, they may be less important than the two conflicts between the goals of the applicant and those of the manager.

As shown in Figure 3.1, the applicant's desire to attract the organization and the manager's desire to select among applicants are often in direct conflict. To make good selection decisions, managers need valid and complete information about applicants. This often comes into conflict with the desire of the applicants to make a favorable impression. How applicants and managers cope with this conflict strongly affects the selection process. The same point can be made about the conflict between

Figure 3.1 *The Attraction–Selection Situation*

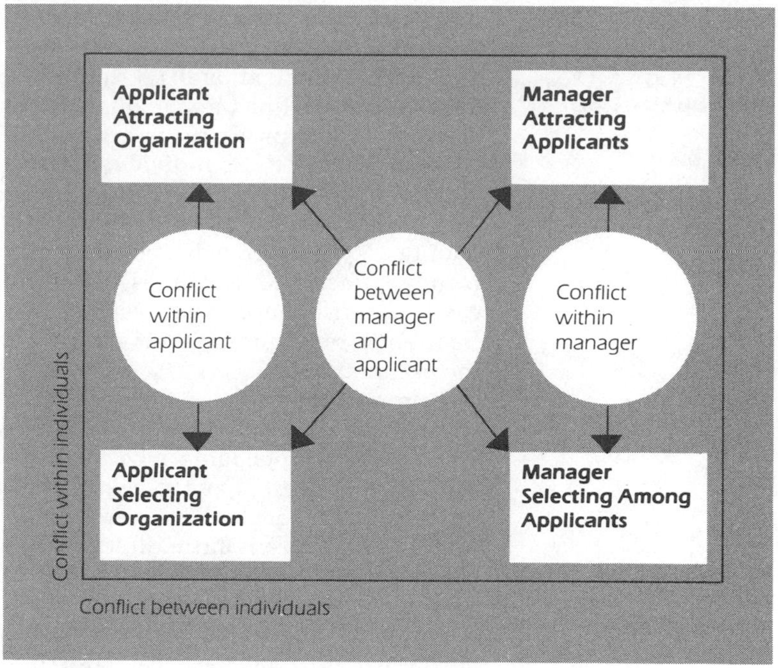

Adapted from Porter, Lawler, and Hackman, 1975.

an applicant's desire to choose the best job and a manager's desire to attract the best applicants. Applicants need complete, valid information about organizations and jobs in order to evaluate them; and managers feel that if they give out negative information about their organization, the jobs they need to fill may become less attractive to the applicants they would like to hire. Thus, whenever a manager attempts to attract an individual and the individual considers whether to join the organization, conflict may be present. This conflict may have a negative impact on the selection process because it will limit the open exchange of information.

Given the conflicts present in the attraction-selection process, is there anything managers can do to effectively manage the process? A considerable body of research evidence suggests that there is (Wanous, 1977a). Although some inherent conflicts occur in the process, the goals of the applicant and the manager are complementary in many ways. It is to everyone's advantage for employees to be effective in and satisfied with their jobs. Further, when managers correctly manage the attraction and selection processes, they can significantly increase their chances of obtaining employees who are effective and satisfied. Let us, therefore, turn to a consideration of what managers can do to make the attraction and selection process effective.

The ideal organizational recruitment program draws in large numbers of qualified applicants who will take the job if offered it and will remain with the organization. At the same time, it does not attract those individuals who cannot do the job or will not be happy doing it. Attracting qualified individuals who become dissatisfied and leave the job is dysfunctional from the manager's point of view because this kind of turnover costs money, time, and resources. Attracting unqualified people is costly because they have to be processed and ultimately rejected, frequently resulting in their forming a negative impression of the organization.

Organizations do a number of things to attract job applicants — advertise, visit schools, provide bonuses to current employees for recruiting applicants who are subsequently hired, and the like. Most of these approaches to recruiting are directed toward impressing on people the rewards associated with holding a particular job. There is little direct evidence that this approach is effective in attracting individuals, although as we discussed in Chapter 2, it should be if it leads to the expectancy that valued rewards are associated with working for the organization. People do seem to apply for and choose those jobs that they feel offer the best mix of rewards.

Evidence indicates that overemphasizing the positive aspects of prospective jobs to applicants can contribute to subsequent problems. It attracts the wrong individuals and creates unrealistic expectations on the part of those who take the jobs, thereby setting the stage for dissatisfaction and quick or early turnover. For example, when compared with job applicants who are given an unrealistic job preview, those who receive a realistic one show higher job satisfaction scores and lower turnover rates after they are on the job (Wanous, 1977a). This suggests that attraction approaches which are based on creating an unrealistic set of expectations are functional for neither the individual nor the manager. What is needed is an attraction process based on the open exchange of accurate information between the applicant and the manager. The most important thing here is a realistic assessment of the job to be filled. Information needs to be provided to applicants on what capabilities the job requires as well as on what satisfactions and dissatisfactions the job provides, so the applicants have a realistic picture.

Information on what the manager expects of people and what kind of management style he or she uses can also be very helpful. One way of providing this information is through a combination of an interview with the manager and separate interviews with people who work for the manager (Gomersall and Myers, 1966). This approach may drive away a few applicants, but in the long run both the manager and the applicant should be better off.

HOW ORGANIZATIONS SELECT INDIVIDUALS

A large number of instruments and approaches are used by organizations to help them decide whom to hire. The most commonly used devices are interviews, psychological tests, and application blanks. Less commonly used are such devices as graphology and tests that simulate the job. The value of all these devices rests on their ability to predict job performance; that is, their validity. Considerable research has been done on just how valid these selection devices are (see Guion, 1965; Dunnette, 1966). The evidence shows that in most situations, no approach leads to highly accurate predictions (Ghiselli, 1966). One reason for this is that it is hard to assess in advance just how motivated individuals will be to perform the job once they take it. In addition, the available measures of capability are not perfect, and the requirements of jobs often change so that a previously valid measure may become invalid.

The interview is probably the most frequently used and misused selection device (Campbell et al., 1970). Almost every employee who is hired by an organization today is given some type of interview. The nature of these interviews varies widely, as does their validity. Psychologists have generally looked on the selection interview with considerable mistrust:

> The personnel interview continues to be the most widely used method for selecting employees, despite the fact that it is a costly, inefficient, and usually invalid procedure. (Dunnette and Bass, 1963)

Despite its problems, managers tend to have a great deal of faith in their ability to make decisions based on interview data. Managers should constantly be aware of the potential invalidity of the interview and, in most cases, use professionally validated approaches when they make selection decisions. This means working with the personnel department to determine what selection devices to use and relying on their expertise to a significant degree.

Unfortunately, there are no simple answers to questions concerning which devices should be used in a particular situation. Different sets of devices usually turn out to be valid in different instances. For example, a valid approach in selecting a salesperson might involve a psychological test, a structured interview with the sales manager, and an extensive written application blank, validated by reference checks. On the other hand, a skilled machinist often is best selected by a well-developed technical skills test. A number of highly technical problems are involved in determining just how valid a selection device is, and the help of a trained professional is needed when selection approaches are being designed. A manager's failure to obtain professional help in designing a selection approach can result in the use of invalid selection devices that are, at best, a waste of time and, at worst, discriminatory and illegal.

Effective management of the selection process can contribute to increases in organizational effectiveness; however, the increases are not easy to obtain, since they require the exchange of valid information. The many conflicts present make it difficult to foster the exchange of accurate data. In many cases, the most effective things a particular manager can do is to be sure that the applicant has a realistic job preview and that the selection process has been validated by a professional.

Entry and Initial Socialization

Once the applicant has taken a job, the complex and often difficult initial adaptation period begins. The new employee and the manager must learn to adjust to each other. The nature of this relationship has been characterized as a sort of "psychological contract" (Levinson et al., 1962). This term means "a series of mutual expectations of which the parties to the relationship may not themselves be even dimly aware but which nonetheless govern their relationship to each other." In some instances the "marriage" settles down into an easy, comfortable relationship. In others, there is an abrupt separation that leaves scars with both parties. In between these two extremes are the majority of cases of individual-organization adaptation: flexible accommodations that result in a never-ending series of compromises — the individual never completely obtaining all he or she wants from the organization, and the manager never obtaining the performance wanted from the individual.

Available evidence is nearly unanimous in indicating that the very early employment period — the first year or even the first few months — is crucial to the development of a healthy individual-organizational relationship (Hall, 1976). One indication of the stressful nature of the early employment period is the relatively high rate (compared to later time periods) of avoidable employee turnover that occurs during it. Studies of college graduates have found that as many as half change jobs within three years of graduation, and that within five years over three-quarters do (Schein, 1978). This indicates that the individual-organization adaptation process breaks down in a relatively high percentage of cases, with consequent costs to both parties.

The key to understanding individual-organization adaptation and contracting lies in the recognition that it is two-way. The individual gives up a certain amount of freedom of action in joining an organization. As part of the psychological contract, he or she implicitly agrees that management will have some legitimate demands it can make (for example, requiring a certain number of work hours per week). The organization and its management actively aids and abets the shaping of the individual's behavior to its needs. This influence process is labeled *socialization*. It is as if the organization is "putting its fingerprints on people" (Schein, 1978). Simultaneously, however, a second process is occurring. The new employee is attempting to exert influence on the organization and his or her manager in order to create a work situation that will provide personal satisfaction. This personalization process can at times come into conflict with the socialization attempts of the organization.

How a manager handles the socialization experience of individuals can have a strong impact on the satisfaction of the relationships between the individual and the organization. A poorly managed process can lead to premature turnover or a psychological contract that involves doing only the minimal amount of work necessary. In the latter case, change can be particularly hard to produce because it involves unlearning an old contract as well as learning a new one. With this in mind, let us turn to a consideration of what methods can be used to promote effective socialization.

METHODS OF PROMOTING SOCIALIZATION

All managers — whether they are in work organizations, religious orders, or prisons — have available a variety of possible means to promote the socialization of new and continuing members. Some methods (such as hazing) are not feasible for managers in most work organizations, but a number of socialization methods can be used. These include designing the selection process to acquaint the individual with the work environment, training experiences, initial job assignments, and the apprenticeship model in which new workers are assigned to older ones. All these approaches can contribute to a positive socialization experience, if they communicate realistic expectations and provide individuals with a positive work experience.

We have already discussed the key roles the selection process and managerial behavior during it can play. Now we will consider what a manager can do to create the right kind of immediate work environment during the early employment period. Three elements of this environment — the job content, the supervisor, and the work group — are critical (Feldman, 1976).

Job Content. Several studies have shown that it is very desirable for managers to give new employees challenging work assignments on which they can experience success (Hall, 1976). One study found that new employees who were fortunate enough to be given relatively demanding jobs in their early organizational careers seemed to be better prepared to perform with greater success on later job assignments. Apparently, an entering employee who is given initially challenging job duties tends to internalize high performance standards and positive expectancies about the rewards that performing effectively can bring (see Chapter 5 for further discussion). On the other hand, an entrant who is placed on a relatively easy first job does not have a chance to experience success (since he or she does not get much credit from anyone for doing such jobs well) and the motivation it produces.

Role of the Supervisor. In many ways, the supervisor *is* the organization to the new employee. If he or she does a good job of performing key tasks, the organization is usually viewed favorably. If a supervisor is ineffective in working with the newcomer, the organization itself is seen negatively. Supervisors need to do three primary tasks well (in addition to assigning the right kind of work) to be effective in dealing with new employees. First, they need to provide the employee with a clear description of the job to be done. Second, they need to be a source of technical information about how to perform the job. Finally, they need to provide the employee with feedback about how well that person is performing (see Chapter 4 for further discussion).

Selecting Supervisors for New Employees. One thing higher level managers can do to see that new members are well supervised is to carefully select the supervisors. In selecting supervisors, it is important to look for individuals who can perform the three primary tasks, but this is not enough. Supervisors must have a high degree of personal security so they will not feel threatened by either the failure or the marked success of new employees.

Often it is difficult to make desirable supervisory assignments for new employees because of other factors. Thus, many entrants are placed with supervisors not able to handle the newcomers' problems. In that case, management must rely on training to heighten the supervisors' awareness of the difficult problems they will face and to provide them with the interpersonal and technical skills they need. An interesting and novel approach to the training of supervisors who themselves are new to a particular job — and who will have to deal with both new and experienced employees — was tried in one manufacturing company (Gomersall and Myers, 1966). In this case, the experienced operators trained the supervisors! This was accomplished by having pairs of operators instruct a new supervisor on such matters as the problems usually faced by the new supervisor and the way the job is viewed by the operators. This approach suggests that recently hired employees who have just gone through the critical entry period may be able to assist in training supervisors to handle new employees.

Work Group. The work group can play a very powerful role in the socialization of new employees. Acceptance by the work group is a key source of social need satisfaction, and as will be discussed in Section III of this book, groups have a powerful influence on the beliefs and attitudes of individuals about what the organization is like and how they should behave. Because the work group is so important, it is crucial that managers assign new employees to work groups that will have a positive impact.

SUMMARY: ENTRY AND SOCIALIZATION

The initial experiences an individual has with an organization seem to be particularly important in shaping the long-term relationship between the individual and the organization. When the organization provides realistic information, challenging work, an effective supervisor, and a supportive work group, the result is a long-term, positive relationship between the individual and the organization. When they fail to provide them, the result is either turnover or a poor individual-organization relationship.

Careers in Organizations

So far in this chapter, we have dealt with how the management of the selection and initial entry period affects organizational behavior. Now we would like to consider how the development of individuals can be managed in ways that will assure that an individual has a rewarding career in the organization and that the organization has the individuals it needs to function in the long term.

Staffing an organization adequately is not simply a matter of having all jobs filled by people who are capable of doing them competently and who are motivated to perform them effectively. The environment in which organizations exist is always changing, and as a result, the skills that are needed to carry out a job one day may not be the right skills another day. In addition, most organizations have life spans that exceed the career of any individual; thus, trained successors, like John deButts, must be available to fill in when jobholders retire, change organizations, or are promoted.

People can be developed through various kinds of training and other experiences. However, people are a unique resource and often prove difficult to develop, maintain, or utilize. They have their own career objectives, which may or may not fit the organization's short- and long-range plans. In the case of John deButts, it looked, at one point, as if a conflict between the organization's plans for him and his personal aspirations might cause him to resign. Finally, efforts to develop individuals may fail because the people are incapable of developing in a given way, the development is poorly planned or administered, or the people do not wish to develop in the way they are asked to.

What can a manager do to ensure that his or her organization's developmental efforts will be successful? Two things can help. First, they can be sure that efforts affecting their subordinates follow the research findings on what makes for a successful training program, and second, they can support the development of a formal career planning and development program in the organization.

TRAINING INDIVIDUALS   If training programs are to promote better performance, they must influence the employee's motivation or the employee's capability to perform the job. Influencing capability, and then performance, is a matter of identifying the changes that are needed and of picking the correct training experience for the individual who is to be trained. The first step requires determining what is to be taught. Managers need to spend considerable time before training starts, analyzing jobs and tasks and looking at behaviors that lead to successful performance of their subordinates' jobs. Unfortunately, this step is not taken by most managers; consequently, training programs often miss their mark (see Campbell et al., 1970).

Once it has been determined what kind of behavior is desired, managers are in a position to assess the individual who is to be trained. Important questions should be asked about the individual. First, is the training needed? To answer this question, managers must know whether the individual does in fact fail to behave in ways that he or she should if the job is to be performed effectively. There are a number of sources of information about this, including the results of formal performance appraisals (see Chapter 4).

If it is determined that the individual needs to learn a new behavior, a second issue arises: Does the individual have the necessary aptitude to learn the new behavior? Frequently, managers can get help in answering this question by checking with the personnel department, which often has ability tests on file for employees. If it doesn't, the personnel department is usually willing to give these tests.

Unless the individual who is to be trained and developed is motivated to learn the new behavior, it is not likely to be learned. This raises the third question that must be considered: Is the individual motivated to learn the behavior? One way to answer this question is by allowing the individual the chance to decide whether or not to go through the training experience. As we will discuss later, giving the individual a choice can be particularly effective if it is part of a systematic effort to involve individuals in planning their careers.

Next, the manager needs to consider how to teach the new behavior. Here again help from the personnel department is in order, since there are usually numerous ways to learn a new behavior or skill. Literally thousands of different management training programs are offered each year in the United States. Often, someone in the personnel department is familiar with the strengths and weaknesses of a number of training approaches and programs and can help identify a suitable one. Larger organizations frequently offer programs of their own, which are adequate for many training needs.

Once the training itself is completed, an important period begins, during which the trainee's supervisor plays a critical role. The supervisor must reward and support the behavior that was learned. If this does not happen, the learned behavior is likely to be quickly dropped (Campbell et al., 1970).

CAREER PLANNING

Career development is a function of a long series of job and training experiences. These experiences are cumulative and influence each other. Since each person has a unique set of background experiences, the same program is likely to impact on people in different ways. Furthermore, a person can make a number of moves in most organizations (John deButts held twenty-two different jobs), and receive many different kinds of training. However, people have only limited amounts of time in their work life; the number of moves they can make is limited as is the number of training programs they can attend.

The career of John deButts presents an interesting example of how an individual is prepared for top management by an organization. Like most managers who make it to the top, he had some powerful sponsors who "looked after him," and he was fortunate enough to have had some jobs that led to higher level managers noticing him. Careful career management is necessary if organizations are to develop individuals. Organizations must look at employees as individuals and systematically develop them in line with their needs for talent. Similarly, managers should consider their subordinates' personal goals and be constantly aware of their development. To help ensure that this happens, many organizations hold managers responsible for reporting each year on the development work they have done with their subordinates.

Organizations often see their development activities as a one-way process — as something they do to the person. This can result in organizations developing people for jobs that individuals do not see as congruent with their career goals. It also causes a great deal of miscommunication. It is not uncommon to find employees who have no idea why they are being transferred to a new job, while the organization views the move as a part of their development for top management. The opposite also occurs frequently. Moves that the organization sees as having no significance are seen by the individual as indicating that he or she has been picked for further advancement. Although, in the short run, this type of misconception may not be dysfunctional, in the long run it can be. The answer to these problems is for managers to make career planning a more open, two-way process in which the individual is actively involved in his or her own career development.

One specific thing that many organizations are doing to help career development be more public and participatory is to publicly post all job openings. This gives individuals the chance to demonstrate their desires for a different job. Some organizations also offer their employees the chance to go through assessment centers in which the employees are given feedback about their capabilities and chances to develop into effective managers.

SUMMARY: CAREERS IN ORGANIZATIONS

Individual development is a vital part of the staffing process in all organizations. Managers can do a number of things to ensure that it is effective. These include being sure that training sessions stress the correct behavior, are given to individuals who can profit from them, and are supported when the individual returns to work. In addition, managers can treat the development of individuals as a two-way communication exchange that is tied to the growth of individuals and is planned on a long-term basis.

Summary: Managing Staffing

What should managers do about staffing the jobs that report to them? Table 3.1 answers this question by summarizing the points made in this chapter. It shows some specific things that managers can do in order to see that the jobs which report to them are correctly staffed. When new employees are to be hired, they need to be sure that valid selection procedures are used. When new employees start work, managers must play a role in aiding the entry process and the initial socialization of new sub-

Table 3.1 *Critical Management Issues in Staffing*

Attraction/selection	Initial entry	Career development
1. Assessment of job to be filled	1. Assign to a task that allows for challenge and success	1. Developing individuals a. identify needed behaviors b. evaluate individual c. design training d. support new behavior
2. Realistic information to applicant	2. Feedback to employee to clarify role and performance expectations	
3. With professional help, gather accurate data about the applicant	3. Assign to a work group that will be accepting and will communicate positive attitudes and beliefs	2. Career planning a. develop systematic plans b. make it an open two-way process

ordinates. Finally, managers should pay continued attention to the career development needs of their subordinates, to be sure that they are receiving the training and development they need and desire.

Suggested Readings

Dunnette, M. D. *Personnel Selection and Placement.* Belmont, Cal.: Wadsworth, 1966.

Hall, D. T. *Careers in Organizations.* Pacific Palisades, Cal.: Goodyear, 1976.

Schein, E. *Career Dynamics.* Reading, Mass.: Addison-Wesley, 1978.

Schneider, B. *Staffing Organizations.* Pacific Palisades, Cal.: Goodyear, 1976.

Chapter **4**

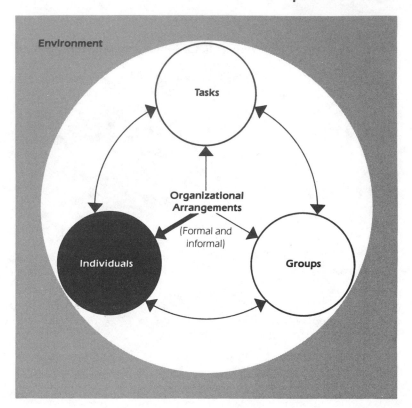

Measuring and
Rewarding
Performance

A little over a year ago, Ted Steele went to work in a research and development lab immediately after he completed his master's degree in physics. He negotiated what he considered to be a fair salary and was told that he would be eligible for a merit salary increase every year. He recently received his monthly paycheck and noticed that it was larger than his previous twelve checks had been. A quick calculation indicated that he apparently had received a 9 percent pay increase. Ted was delighted but also a little bit confused. What had happened, he wondered. Was it a merit increase? Was it because he had been performing his job well? Perhaps it was just a computer error.

For the next couple of weeks, Ted spent a considerable amount of time wondering what, if anything, he should do about his increase. Different thoughts occurred to him. If he asked about it and it had been an error, maybe it would be taken away. Ed and Fritz joined the organization at the same time; what did they receive? How did his boss feel he was doing so far?

Finally, Ted decided to do something which for him was risky and quite different. He asked Ed and Fritz if they had received a raise. Both seemed relieved and readily confided in him that they had received smaller ones. In some ways this information just piqued Ted's curiosity more. He thought Ed and Fritz were performing about as well as he was; why didn't they get the same raise? Finally, he decided he simply had to raise the issue with his boss, Chris Taylor. He had to know what Chris thought of his work and if, in fact, his pay increase indicated that the company did reward merit.

Chris greeted Ted warmly and then asked Ted why he had come to talk to him; an awkward silence followed. Suddenly Ted felt very nervous, but eventually managed to say that he wanted to talk about his pay raise. Chris looked surprised, paused for a moment, and then said, "Oh yes, I have been meaning to talk to you about that. I recommended you for a merit increase a few months ago. By now I imagine you have received it." As comforted as Ted was to find out that it was not a clerical error, he still was not satisfied. He pressed on, "You say it is a merit increase. Does that mean I am performing satisfactorily?" Chris responded, with a hint of irritation in his voice, "I thought you knew that we are pleased with your work so far. We talked about that several months ago when I reviewed your performance." Ted was not sure what Chris was talking about, since he did not remember any performance review, unless Chris was referring to the discussion they had by the water cooler on how he had done on developing the new fuel metering device.

Before Ted could ask him another question, Chris asked Ted how things were going on one of his projects. A thirty-minute technical discussion followed. Finally, Ted decided to make one last try at getting some information about the company's pay plan. He asked Chris what pay raises he might expect in the future if he continued to perform well. Chris looked startled by the question. Then he gave a long rambling answer in which he stressed the complexities of the pay system, that there were no guarantees, and that although merit is important, "other things must be considered." Ted left Chris's office thinking he probably never should have raised the pay issue, still wondering what he had done to earn a merit pay raise, and resigned to the fact that he probably never would know.

THE PERFORMANCE appraisal and reward systems in organizations can be effective tools for managing organizational behavior because they distribute rewards that are important to people (such as increases in pay and promotions). When managed properly, they can play an important role in motivating employees to perform well, for they can directly impact on the people's expectancies about the consequences of performing effectively. They can also motivate people to develop their capabilities by providing feedback and by rewarding skill development. In addition, they can play a key role in attracting and retaining competent employees because they determine the rewards people receive and thus influence how satisfied people are with their jobs. The mere existence of a formal performance appraisal system and a merit pay plan, however, by no means guarantees that positive results will be obtained. In fact, as the example of Ted points out, sometimes such plans can do as much or even more harm than good. In this chapter, we will focus on the issue of how performance appraisal and the distribution of rewards can be effectively managed.

Measuring Performance

In a real sense, the performance of everyone in an organization is constantly being appraised — by the individual as well as by superiors, peers, and subordinates. Evaluation is an inevitable consequence of the way organizations are structured and the always-present tendency of individuals to judge each other. Making individuals responsible for the performance of tasks makes the assessment of how an individual performs both possible and necessary. It makes it possible because it identifies the results for which the person is responsible; it makes it necessary because organizations need information on how well jobs are being done if they are to be controlled and directed effectively.

Much of the evaluation that takes place in organizations is informal, but some of it is part of the formal performance evaluation systems that most organizations have. In this chapter, we are going to focus on the use of formal performance evaluation systems for motivating performance and for human resources management. When managed properly, performance evaluations can influence the motivation and behavior of individuals.

When rewards like pay are tied to performance, they can motivate performance. The first step in tying pay to performance is the measurement of performance. As was pointed out in Chapter 3, organizations need to do more than motivate employees to perform well; they need to plan and program the development of their human resources. Without adequate information on the capabilities and performance of employees, this is impossible to do. It is also impossible to counsel employees on career development in such a way as to fit in with the plans of the organization.

Because the performance motivation and human resources management functions of performance appraisal are so important, it is not surprising that most organizations have formal appraisal programs. However, study after study has pointed out that, as was true in the case of Ted, the process is done poorly in most organizations (Campbell et al., 1970). Neither the organization nor the individual tends to be satisfied with it. First, we will consider what the major problems are, and then discuss some things that managers can do to improve the process.

PROBLEMS IN PERFORMANCE APPRAISAL

Conflicts in the Appraisal. Because the major functions of performance appraisal are in conflict with each other, it is difficult to do effective performance appraisals. Appraisal for performance motivation needs to focus on objective evaluation of the employee in relation to other employees so that rewards can be given according to performance. Appraisal for development and counseling needs to focus on the strong and weak spots of the individual's performance from the point of view of how performance can be improved. These can call for different discussion emphases and can have different effects on the employee. Considerable evidence exists that individuals want and seek out feedback about their performance (see Festinger, 1954; Pettigrew, 1967), since it helps them learn more about themselves. Ted is no exception here. The performance appraisal represents an opportunity to get feedback that helps employees evaluate their own performance and learn how they are progressing in their own development. However, the individual must be open to feedback and willing to discuss his or her performance in a nondefensive manner for a useful appraisal to take place.

When the performance evaluation is crucial in determining the rewards an individual will receive, employees have a reason for defending their performance and presenting themselves and their performance in the best possible light. There are a number of examples in the management literature of employees giving invalid data about their performance in order to look good. For example, the classic Western Electric studies (Roethlisberger and Dickson, 1939) point out how employees manage the kind of production reports that go outside their work group. The employees studied were on a pay incentive plan, and they wanted to show a consistent daily production figure. They did this by not reporting what they produced on some days and reporting things as having been produced that never were on other days.

Because of the dual functions of performance appraisal, reward distribution, and counseling, employees often have conflicting objectives when taking part in it. On the one hand, they want to look as good as possible in order to maximize rewards, while on the other, they want accurate and helpful performance feedback (Meyer, Kay, and French, 1965).

A second major conflict in performance appraisal is between the organization's need for complete data and the individual's desire for rewards. It often is not in the best interest of the individual to provide such data. The conflict then is over the exchange of valid information. As long as the individual sees the appraisal process as having an important influence on rewards, the potential for this conflict will be present. In the case of the good performer, the conflict is negligible, but in the case of the poor performer, it is substantial.

The Vanishing Appraisal. Because of the conflicts present in performance appraisal, both the superior and the subordinate often have ambivalent feelings about holding performance evaluation sessions. From the superior's point of view, being in the position of evaluating someone's performance and giving feedback can be unpleasant. If the evaluation is more negative than the individual expects, the situation is almost certain to end up in a disagreement about whether the measure of performance was valid. Subordinates want the feedback that the performance appraisal process yields, yet may be ambivalent about receiving it. Subordinates do not want just any kind of feedback; they want something positive and constructive that will help them reach their goals. Subordinates also experience stress because of their conflicting desires for valid feedback and for rewards.

Because both superiors and subordinates have ambivalent attitudes about performance appraisal, a phenomenon called the "vanishing performance appraisal" occurs in many organizations. The case of Chris and Ted is typical of this problem; the boss thinks the appraisal has taken place, while the subordinate does not think it has occurred. This is because the subordinate's need for constructive feedback has not been met.

Unheard Feedback. Several studies have shown that subordinates tend not to "hear" criticism, and respond negatively when it is given (Meyer, Kay, and French, 1965). When presented with a long list of criticisms, subordinates tend to remember only the first few remarks. The rest are never heard, because the subordinates are busy thinking up arguments to refute the first few criticisms that are presented. Research also suggests that, rather than serving as a stimulant to more effective behavior, criticism can have a negative effect on future performance.

Thus, rather than serving as facilitators and motivators of good performance, many performance appraisal sessions appear to have just the opposite effect; they decrease performance.

Invalid Appraisal Measures. Numerous studies of performance evaluation have pointed out that it often fails to produce valid data about employee performance levels. The typical performance evaluation ratings done by a superior seem to be full of biases and errors (Campbell et al., 1970; Kane and Lawler, 1979). For example, when asked to rate subordinates on a number of traits (such as dependability and attitude), supervisor ratings show a "halo effect," such that a given subordinate tends to be rated the same on all traits even though that individual may actually be higher on some than on others. It has also been shown that some superiors tend to rate everyone high, while others tend to rate everyone low, a fact that further serves to reduce the accuracy and usefulness of performance ratings.

MAKING PERFORMANCE APPRAISAL EFFECTIVE

Our discussion of the problems with performance evaluation should not obscure the fact that it can lead to a number of positive outcomes for both the individual and the organization. It can produce valid performance data, which can be used as a basis for motivating and rewarding employees, for long-range planning, and for training and development activities. Therefore, the critical question is, What factors determine whether the net effect of performance appraisal will be negative or positive?

Results Emphasis. The work effectiveness of any individual can be evaluated from two perspectives. It can be looked at as the activities the person performs, and it can be looked at as the results of the activity. Some performance evaluation systems can and do focus exclusively on results; others focus exclusively on activities. Focusing on either activities or results to the exclusion of the other produces undesirable consequences because it causes individuals to emphasize that which is measured to the exclusion of that which is not measured (that is, great form with no results, or results at any cost). Any performance measurement system that is going to have a constructive effect on both motivation and development must measure both activities and results. What is more, it must measure all the results and activities that the person needs to perform; otherwise the unmeasured areas are likely to be neglected.

Responsiveness of Measures. Performance measures vary in the degree to which they can be influenced by the behavior of the person whose performance is being evaluated. An individual's reaction to being evaluated and rewarded on the basis of a particular measure and the usefulness of the measure to the organization is largely determined by how much it is influenced by the actual job performance of the individual. For motivation to be present, the individual has to feel that his or her performance influences the measure. Most measures, to some degree, can be influenced. Profits, for example, are affected by factors over which many employees have no control, but they are also influenced by some controllable things. The same can be said for the production of an automated assembly line or the sales volume of a salesperson. There is no magical formula that says how much an individual should be able to influence a measure if it is to be used as a basis for performance appraisal. What can be said is that the less measures can be influenced, the more risk there is of problems appearing in the appraisal process.

Subordinate Participation and Involvement. The traditional performance appraisal model has been one in which at the end of the year the superior has *told* the subordinate how the subordinate's performance was appraised. A number of writers have pointed out that there are many problems with this approach (for example, subordinate defensiveness — the boss playing God). McGregor (1957) has argued that subordinates should take an active role in establishing performance goals, in deciding how performance is to be measured, and in appraising performance against the goals. The advantages of this approach appear to be multiple. It assures that *both* the superior and the subordinate are in agreement with respect to what needs to be done. It also gives the subordinate a chance to influence how performance will be evaluated, thereby increasing commitment to the appraisal process. Finally, it helps ensure that in the eyes of the subordinate, whatever goals and objectives are agreed to are reasonable and can be achieved, since subordinates are unlikely to develop unrealistically high goals. As will be discussed below, there are some important motivational advantages to setting moderately difficult goals.

One final word is in order here. None of the individuals who advocate subordinate participation advocate superior inaction. Quite the contrary, they stress that the superior must actively manage the process to ensure that reasonable goals are set and that the organization's needs for performance are met.

Goal Difficulty. The establishment of goals can have a strong impact on the effectiveness of the performance appraisal. Goals that are set at the right level can have a very positive effect, but those that are set at the wrong level can have a negative effect. Goals that are perceived as too difficult can lead to employees giving up or producing invalid data in order to look good. On the other hand, goals that are too easy to accomplish are not especially effective, since they tend to motivate individuals to reach them and not to perform at higher levels. A great deal of research on achievement motivation shows that motivation is highest when people see themselves as having about a 50/50 chance of reaching a goal. In 50/50 cases, good performance becomes attractive, since it represents a challenging but attainable objective which, if reached, will produce feelings of accomplishment and satisfaction.

Thus, it seems that the establishment of moderately difficult goals should be an important part of performance appraisal systems. The advantages of this include better performance motivation and increased superior-subordinate understanding about what the subordinates will be doing. The major risk of setting goals is that they will be either too easy or too difficult. No simple formula can prevent this from happening. It is up to individual managers to know the situation well enough to manage the goal-setting process skillfully so that this will not happen.

A Continuous Process. Performance appraisal cannot be a one-meeting-a-year event; too many things must be accomplished, and it leads to the meeting becoming too important and potentially traumatic. Further, if people are to perform their jobs effectively, they need ongoing feedback and coaching. Thus, most studies of appraisal effectiveness recommend continual coaching by the supervisor as well as formal appraisals during the year.

The issue of how much to separate or combine the various appraisal functions is a crucial one in structuring appraisal sessions. The alternatives range from having all the functions of the appraisal system built into the same session to having completely separate appraisal systems. Either of these extremes appear to be unsatisfactory. When everything is combined into a single session, it has been demonstrated that many important things tend to get neglected (such as development and training). Having completely separate sessions ignores the natural spillover from one to the other. One possibility is to have relatively separate sessions; that is, sessions separated by time for the different functions. If development discussion sessions are held after the reward decisions have been made and communicated, it may be possible to talk about development needs without the question of salary lurking too strongly in the background. The developmental sessions should provide the individual with a chance to get performance reports in a relatively nonevaluative setting and offer the opportunity for planning future developmental activities. These are functional outcomes for both the individual and the organization. At best, achieving these outcomes is no easy task but they may be obtained if the conditions are right and the process managed effectively.

Observable Behavior. In an effort to measure both results and activities, some performance appraisal systems rate or evaluate individuals on traits like friendliness, consideration, or attitude. This approach has consistently been shown to be ineffective and to lead to defensive behavior. The problem is that traits like these are too vague, and as a result, there is little agreement about what they mean in behavioral terms. Supervisors and subordinates often end up debating the meaning of the terms rather than talking constructively about the subordinate's behavior. Because trait ratings are not tied to behavior, it is difficult to set goals and objectives for the future, and this serves to reduce the motivational potential of the process. Discussions involving traits rarely lead to a clear agreement between superiors and subordinates on what is to be accomplished and on how performance is to be measured. Trait ratings also do not form a good basis on which to plan developmental activities. How do you train someone to have a better attitude or to be more dependable?

Instead of having superiors rate their subordinates on a number of separate traits, some organizations simply ask for a single rating of overall job performance. Overall or global ratings can be done validly by some superiors and they have additional advantages: (1) employees are compared with their peers and relative standing is apparent; (2) global ratings include a number of behaviors and tend to be rather inclusive; and (3) superiors are willing to make such ratings. Because of their advantages, global ratings are often useful as one basis for making raise and promotion decisions. However, they are not useful in providing feedback and in forming the basis for developmental counseling. Like trait ratings, they are far removed from actual behavior. They also, like trait ratings, often produce defensiveness on the part of the person who is evaluated. In addition, they do not tend to produce better superior-subordinate communication or well-defined objectives.

Based on the research on trait rating, it seems apparent that to be effective, performance measurement must be based on clearly defined, observable behavior. This means that rather than focusing on dependability, it needs to focus on what dependability means in a particular work situation. If it means not being absent, this needs to be stated, and it needs to be stated how it is measured. The only way that appraisals can produce valid data that are useful to both the individual and the organization is to have them focus on measurable behavior.

Management by Objectives. In recent years, programs stressing Management by Objectives (MBO) have provided an alternative to the various rating approaches. These programs typically involve superiors and subordinates agreeing on specific performance objectives and how achievement of the objectives is to be measured. This is followed at the end of an established time period by a meeting in which performance is evaluated against the objectives. This method has considerable appeal, since it is based on specific behavioral objectives and, when successfully implemented, can lead to goals that are moderately difficult and comprehensive.

Despite its advantages, MBO is not the answer to all performance evaluation problems. No system will ever do this; too many conflicts are present in performance evaluation, and the measurement of performance is too complex an issue. As a general rule, objectives-based approaches are superior to the traditional trait-rating approach. However, it is not clear that they are always superior to a global-rating approach. For many jobs it is extremely difficult to apply objective performance measures. In still other instances, a few measures can be developed, but in many performance areas, measures cannot be developed. In these cases, global ratings may prove to be more useful. In addition, objectives-based measures often are not helpful when promotion and pay decisions have to be made. Because they are frequently based on individuals setting goals that are applicable to their situation, objectives vary in content and difficulty. This makes it very difficult to compare the performance of individuals. Thus, they often do not produce the kinds of comparisons between people that are most helpful in making pay and promotion decisions. Finally, research has shown that it takes considerable skill on the part of both the superior and the subordinate for the objectives approach to be effective. This means that, in most cases, training is required and it takes time to develop an effective system.

SUMMARY:
PERFORMANCE
APPRAISAL
EFFECTIVENESS

Our discussion of what contributes to an effective performance appraisal system suggests that if it is to fulfill its multiple objectives, it must involve a certain kind of process and it must use the correct types of measures. On the process side, the program needs to stimulate active participation on the part of the subordinate and the supervisor and frequent communication at the beginning, during, and at the end of the time period that is covered by the appraisal. This rules out the all too typical year-end session in which the superior *tells* the subordinate how well he or she has performed.

One of the most important determinants of the effectiveness of any appraisal system is the type of measures used. We have stressed the importance of using behavior-oriented measures that are inclusive, can be influenced, and that incorporate moderately difficult goals. It is interesting to contrast this prescription with what research says is done in most organizations — trait rating.

Table 4.1 summarizes what we have said so far about the different measurement methods. It shows that objective-oriented performance measures tend to be the best on an overall basis, although the approach does have the "comparison" problems mentioned above. Both the objectives-oriented and the single global rating have some merit, but these also have a number

Table 4.1 *Evaluation of Three Approaches to Measuring Performance*

	Traditional trait rating	Single global rating	Behavioral objectives-oriented evaluation
Acceptability to superior and subordinate	Poor	Moderate	Good
Counseling and development information	Poor	Poor	Good if it includes activities measures
Salary and reward administration	Poor	Moderate to good	Moderate
Motivation based on goal setting	Poor	Poor	Good
Clarification of job objectives	Poor	Poor	Good

Adapted from Porter, Lawler, and Hackman, 1975.

of deficiencies. The traditional trait-rating approach seems least defensible, and should not be used by any manager who is concerned about effectively managing organizational behavior.

Extrinsic Rewards

What role should such extrinsic rewards as pay and promotion have in managing organizational behavior? Organizations can use extrinsic rewards to do three things that contribute to organizational effectiveness: (1) motivate employees to join the organization, (2) motivate employees to come to work, and (3) motivate employees to perform effectively. The considerable amount of research that has been concerned with each of these functions of reward systems is summarized in the rest of this chapter. As we shall see, this research shows that although rewards can perform these functions, they often do not.

REWARD SYSTEMS AND ORGANIZATIONAL MEMBERSHIP

A great deal of evidence shows that the rewards an organization offers directly influence the decisions people make about whether to join it as well as their decisions about when and if to quit (see Lawler, 1971 and Hall, 1976 for reviews), as is predicted by expectancy theory. All other things being equal, individuals are attracted to and remain in those organizations that give the most desirable rewards. Many studies have found that turnover is related to satisfaction with the extrinsic rewards a person receives (Porter and Steers, 1973). Admittedly, extrinsic reward satisfaction is only one influence on turnover, but it is an important one because individuals who are presently satisfied with their rewards expect to be satisfied in the future and, as a result, want to stay with the same organization.

As was discussed in Chapter 2, satisfaction with rewards is a function of several factors. Undoubtedly, the most crucial determinant is how much a person receives. However, extrinsic reward satisfaction is not solely determined by the amount of reward. A great deal of research has shown that people's feelings are very much influenced by what happens to others like themselves (Patchen, 1961). People compare what others do and what others receive with their own situations. These comparisons are made both inside and outside the organizations they work in, but are usually made with people in similar situations. In the case of Ted, he made them inside the organization with two people who were hired at the same time, a common comparison. As a result of these comparisons, people reach conclusions about what rewards they should receive. When the overall comparison between their situations and those of others is favorable, people are satisfied. When the comparison is unfavorable, they are dissatisfied and may quit.

In practice, organizations need to do a number of things if they are going to distribute extrinsic rewards in general, and pay in particular, in an effective manner. First, they need to know what their competitors are doing. In most cases, salary survey data are helpful and available. Second, they need a good system for evaluating jobs so that they can be sure that the people who perform more demanding jobs are rewarded more highly. Job evaluation systems are often difficult to construct and maintain, but they are crucial if an organization is going to have a rational, defensible pay structure. It is often a necessary ingredient in making comparisons to the outside market as well, since it is one way to ensure that similar jobs are being compared. Finally, organizations need a performance appraisal system that identifies the better performers and a reward system that rewards them proportionately. If an organization does not identify its best performers and reward them accordingly, it may have a problem retaining them even though its average pay levels are competitive. Good performers must be rewarded more highly if they are to be attracted and retained.

EXTRINSIC REWARD AND ABSENTEEISM

Absenteeism, like turnover, is expensive because, among other things, it leads to overstaffing and inexperienced individuals doing the jobs of those who are absent. Thus, it makes sense for organizations to adopt reward policies that minimize absenteeism. What kind of reward policies will do this? One answer can be found in the research on satisfaction, which has shown that absenteeism and satisfaction are related. When the place of work is pleasant and satisfying, individuals attend regularly; when it is not, they do not. This seems to occur because satisfied individuals see work as more attractive than the alternative ways they have available to spend their time.

Several studies have also shown that, as would be predicted by expectancy theory, absenteeism can be reduced by tying pay bonuses and other rewards to attendance. This approach is costly, but sometimes it is less costly than absenteeism. It seems to be an especially useful strategy in circumstances where both the work content and the working conditions are poor and do not lend themselves to meaningful improvements. The other approach that organizations can take is to punish employees for being absent. This can have an effect on attendance if it is fairly and consistently done because it makes coming to work more attractive than not coming. Thus, reward systems policies are one of several ways to influence absenteeism, but they are likely to be effective only if an organization is willing to tie important rewards to coming to work. In many ways, this is easier to do than tying rewards to performance because attendance is more measurable and more visible.

REWARD SYSTEMS AND PERFORMANCE MOTIVATION

When certain specifiable conditions exist, reward systems have been demonstrated to motivate performance. What are those conditions? They were mentioned in our discussion of expectancy theory and motivation: Important rewards must be perceived to be tied to effective performance. Stated another way, organizations get the kind of behavior that is seen to lead to valued rewards. At first glance, it may seem to be simple for a manager to relate valued rewards to performance, but in fact it often is very difficult to accomplish. This is true because it requires good measures of performance, the ability to identify which rewards are important to particular individuals, and the ability to control the amount of rewards an individual receives. None of these things are easy, a fact that has led some to conclude that many managers should not try to relate rewards to performance. In the discussion to follow, we will first describe the characteristics of the major rewards organizations can use, and then discuss how and when one of them, pay, can be related to performance.

Characteristics of Extrinsic Rewards. For reward systems to operate as effective motivators of behavior, there are four identifiable characteristics that the rewards themselves should have. These include (1) importance, (2) flexibility, (3) frequency with respect to administration, and (4) visibility. From the point of view of the organization, it is also desirable if they have a fifth characteristic, low cost.

A reward must be important to some individual or group if it is to influence behavior and satisfaction. The first question that needs to be asked about any reward, then, is whether it is valued by the individuals involved. A reward system that relies solely on generally important rewards is inevitably going to miss some employees. Even rewards that are important to most employees are not important to everyone. This creates the need for individualizing rewards (Lawler, 1974) so that employees will receive the rewards they desire. In some cases, this can be accomplished by giving people the choice of which extrinsic rewards they will receive. For example, some companies allow workers who have finished their daily production quota the choice of going home or receiving extra pay.

If rewards are to be tailored to individuals, they must be flexible with respect to the amount given and whether they are given to everyone in the organization. Unless flexibility is present, it is impossible to vary rewards according to the performance of individuals, and equity and performance motivation cannot be achieved.

Related to the issue of flexibility is the issue of frequency. Giving rewards frequently is often helpful for sustaining motivation and satisfaction. The best rewards are those that can be given frequently without losing their importance.

The visibility of rewards is important because it influences the ability of the reward to satisfy esteem and recognition needs. Low-visibility rewards cannot satisfy these needs and, therefore, are often less valued by employees. Visibility is also important in clarifying the relationship between rewards and performance, a key ingredient in motivation.

Table 4.2 presents an evaluation of the common rewards used by organizations based on their importance, flexibility, visibility, frequency, and cost. As can be seen from this table, none of the rewards rate high on all of the criteria. Interestingly, pay seems to possess all the characteristics necessary to make it the perfect extrinsic reward except one — cost. Promotion and dismissal are

Table 4.2 *Evaluation of Extrinsic Rewards*

	Average importance	Flexibility in amount	Visibility	Frequency	Dollar cost
Pay	Moderate to high	High	Potentially high	High	High
Promotion	High	Low	High	Low	High
Dismissal	High	Low	High	Low	High
Status symbols	Moderate	High	High	Low	Moderate
Special awards, certificates, and medals	Low	High	High	Low	Low
Fringe benefits	High	Moderate	Moderate	Low	High

low in flexibility. They cannot be easily varied in amount according to the situation. Also, they cannot be given very regularly. This makes it difficult to tie them closely to performance over a long period of time. These rewards also tend to be expensive. Their high cost is not as visible and obvious as is the cost of pay, but it is real. Special awards, certificates, and medals are examples of rewards with quite a different set of characteristics. They are high in flexibility and visibility. However, they can only be given a few times before they lose their value. And because many people do not value them at all, their average importance is relatively low.

The major message in Table 4.2 for managers is that they must carefully diagnose each situation and use the reward or rewards that are appropriate. No one reward or class of rewards meets all the criteria for being a good extrinsic reward. The one that stands out as having the most potential is pay. Because of its strengths and widespread use, we will discuss it in more detail.

Methods of Relating Pay to Performance. A variety of approaches for relating pay to performance have been tried and some clearly are more effective in motivating performance than others. However, none is perfect and none is universally applicable. Effective management of the pay performance relationship depends on picking the right approach and administering it in a credible manner.

Pay plans can be classified according to where they fall on three dimensions: (1) the organizational unit where performance is measured for reward purposes (individual, group, or organization-wide basis); (2) the way performance is measured (measures typically vary from subjective — for example, superiors' judgments or ratings — to objective, for example, costs, sales, or profits); and (3) what rewards are offered for successful performance (salary increases or cash bonuses). Table 4.3 presents a breakdown of various pay plans on these three dimensions. This classification system yields eighteen different types of pay incentive plans, many of which have no commonly accepted name and are not widely used. The more commonly used ones are identified by name in the table.

Table 4.4 provides an effectiveness rating for each plan on three criteria. These ratings attempt to summarize what has typically happened when each kind of plan has been used. First, each plan is evaluated on how effective it is in creating the perception that pay is tied to performance. Second, it is evaluated on whether it results in the negative side effects that often are produced by pay-for-performance plans. These include punishment of good performers (discussed further in Section III), defensive behavior, and giving false data about performance.

Table 4.3 *Classification of Pay Incentive Plans*

	Performance measure	Reward offered	
		Salary increase	Cash bonus
Individual plans	Productivity Cost effectiveness Superiors' rating	{Merit rating plan	{Sales commission Piece rate
Group plans	Productivity Cost effectiveness Superiors' rating		Group incentive
Organization-wide plans	Productivity Cost effectiveness Profit	{Productivity Bargaining	Scanlon plan Profit sharing

Adapted from Lawler, 1971.

Third, each plan is evaluated on the degree to which it contributes to teamwork and cooperation by rewarding cooperative behavior. (These issues will be considered further in Section III.) All the ratings range from 1 to 5; a 5 indicates that the plan is generally high on the factor, and a 1 indicates that it is low.

A number of trends appear in the ratings. On the criterion of tying pay to performance, individual plans tend to be rated highest, group plans are rated next, and organization-wide plans are rated lowest. This is because in group plans, to some extent, and in organization-wide plans to a great extent, the pay of individuals is not a direct function of their behavior. It is influenced by the behavior of others and, in the case of some types of performance measures (for example, profits), by external conditions.

Bonus plans are generally rated higher on tying pay to performance than pay raise and salary increase plans. Under bonus plans, a person's pay may vary sharply from year to year in accordance with recent performance. This does not usually happen with salary increase programs, because organizations seldom cut anyone's salary. As a result, pay under a salary increase plan reflects not only recent performance but also performance over a number of years.

Finally, approaches that use objective measures of performance are rated higher than those that use subjective measures. In general, objective measures enjoy higher credibility; employees will often accept the validity of an objective measure, such as sales or units produced, when they will not accept a superior's ratings like the ones that were given to Ted, Ed, and Fritz. Thus,

Table 4.4 *Ratings of Various Pay Incentive Plans*

		Tie pay to performance	*Produce negative side effects*	*Encourage cooperation*
Salary reward				
Individual plan	Productivity	4	1	1
	Cost effectiveness	3	1	1
	Superiors' rating	3	1	1
Group	Productivity	3	1	2
	Cost effectiveness	3	1	2
	Superiors' rating	2	1	2
Organization-wide	Productivity	2	1	3
	Cost effectiveness	2	1	2
Bonus				
Individual plan	Productivity	5	3	1
	Cost effectiveness	4	2	1
	Superiors' rating	4	2	1
Group	Productivity	4	1	3
	Cost effectiveness	3	1	3
	Superiors' rating	3	1	3
Organization-wide	Productivity	3	1	3
	Cost effectiveness	3	1	3
	Profit	2	1	3

Adapted from Lawler, 1971.

when pay is tied to objective measures, it is usually clearer to employees that pay is determined by performance. Overall, then, the suggestion is that individually based bonus plans that rely on objective measures produce the strongest perceived connection between pay and performance.

Ratings of the degree to which pay plans contribute to negative side effects reveal that most plans have little tendency to produce such effects. The notable exceptions here are individual bonus and incentive plans at the nonmanagement level. These plans often lead to situations in which social rejection and ostracism are tied to good performance, and in which employees present false productivity data and restrict their production. These side effects are particularly likely to appear where trust is low.

Group and organization-wide plans are best at encouraging cooperation. Under these plans, it is generally to everyone's advantage for an individual to work effectively because all share in the financial fruits of an individual's higher performance. This is not true under an individual plan. Thus, good performance is much more likely to be supported and encouraged by others when group and organization-wide plans are used. In short, if people feel they can benefit from another's good performance, they are much more likely to encourage and help other workers to perform well than if they will not benefit and might even be harmed. As will be discussed in Section III, this point has important implications for how pay should be managed when work has been designed for groups to perform on a cooperative basis.

From this short review, it should be clear that no one performance pay plan represents a panacea. Unfortunately, no one type is strong in all areas. Thus, it is unlikely that any organization will ever be completely satisfied with its approach. Perhaps the most important conclusion arising from the research on different performance pay plans is that the effectiveness of all pay plans varies according to a number of situational conditions. For this reason, a plan that works well for one organization often is unsatisfactory for another. The challenge in managing organizational behavior, therefore, is to pick the best plan in light of what type of impact is desired.

Should Organizations Relate Rewards to Performance? There are conditions under which extrinsic rewards probably should not be used to motivate performance because the dysfunctional consequences outweigh the positive ones. We have already mentioned a number of conditions that must be present if rewards are to motivate performance, but it is worth summarizing them here: (1) important rewards can be given, (2) rewards can be varied depending on performance, (3) performance can be validly and inclusively measured, (4) information can be made public about how the rewards are given, (5) trust is high, and (6) superiors are willing to explain and support the reward system in discussions with their subordinates.

If many of these conditions do not exist, it typically is better not to attempt to use extrinsic rewards as motivators. Putting performance-based pay into an organization where the conditions are not right (for example, where good superior-subordinate relations do not exist and trust is low) may only make the situation worse. When reward decisions are tied to a performance appraisal method that is defective, a number of negative things can happen. The subordinate's stance toward the appraisal can change. Suddenly, it becomes a contest in which he or she has to present a good case for a raise, for promotion, or whatever. In other cases, it may lead to the subordinate providing invalid data about what performance levels are possible so that objectives will be set low (Whyte, 1955). In still others, it may lead to the subordinate producing invalid data about past performance or to performing in a dysfunctional or bureaucratic way simply because it is measured.

We have seen that rewards have the power to influence some very important behaviors. Thus, they can be a powerful managerial tool. Using them effectively, however, is difficult and requires careful analysis and planning. This is especially true when using pay as a motivator of performance. Only if certain conditions exist should pay be used as a motivator. The choice of a plan to tie pay to performance also requires considerable analysis, since no one plan is right for all circumstances. If pay cannot be related to performance, it does not mean that motivation must be low, however. As will be discussed in the next chapter, jobs can be designed in ways that make them motivating even when extrinsic rewards are not tied to performance.

Suggested Readings

Lawler, E. E. *Pay and Organizational Effectiveness*. New York: Mc-Graw-Hill, 1971.

——— "Reward Systems." In *Improving Life at Work,* edited by J. R. Hackman, and J. L. Suttle. Pacific Palisades, Cal.: Goodyear, 1977.

Nash, A., and Carroll, S. *The Management of Compensation*. Monterey, Cal.: Brooks/Cole, 1975.

Patten, T. *Pay: Employee Compensation and Incentive Plans*. New York: Free Press, 1977.

Chapter 5

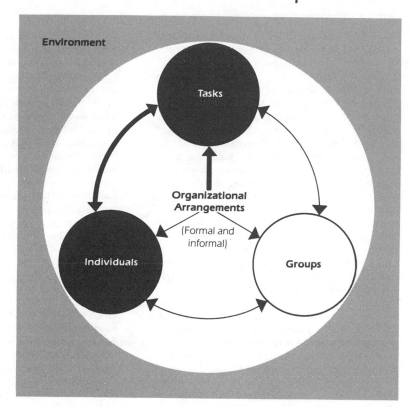

Job Design

Managers at Kless Bider & Associates, a large consulting firm, have been concerned about the performance of some of their research assistants. The firm does projects that involve data collection and analysis for reports to clients, and is organized into a number of departments, each of which provides services to different industry groups (heavy manufacturing, consumer goods, health care, and so on). Each department includes partners, group managers, consultants, and research assistants. The research assistants (about 5 in each department) provide support services to the professional staff, mainly related to data processing. They aid in data collection, building of data files on the computer, data management, data analysis as directed by senior staff, and report production. Recently, top management has noted that there have been problems with the research assistants in some of the departments. In some areas, performance is low, people seem "turned off" to their jobs, and much time and money appears to be wasted by the research assistants. Since all of the research assistants have roughly the same training and educational backgrounds, are well qualified to do their jobs, are paid on the same pay scale, and have identical fringe benefits, it is puzzling why the differences exist in performance.

Some people think that a clue to the problems may be the way in which the work is organized. Three of the departments illustrate some of these differences. In the health care department, when a consultant has a project and needs assistance, he or she calls on a research assistant and gives that person a specific task. For example, having collected some data which were keypunched onto computer cards, the consultant might direct the research assistant to build a computer file which has the data in it in a particular order with specific types of labels, and set up in a certain way. Next, the consultant might contact another research assistant to take the file and perform certain statistical analyses on the data according to specific instructions. In fact, over time in the health care department, the consultants have found it easiest to identify specific individuals who are specialists. So one research assistant only builds files, another only does certain kinds of analysis, another only prepares data for input to files, and so on.

In the department that consults to heavy manufacturing companies, the work is set up very differently. When a consultant begins working on a project, a research assistant is assigned. The consultant meets with the research assistant and explains what the project is all about, and what kinds of end products (analyses) will be needed. The research assistant then helps in designing the data collection, takes the raw data and determines what kinds of files to build, and so forth, in order to produce the finished product. The research assistant thus does a number of different tasks, decides how some of the tasks will be done, and follows the project through its different phases.

In the department that consults to consumer goods companies, the work is organized a third way. The research assistants are a close-knit and well-functioning group. When a new project appears, the group considers it at one of its weekly meetings. The group members discuss the project, discuss their different work loads and interests, and then make decisions about who will do what parts of the work. In some cases, the project work will be divided up among individuals (although different people rotate and do different tasks frequently) while in other cases, one person will follow a project all the way through.

IN OBSERVING these three departments, it has been noted that the health care department has been experiencing many problems with its research assistants, while the other two groups have had few problems. Why is the health care department the one with problems? As we will see, the reason for this probably can be found in the way the research assistants' jobs are designed. So far, we have attempted to understand individual behavior in organizations by looking at the characteristics of individuals and how the formal rewards system in an organization can create expectancies that determine individual behavior. Now we want to look beyond the formal and explicit rewards systems in organizations at another important source of outcomes (desired or undesired): the job that an individual performs. A person's job, depending on how it is structured, can lead to the development of different types of expectancies. On some jobs, expectancies might be created that the harder I work, the more I will be bored, fatigued, tired, and so on. On the other hand, another job might create the expectancies that the harder and more effectively I work, the more I will obtain feelings of accomplishment, the more opportunities I will have to be creative, and the more I will get to test myself against important challenges. For most people, the first job is not going to motivate them to work hard, while the second job will motivate them to perform well.

The jobs that people perform are perhaps one of the most important sources of expectancies and, thus, motivation in organizations. While individuals may experience rewards systems, group pressures, or the actions of a supervisor from time to time, an individual *constantly* and *continually* experiences the consequences of performing his or her individual job well or poorly. It is the point in the organization where individuals see the most direct connection between how they do their work and what outcomes they receive.

Given the importance of jobs for motivating performance, it is important to understand how the nature of jobs and the design of work affects the behavior of individuals in organizations. It is also important to understand what the possible alternatives are for designing work, what the strategies for work design are, and what issues need to be considered when contemplating the design or redesign of jobs in organizations.

This chapter is aimed at exploring a number of these critical issues. First, three different *approaches to work design* will be discussed in detail. Specifically, conceptions of work design coming out of scientific management, individual job enrichment, and autonomous work groups will be discussed. Second, some of the issues in choosing *appropriate work designs* will be reviewed, with the goal of providing a set of decision rules for choosing among alternative work design approaches.

Approaches to the Design of Work

The research on work design all points to the conclusion that there is no one best way to design work or structure jobs. Different situations provide different constraints and opportunities. Given different types of organizations, technologies, and individuals, different job design approaches are most appropriate. Before discussing where such approaches are most applicable, it is important to understand what some of the ways are of thinking about the design of work.

SCIENTIFIC MANAGEMENT

The design of tasks and jobs was central to the notion of scientific management, as developed by F. W. Taylor:

> Perhaps the most prominent single element in modern scientific management is the task idea. The work of every workman is fully planned out by the management at least one day in advance, and each man receives in most cases complete written instructions, describing in detail the task which he is to accomplish. . . . This task specifies not only what is to be done but how it is to be done and the exact time allowed for doing it. (Taylor, 1911)

The principles underlying the scientific management approach to work design may be summarized as follows:

1. Work should be studied scientifically in order to break it down into small, easily mastered tasks.
2. The work to be done should be studied scientifically to determine how each segment of the work should be done most efficiently. Once this is determined, every worker is expected to adopt the standardized approach.
3. Employees selected for the work should be as perfectly matched to the demands of the job as possible. Workers must, of course, be physically and mentally capable of the work, but care should be taken as well to ensure that they are not over-qualified for the job.
4. Employees should be trained very carefully by managers to ensure that they perform the work exactly as specified by the prior scientific analysis of the work. In addition, many planners and supervisors are kept near the worker to make certain

that the person is, in fact, performing the work exactly as expected, and that there are no distractions or activities the worker must attend to other than productive work itself.

5. Finally, to provide motivation for the employee to follow the detailed procedures and work practices that are laid out and constantly enforced by supervisors, a substantial monetary bonus should be established to be paid on successful completion of each day's work.

The appeal of the scientific management approach was strong when it was introduced at the beginning of the century, and it continues to be. Indeed, it spawned a whole new technological and research culture aimed at providing the kinds of skills and data necessary for successful implementation of the scientific management philosophy. For example, large research efforts have been aimed at describing and analyzing jobs to provide a systematic basis for selecting, training, evaluating, and compensating employees. New occupational groups have emerged as a result of the scientific management approach, such as methods engineers, who plan the most efficient means of accomplishing work from a technological perspective, and time and motion analysts, who study in detail the specific operations that must be carried out by a worker and establish time standards for each work segment.

Many managers find scientific management appealing because it promises increased organizational effectiveness. Jobs designed according to these principles tend to be specialized (the worker does one particular task) and standardized (done in the same manner all the time). Under such a system, mistakes are unlikely, it is argued, because each worker is doing one part of the production process — and only one part — in the best way. This should lead to high quality because every worker can easily become an expert. In addition, such jobs increase management control over workers. A supervisor need only glance at a worker to know whether he or she is performing effectively. Assuming the worker is at his or her work station or machine and doing the simple repetitive task, production should proceed according to plan.

The benefits also seem clear to the organization. Since there is little training investment in workers, they can be replaced without a great deal of expense to the organization. This serves also to increase the company's power over the labor force, since the threat of being fired can be very real and immmediate to most workers. In summary, a solid case can be made for the economic advantage of having simple, standardized, and relatively routine jobs.

Despite the supposed economic advantages of simple, routine, standardized jobs, problems occur with this approach to job design. Both managers and behavioral scientists have noted that many employees dislike such jobs intensely and find them non-motivating. A growing body of research shows that the more jobs are simplified and routinized, the more workers experience dissatisfaction. In many cases, workers find that their needs for growth, challenge, recognition, and stimulation, are not met by this kind of job.

When jobs do not meet individual needs, people develop different responses to working. Some individuals, experiencing jobs as boring, monotonous, and thus fatiguing, respond by not working as hard or as effectively as they might (Scott, 1966). Where the job is debilitating, individuals may compensate by being absent or away more frequently. When people feel that they have options for other jobs that will meet their needs more adequately, they may leave the organization. In other cases, they may attempt to change the workplace so that their needs will be met. Sometimes this may result in new ideas or innovations, but more often, people engage in other activities (such as horseplay, sabotage, theft, drug or alcohol usage to name a few) that provide stimulation and meet individual needs in the workplace (see, for example, Roy, 1959).

Management sometimes responds to these effects of the scientific management approach by creating rules, additional supervisors, stricter procedures, and other controls to ensure that the work gets done as it is supposed to. This can result in making the work even more confining or constraining and in exacerbating the situation.

In summary, it is not always true that designing jobs that are efficient from an engineering point of view — standardized, specialized, simplified — will result in lower costs. There may be so many direct and indirect costs to the organization associated with how employees react to such jobs that the "efficient job" may be less effective than other design approaches.

If we look back to the Kless Bider case at the opening of this chapter, we see that in many ways the research assistant's job in the health care department resembles a scientific management approach. This is not surprising, since this approach to work design has become so ingrained that it is almost the automatic approach to design. Our natural inclination, given a large task and a set of people to do the work, is to break it down into its component parts in a consistent manner and assign one individual to do each part of the job, ideally the part that he or she can do best. Given the consequences of this approach that we have noted, it is not surprising that this department is experiencing problems of low performance and high dissatisfaction. The question, then, is, What is it about the way in which the work is organized in the other two departments — heavy manufacturing and consumer goods — that has led to more effective patterns of behavior? The answer lies in examining some alternative approaches to the design of work.

INDIVIDUAL JOB ENRICHMENT

The job enrichment approach has focused on identifying those aspects of work that make jobholders want to work hard, work more effectively, and feel better about themselves and the work they do. Much effort has been expended in the last fifteen years on developing approaches to both understanding and changing the specific elements of jobs that have implications for the motivation and satisfaction of the jobholder (Herzberg, 1966; Lawler, 1969). While there are a number of different approaches, they are similar in that they all look at those job elements that enrich the job in ways that enable the jobholder to meet more of his or her higher-order needs through effective working.

One of the approaches to individual job enrichment that has been extensively tested and used is the job characteristics model (Hackman and Oldham, 1975). The model is based on the view that three key *psychological states* are critical in affecting a person's motivation and satisfaction on the job. The first of these is *experienced meaningfulness,* or the degree to which one experiences work as important, valuable, and worthwhile. A second is *experienced responsibility,* or the extent to which the individual feels personally responsible and accountable for the results of the work he or she performs. The third is *knowledge of results,* or the extent to which the individual understands on a regular basis how effectively he or she is performing in the job. The more these three states are experienced by an individual performing a job, the more the person will feel internal work motivation — a motivation based on the job rather than on external rewards provided by others — in other words, the more that person will feel good as a result of performing well and feel unhappy when performing poorly. Thus, as a person works effectively, that individual will experience having done something meaningful for which that person was responsible, and know that it was done effectively. To the extent that these are desirable outcomes for the individuals, they will be motivated to perform well.

Research has identified a number of specific job design characteristics that lead to these psychological states. Table 5.1 provides a listing and brief description of each of these job characteristics. As is shown in Figure 5.1, the first three characteristics — skill variety, task identity, and task significance all lead to increased feelings of meaningfulness. When individuals can do things that result in a whole piece of work with a visible outcome and where that work has a significant effect on other people, the work is experienced as meaningful. The fourth job characteristic, autonomy, is directly related to feelings of responsibility for the work. The more people have control over how they do their work, the more responsible they feel. The final dimension, feedback, is clearly and directly related to knowledge of results by the individual jobholder.

Using the job characteristics model, it is possible to compare

Conclusion intro (c).

Table 5.1 *Key Job Characteristics for Work Design*

Skill variety	The degree to which the job requires a variety of different activities in carrying out the work, which involves the use of a number of an individual's skills and talents.
Task identity	The degree to which the job requires completion of a "whole" and identifiable piece of work—that is, doing a job from beginning to end with a visible outcome.
Task significance	The degree to which the job has a substantial impact on the lives or work of other people—whether in the immediate organization or in the external environment.
Autonomy	The degree to which the job provides substantial freedom, independence, and discretion to the individual in scheduling the work and in determining the procedures to be used in carrying it out.
Feedback	The degree to which carrying out the work activities required by the job results in the individual's obtaining direct and clear information about the effectiveness of his or her performance.

the research assistant's job in the heavy manufacturing department with the health care department in the Kless Bider case described earlier. In the heavy manufacturing department, each individual gets to do the support work for an entire project all the way through to completion. This involves doing a number of different activities as opposed to the same activities (that is, file building) over and over again, so *skill variety* is higher. By doing a whole project rather than pieces of different projects, the job has much higher *task identity*. To the extent that it is now clearer what the work is about and what consequences it has, *task significance* may also be higher. The individual research assistant also can decide how the different pieces of work should be done and in what order, so *autonomy* is higher. Since the research assistant works on the complete project rather than handing the work to someone else, feedback about how well previous stages of the work were done is readily available.

It appears, then, that the research assistant job as designed in heavy manufacturing, when compared to the same job as designed in the health care department, has higher levels of experienced meaningfulness, responsibility, and knowledge of results for jobholders, and thus, higher levels of internal work motivation.

The job characteristics model has one additional and very important feature. As mentioned earlier, different people come

Figure 5.1 *The Job Characteristics Model of Work Motivation*

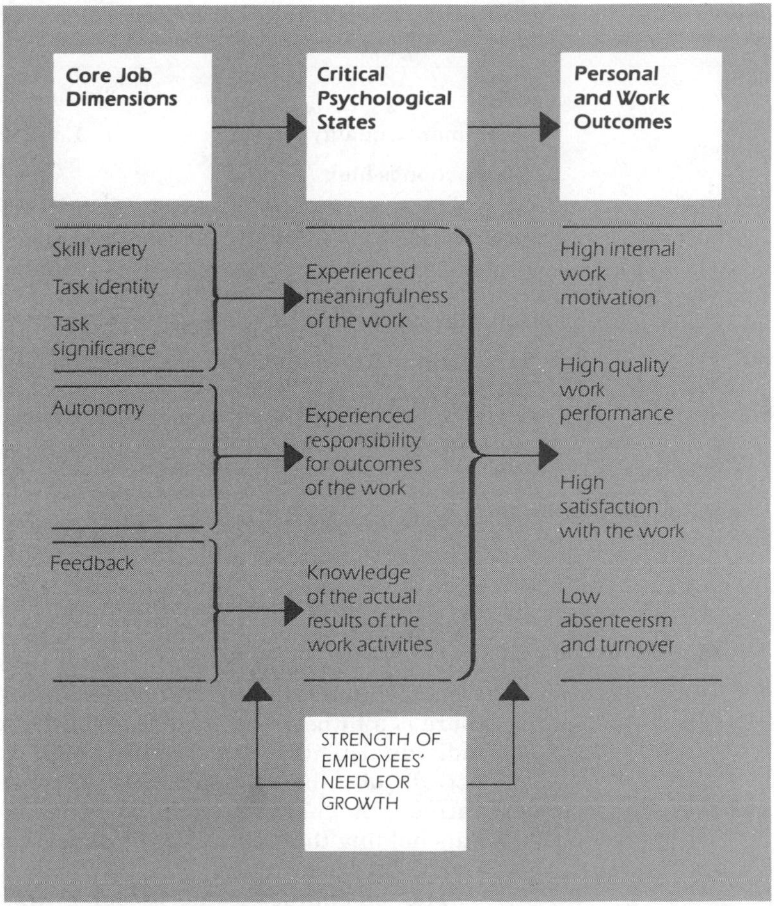

Core Job Dimensions	Critical Psychological States	Personal and Work Outcomes
Skill variety Task identity Task significance	Experienced meaningfulness of the work	High internal work motivation
Autonomy	Experienced responsibility for outcomes of the work	High quality work performance High satisfaction with the work
Feedback	Knowledge of the actual results of the work activities	Low absenteeism and turnover

STRENGTH OF EMPLOYEES' NEED FOR GROWTH

Adapted from Hackman and Oldham, 1976.

to work with different capabilities and needs. Consequently, what may be good job design for one individual may not be good job design for another. The model incorporates this by showing the relationship between job characteristics and individual responses to jobs as being moderated by the strength of an individual's need for growth. In other words, where individuals have high needs for growth, creativity, challenge, and such, they are likely to respond positively to jobs that provide more meaningfulness, responsibility, and knowledge of results. Where these needs are at low levels, they may not respond positively.

One way of thinking about the role of individual differences

Table 5.2 *Matching Individuals and Jobs*

| Degree of job enrichment | Intensity of desire for job enrichment | |
	High	Low
Enriched	"Match" 1. Performance quality is high. 2. Satisfaction is high. 3. Absenteeism and turnover are low.	"Mismatch" 1. Employee is overwhelmed and possibly confused. 2. Performance is poor. 3. Absenteeism and turnover are high.
Simple	"Mismatch" 1. Employees feel underutilized. 2. Job satisfaction is low. 3. Absenteeism and turnover are high.	"Match" 1. Employees can be motivated by pay incentives in the absence of intrinsic motivation. 2. Performance is high.

Adapted from Wanous, 1977b.

in needs and the response to different job designs is to think of a fit or match between the demands and rewards of the job on one hand and the abilities and needs of the individual on the other. Work behavior and individual feelings are most positive where there is a fit between the nature of the job and the nature of the individual. This is depicted in Table 5.2. The implication is that not all jobs should be enriched or designed to be high on the various job characteristics, and that the nature of the individuals holding that job should be a factor in determining how a job should be designed.

The job characteristics model of work design has been tested in great detail (Hackman and Oldham, 1976), and the research on it provides support for it. In particular, people who work on jobs that score high on the core job dimensions are more motivated, satisfied, and productive than people who work on low-scoring jobs. The responses to jobs high on these dimensions tend to be markedly positive for individuals who have strong needs for growth. Thus, the model appears to be a useful tool for thinking about designing work.

PRINCIPLES FOR DESIGNING ENRICHED JOBS

If jobs high on core job dimensions tend to create higher levels of motivation and satisfaction, then an important question is, How can work be designed in a way that will build these characteristics into jobs? Working from the model presented in Figure 5.1, a number of job design principles have been identified (Hackman et al., 1975). These principles can serve as a guide for both the design and redesign of jobs (see Figure 5.2).

Forming Natural Work Units. This involves identifying different tasks that need to be done, grouping those tasks together into natural and meaningful categories, and then assigning those groups of tasks to individuals. For example, a research assistant might be asked to do work on all of the projects that come from a certain group of consultants, or to do the file creation and management for a particular kind of project. Creating natural units of work increases the individual's ownership of the work and, thus, increases task identity and task significance.

Combining Tasks. A similar approach is to combine different tasks to create larger whole tasks. For example, in the heavy manufacturing group, the research assistant's job has been redesigned to combine the different tasks of data collection, file preparation, analysis, and so on, to create a whole task of research support for an entire project. This has the effect of increasing the variety of the work while also increasing task identity.

Figure 5.2 *Principles for Changing Jobs*

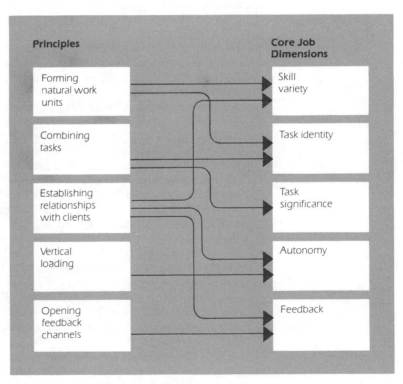

Adapted from Hackman et al., 1975.

Establishing Relationships with Clients. Direct communication can be established between the individual worker and the various clients or users of that individual's work. For example, the research assistants might be given much more opportunity to interact with the Kless Bider clients as they use the results of the analyses. When problems or questions arise, the clients could talk directly with the research assistant who did the work rather than communicating through the consultants. Direct relationships improve the work by creating feedback. Dealing with clients is a new and different task, so variety increases. To the extent that individuals are given responsibility for dealing with and responding to client needs as they see fit, autonomy is also increased.

Vertical Loading. Vertical loading involves changing the job to include planning, deciding, and controlling of work as well as doing it. Vertical loading can be done by having individuals set goals for work performance, by doing their own problem solving or trouble shooting, or by making decisions about how work procedures will be done and in what sequence. The research assistant's job in the heavy manufacturing group and particularly in the consumer goods department is vertically loaded, since the research assistants now are much more involved in making decisions about how the work will be done. Vertical loading has a strong impact on autonomy.

Opening Feedback Channels. A final design principle is to design work so as to provide individuals with feedback about how they are performing directly as they do the job (as opposed to finding out from management, or just from clients). Having people do their own quality control, for example, provides them with more information on how they are performing. In the research assistant situation, by creating a total task, the research assistant in each stage makes use of his or her work in earlier stages of the project. If mistakes are made in creating a data file, it is apparent when that research assistant attempts to use the file for doing statistical analysis. By doing the work, the person is getting feedback on performance, which leads to a job that is higher on feedback and, in turn, leads to increased knowledge of results.

DESIGNING WORK FOR GROUPS — THE AUTONOMOUS WORK GROUP APPROACH

A third approach to the design of jobs is to design work for interacting groups, or work teams. Research and experimentation with different work designs for groups (for example, Rice, 1958; Trist et al., 1963; Davis and Trist, 1974) has indicated that jobs can be effectively designed to take advantage of the dynamics that occur within groups.

As will be seen in the section to follow, groups are an important element in organizations. Groups can greatly influence the behavior of individuals, and work teams have the potential of performing work more effectively than individuals. The question is, How can work be designed to take advantage of the potential effectiveness of group as opposed to individual effort?

If jobs for group members were designed based on the job enrichment principles listed above, the motivation and satisfaction of group members should be increased. A number of work design principles have been identified that point out how this can be done (Hackman, 1976).

A Whole Task. The work should be designed so that the group has an entire task to perform, and so that the members will experience the accomplishments of the whole group as meaningful. By doing this, individual group members can have task significance, task identity, and feedback beyond that provided by their own individual job. The work of the entire group thus becomes a source of internal rewards.

Training for Rotation. Individuals should be trained so that they can perform several of the jobs needed by the group to complete the whole task. In some cases, each individual is trained to do every job in the group. The cross-training and rotation of work adds variety. By working on different jobs, the individual also may get a better sense of the entire work process, adding to task identity.

Autonomy. The group should have the freedom to make important decisions about how it will perform its job. In particular the group should be able to make decisions about methods, scheduling, assignments, etc. In some cases the group may also make decisions about hiring new members, promoting people out of the group, and other related matters. Obviously, autonomy is increased by this, and the decision-making activities add an element of variety to the job. The group is also free to change job designs and thus influence other core characteristics of work.

Group-Based Rewards. A final element of this design approach involves the design of reward systems that will be consistent with the task design itself. Rewards should be based on the performance of the total group, rather than on individual performance. In this way, external rewards are consistent with the internal work motivation that is created by the job design.

The core of this design approach is that a group is given a whole task and has a good deal of autonomy in deciding how to do the work. Therefore, this approach is called the *autonomous work group* approach to job design. The effectiveness of an autonomous work group is influenced, of course, by the design of its work, but it is also influenced by the characteristics of the group itself, such as who is a member of the group, how the group members work together, the patterns of communication among group members, and so on. Such characteristics of the group are important factors in the design and management of work teams. These factors will be considered in Chapter 8, after we discuss a number of basic concepts about group behavior and functioning in Chapters 6 and 7. At this point, it is sufficient to note that another alternative for work design is to create jobs for groups rather than for individuals.

In many ways, the third department in Kless Bider, the consumer goods department, reflects a group-oriented design approach. The group gets a whole task and autonomously decides how it will divide the work to be done. Different individuals are qualified to do different jobs, and they frequently rotate positions. Except for compensation, therefore, the research assistants function as an autonomous work group within that department.

**SUMMARY:
DESIGN CHOICES**

Three major approaches to work design — scientific management, individual job enrichment, and autonomous work groups — have been presented and discussed. As was mentioned earlier, they provide alternatives for design. No one approach is the most effective in all instances. The critical task then is choosing the appropriate work design.

Issues in Choosing Work Designs

At Kless Bider, several work designs have emerged over time almost by accident. An alternative would be consciously and deliberately to design work that is consistent with one of the three approaches discussed above. How would one go about deciding what is the right design? While there is no simple set of decision rules, a number of key issues need to be considered as they affect the choices among design approaches.

**INDIVIDUAL
DIFFERENCES**

The job design model discussed here puts an emphasis on the consistency between individual needs and different job designs. When considering the design or redesign of work, thought needs to be given to the individuals performing the work. If these individuals appear to have strong needs for growth (including needs for learning, challenge, opportunity for creativity, and so on), then job enrichment approaches should be used. Where these needs are not evident or strong, more traditional designs can be used. A second factor is the degree to which individuals have strong social needs — to be with others, interact with others, and establish positive relationships with others. When these needs are present, group designs as opposed to individual designs are indicated.

In addition to individual needs, it should be obvious that there should also be a consistency between individual capability and the nature of jobs. Enriched jobs (either group or individual) demand more from the individual. Thus, both the capabilities and needs of individuals should be considered.

A second factor concerns the physical setting and characteristics of the work, including the nature of the work, the type of technology, and the costs involved in changing the work. First, some work technologies greatly limit the kinds of work designs that can be employed. In heavy industry, the technology may be such that very little flexibility is provided for changing individual or group job designs. Second, cost issues must be considered when designing jobs. The scientific management approach to work design creates efficient work procedures; enriching a job may make them less efficient. This efficiency loss is acceptable when the gain that comes from increased motivation and satisfaction is equal to or greater than that loss. When the efficiency loss is very great or the enrichment gains are few, it may be prohibitively costly to create enriched jobs. Third, there is the cost of change in job designs. Existing designs represent investment of money by the organization. Where the technology is not very flexible and involves major investments of capital, the costs of change may be great. One of the best opportunities for innovative job design is where a new work setting (a new plant, office, or facility) is being designed. In fact, some of the more notable work design experiments have involved such new settings (Lawler, 1978).

As is clear from the organizational framework used throughout this book, tasks and jobs exist within the context of an organization. Individuals doing jobs are the core of organizational behavior, but they do not stand alone. They are surrounded by groups, by leaders or managers, by the organization's structure, and by patterns of interacting. An important concern, then, is how different job designs might or might not fit within larger patterns of organizational design and behavior.

The three different job design approaches that have been considered are consistent with different approaches to management and organizational design. The scientific management approach, for example, puts an emphasis on the separation between controlling (making decisions) and actually doing the job. Those who do the job are not involved in making critical decisions and must follow predetermined procedures, approaches, and rules. On the other hand, both the individual job enrichment and the autonomous work group approaches involve the decentralization of decision-making so that those who do the work are given the opportunity to make decisions about how the work is done (this is the critical issue in autonomy, for example). They call for less formalization of work procedure and more flexibility in how individuals perform the work. Problems obviously can emerge, therefore, when the design of individual or group jobs is inconsistent with the design and climate of the larger oganization (Porter, Lawler, and Hackman, 1975.)

MAKING A CHOICE OF JOB DESIGNS

Given these factors, it is possible to identify some basic guidelines for making choices among different job design strategies (see Table 5.3). One would use scientific management approaches when individuals have relatively low growth and social needs and relatively low levels of skill or ability. Such approaches would be indicated where the technology does not permit enriched designs, where efficiency losses would be great, or where the costs of changing existing technology are great. Finally, scientific management approaches would be consistent with a centralized structure and very directive (nonparticipative) management styles.

Individual job enrichment would be used where individuals have relatively high needs for growth. To the degree that enriched jobs require more capability, such approaches should be

Table 5.3 *Some Guidelines for the Choice of Alternative Job Design Strategies*

	Job design strategies		
Choice factors	Use SCIENTIFIC MANAGEMENT APPROACH when:	Use INDIVIDUAL JOB ENRICHMENT when:	Use AUTONOMOUS WORK GROUPS when:
Individual differences	Individuals have relatively low needs for growth, relatively low social needs, and low skill levels	Individuals have relatively high needs for growth and higher skill	Individuals have relatively high needs for growth, relatively high social needs, and high skill
Technology and cost	Technology constrains job designs or makes enriched designs costly and inefficient; where costs of changing existing technology are great	Technology is such that efficiency losses from enrichment are not great, where enrichment gains would be great, where technology is flexible, or in new work settings	Technology is such that efficiency losses from enrichment are not great, where enrichment gains would be present, where individual jobs would be low on core dimensions, where there is high interdependence and where technology is flexible, or new work settings
Organizational structure and climate	Structure is highly centralized and climate is very directive	Where climate is participative	Where structure is decentralized and climate is participative

used with individuals who have higher skill levels or the potential for developing increased skills. Job enrichment will be most effective where the work technology is such that efficiency losses from enrichment are limited, or when the gains from enrichment outweigh the efficiency losses. Similarly, job enrichment is most feasible where changing the technology is not costly or where a new work setting is being created. Finally, job enrichment fits into a participative and somewhat decentralized organizational structure.

The autonomous work group design should be used in situations where the nature of the individuals, the technology, and the larger organization are consistent with the principles of group work design. Individuals should have high growth needs as well as high social needs for this approach to be most effective. Similarly, since job rotation is also involved, individuals must have the ability to learn a number of different jobs.

Autonomous work groups can be used where cost and technology factors are similar to those that indicate individual work design. However, some other technology factors are specific to group work design. Group work design can be used where the technology makes the design of enriched individual jobs impossible. Some tasks cannot be done alone (such as putting together a truck), and if the task were broken down into individual jobs, they would be very low on the core job dimensions. Thus, a group approach is needed if any meaningful work is to be created. A second work technology factor concerns the nature of the interdependence among people performing jobs. Where different sets of jobs are interdependent (that is, one person cannot do his or her job if other persons do not do theirs), then the creation of work teams is a natural extension of the inherent work demands, which require that people work together and coordinate their efforts. For jobs that are independent in nature, there may be no real basis for forming a work team, and individual job enrichment is the preferred approach.

Autonomous work group designs inherently move decision-making down and out in the organization, increase participation, and reduce direct control by upper level management. Thus, such approaches should be used where the organizational structure is relatively decentralized and where participation in decision-making is an accepted approach to management.

DIAGNOSIS OF POTENTIAL DESIGN-BASED PROBLEMS

While the above factors provide some basis for choice, other elements need to be considered. When thinking about the design of work, perhaps the first and most critical step is diagnosis. The specific question is whether factors related to job design are actual or potential problems. Looking at existing jobs, the questions are whether motivation and satisfaction are problems among job holders, whether the job characteristics (variety, task identity, significance, and such) are indeed low, and what aspects of the job are causing problems. Many kinds of performance problems exist that are not rooted in the design of work. Problems may arise because of inadequate individual skills or abilities, poorly designed pay systems, ineffective leadership, and so forth. In these circumstances, to invest time and effort in the redesign of work may be futile. Thus, there is a need to diagnose the work situation to determine whether problems exist, and whether those problems are related to the design of jobs.

THE PROCESS OF MAKING THE CHOICE

All of the above factors — individual differences, technology and cost, organizational structure and climate, and, finally, available diagnostic data — need to be considered when jobs are being designed or redesigned. Many situations, however, are not clear cut; there is no obvious best job design to use. It remains the job of the manager to weigh the different factors and the tradeoffs involved in using different job designs, and based on those tradeoffs, to make a decision. The manager, however, can find help elsewhere. The people in the organization who will perform the jobs to be designed or redesigned have important information. Therefore, it is valuable and useful to involve job holders in the diagnosis of current jobs, in the discussion of job design strategies, and in the design of specific job features.

A final point which needs to be made is that jobs are designed all the time in organizations. The view often held is that jobs are designed by engineers who sit with blueprints and drawings and determine what jobs will look like. While this is certainly true in many cases, much work design also occurs during the day-to-day process of managing organizations. This is particularly true in professional, technical, managerial, and other jobs less directly tied to physical work technologies. In these situations, the design of work becomes a management function. For example, in the Kless Bider example, managers in the three groups, through their actions, encouraged the development of three patterns of work design. This was not an explicit choice; no work design meetings or conferences were held; rather, the designs emerged over time. When such designs emerge over time, little thought is given to the consequences of different work arrangements.

In the absence of explicit job design, the traditional approach to job design usually is taken because it has become so deeply ingrained in our thinking about work, jobs, and management. Faced with a task and a set of people to do it, as in the research assistant example, it is natural to think about dividing the task into distinct subtasks, specifying how those are done in a consistent manner, identifying who is most skilled to perform each, and then assigning those best skilled to do one subtask, with a manager or supervisor to do the coordination that is necessary so that all combine to create a total task. Given the general acceptance and use of such approaches, it is not surprising that too many jobs are designed that have low variety, low task identity, low autonomy, and low feedback.

Summary: Job Design as a Management Process

We have stressed that the design of work is an important factor that influences how employees feel, how they perceive the work situation, and thus, how they behave. The job that a person does has a central influence on behavior. In addition, three different approaches to thinking about and designing work have been discussed — scientific management, individual job enrichment, and autonomous work groups. The point has been made that no one approach to designing work is best for all situations and that a number of issues need to be considered as choices are made among different job designs.

In reality jobs are designed all the time. The manager modifies job design on a day-to-day basis. The design of work is potentially another tool that the manager has to motivate effective organizational behavior. To rely on traditional work designs is to throw that tool away or to misuse it. The principles that were mentioned for designing enriched individual jobs or autonomous work teams can be applied to many work settings with relatively little effort. The important learning is that managers need to think about work design and actively participate in the design of work for individuals and groups as a basic part of building and managing organizations.

Suggested Readings

Cherns, A. "The Principles of Sociotechnical Design," *Human Relations*, 1976, *29*, 783–792.

Hackman, J. R., and Oldham, G. R. *Work Redesign*. Reading, Mass.: Addison-Wesley, 1979.

Hackman, J. R., and Suttle, J. L. *Improving Life at Work*. Pacific Palisades, Cal.: Goodyear, 1977.

Herzberg, F. *The Managerial Choice*. Homewood, Ill.: Dow Jones-Irwin, 1976.

Section III

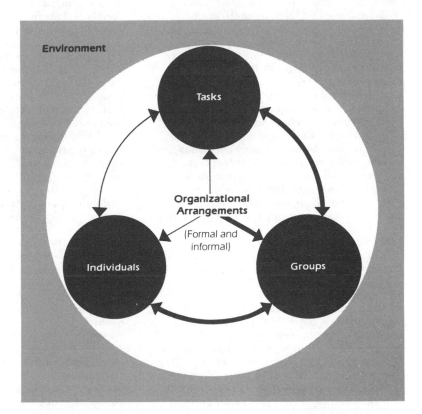

Group
Behavior in
Organizations

OVERVIEW / When we think about organizations, most of us picture a collection of individuals, each of whom has his or her own job, supervisor, and career. And when we attempt to explain why people behave as they do in organizations, we talk about the relationships between individual characteristics (for example, personal needs and job-related skills) and organizational practices (for example, compensation plans and how jobs are designed). Such relationships between individuals and organizations are of great importance, and were the focus of the previous four chapters.

Yet views of organizations that emphasize individual-organization relationships overlook one very important fact: Much of a person's work time in an organization is spent with other people, as a member of various formal and informal groups. In this section, we will explore the importance of groups in understanding organizational behavior, and show how a good portion of the manager's job has to do with the design and management of various kinds of groups in organizations.

We begin by examining the nature of groups and how they operate. Chapter 6 will explore the diverse kinds of groups that exist in organizations and analyze the purposes that groups can serve for their members and for the broader organization. We give special emphasis to an issue that is of paramount importance to any manager who deals with groups: why some groups are very significant in the lives of their members and powerful in affecting organizational productivity, while others groups are so impotent and irrelevant that they can safely be ignored. Chapter 6 concludes with a framework for classifying different types of groups with which a manager must deal.

After this introductory material, we will turn, in the next three chapters, to the specifics of dealing with groups in organizations. Chapter 7 will analyze the dynamics of group influences on individual organization members. Like formal reward systems and the design of jobs, groups provide motivation and satisfaction to individuals and influence their on-the-job behavior. In Chapter 7, we will attempt to identify those factors that make the most difference in determining whether groups foster or inhibit the work motivation and satisfaction of their members.

One of the most important organizational issues having to do with groups is how well they perform tasks. In Chapter 8, a model of task group effectiveness will be presented. Design factors are identified that can be used to diagnose group functioning as well as to improve group performance.

Finally, the organization, and in particular managers, can have a great influence on how groups develop, how they influence individual behavior, and how they perform work. Chapter 9 will build on Chapters 6-8 and will develop a set of strategies for managers to use in effectively leading different types of work groups.

Overall, Section III highlights the importance of groups in organizational behavior. It shows that groups, when well understood and well managed, can serve both the needs of individual members and those of the organization in which they exist.

Chapter **6**

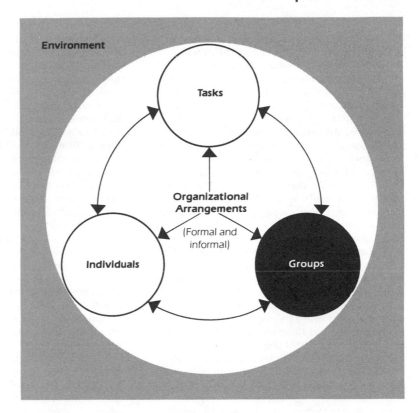

Groups in Organizations

Arnold Tanner is a member of a five-person team that assembles and codes information needed to effect the legal transfer of stocks in a large metropolitan bank. He also serves on a temporary, cross-departmental task force that was formed to redesign computer procedures to speed up the processing of stock transfers and reduce the error rate. In addition, he is one of a dozen younger members of the organization who support one another in attempting to change certain organizational policies that they find unnecessarily restrictive. This group (known informally as the "Dirty Dozen") lunches together on a regular basis, and about once a week the members get together socially away from the bank.

Wilma Schaeffer is an assistant vice-president in the same bank. She is charged with coordinating the work of several sections of the stock transfer department, and created the task force of which Arnold is a member. She serves on numerous management committees (some formal and some temporary) and spends about half of a typical work day in meetings of various groups. Most important to her (and most time consuming) is her membership on the management council, which is chaired by a vice-president and charged with overall responsibility for running the securities division of the bank. Wilma also serves on the bank's affirmative action committee, and is an active member of the Women's Financial Caucus, a group of women managers from a variety of financial organizations who want to increase the opportunities for women to obtain high-level managerial positions within the financial community.

Ralph MacDonald is a clerk in the securities division of the bank. He spends most of the day at his desk coding information from stock transfer requests onto computer processing forms. Ralph has nothing to do with the bank or other bank personnel when he leaves in the evening. He is a member of no formal bank committees, and his work requires minimal coordination and cooperation with other people. Recently, Ralph was informed that he had been selected to participate in a training program in which a number of experienced clerks will be instructed as a group in new procedures to be used in a revised computer system for processing stock transfers. The training will take three hours a day for three weeks, and because he dislikes working in groups, Ralph is apprehensive about the program. Ralph identifies himself with only one group in the organization, other "back room clerks" who are male, middle-aged, and white. His membership in that group, however, does not extend much beyond the exchange of critical comments about managerial practices or about the increasing numbers of younger clerks (especially members of minority ethnic and racial groups) who have been hired into the department in recent years.

GROUPS ABOUND in the bank where Arnold, Wilma, and Ralph work, as they do in all organizations. We can get some solid clues about what life is like at work for these three individuals by simply noting the groups they are in. Moreover, to change the attitudes or behavior of these individuals, we would have to take their group affiliations into account — and we might even want to use the groups as part of our change strategy.

If a manager wants to use groups to influence behavior in organizations, what does he or she most need to know? Here are some questions that we believe to be of special importance and that will be addressed in this section.

□ To what extent are the beliefs and attitudes of individuals affected by the work groups to which they belong? How can groups be set up and managed so that their effects on members are as constructive as possible?

□ How do groups influence the productivity of their members? Are there things a manager can do to increase the chances groups will foster high productivity and high quality work? How should a manager deal with groups that enforce norms of low productivity?

□ When changes in work procedures or organizational policies are to be introduced, what determines whether a group will support or resist those changes?

□ When work is designed to be done by a group, how should the group be set up and managed to increase performance effectiveness?

This chapter establishes a framework for examining these questions. To begin, we need to understand the diverse kinds of groups that exist in organizations, and the different purposes that they can serve.

The Diversity of Groups in Organizations

Groups are so much a part of everyday life in organizations that we often fail to notice them. If you were to walk through an organization looking for all possible groups, you probably would be surprised at how many there are — and also at how *different* they are. You might, for example, see:

Work groups, in which a number of employees work interdependently to generate a single group output. The five-person team of which Arnold is a member is a work group with a clerical task. For other technologies, a work group might be responsible for assembling an automobile transmission, for caring for a defined group of patients in a hospital, or for maintaining a twenty-mile segment of a public highway. A special type of work group is the "autonomous work group," discussed in Chapter 5.

Interdisciplinary teams, in which individuals (who may have their primary organizational responsibilities elsewhere) are brought together to solve a problem or perform a task that requires a diversity of expertise. Interdisciplinary teams are a type of work group, but usually have a short life span, or are brought together only when needed for a specific problem. The task force to redesign computer procedures of which Arnold is a member is an example of this type of group.

Management groups, in which responsibility for managing an organizational unit is shared to some extent by group members. The management council of which Wilma is a member is an example of a management group that deals with specific managerial tasks and problems under the direction of the person who is officially responsible for the organizational unit (in this case, the vice-president of the securities division). In other cases, the management group itself may have final decision-making responsibility, as in some organizations where top management is carried out by an "Office of the President," composed of three or four individuals who share responsibility for the executive management of the organization.

Training groups, which are formed for a specific educational purpose and have a short life span. The group about which Ralph is apprehensive is an example of a short-term, low-intensity training group. Other training groups may be considerably more intense, such as an off-site, two-week program in which managers explore in depth their relationships to one another and attempt to develop better ways of dealing with one another at work.

Informal groups, not formed by the organization, in which individuals with shared interests, aspirations, or concerns interact with one another to seek common goals. The group of white male securities clerks of which Ralph is a member is an example of such a group; so is the "Dirty Dozen" group of young employees of which Arnold is a member. A common example of an informal group is a group of production employees in industry who informally agree to control the individual productivity of group members to make sure that organizational rewards are equitable (or sometimes even identical) for all. Informal groups can be a powerful force in an organization, and indeed sometimes form the basis for a larger "invisible organization" that can affect the potency and the effectiveness of the formal organization.

Demographic groups, consisting of members who share personal attributes such as age, gender, race, or ethnicity. Members of demographic groups may not even interact with one another on a regular basis, but still serve as a powerful point of reference for their members — for example, "the women in this company," or "the black faculty members in the university." Both Wilma (a woman manager in an organization that does not have many) and Ralph (a middle-aged white clerk in a unit that is changing in age and racial composition) are members of demographic groups. As Ralph's experience indicates, demographic groups often turn into informal groups that members use to seek shared goals through collective action.

As is the case for Wilma, Arnold, and Ralph, organization

members usually are members of several groups in an organization simultaneously (not to mention their memberships in family, recreational, or service groups outside the organization). Membership in multiple groups provides a diversity of stimulation to individuals, and a number of comfortable social "homes" for them.

Sometimes, however, multiple group memberships generate conflict and personal distress, especially when a person strongly values membership in more than one group and these groups place directly conflicting demands on the person. Wilma, for example, cares very much about the goals of both the management council and the bank's affirmative action committee, and desires to be accepted as a central member of both groups. At the moment, however, the management council is pressuring her to hire an *experienced* new supervisor for an opening in her section. Because of a history of sex discrimination in the bank all available candidates who have relevant managerial experience are male. Wilma discussed her distress regarding this matter at the last meeting of the Women's Financial Caucus, and received a great deal of support for continuing the search for a qualified woman candidate — even if it would mean an increase in pressure from her colleagues on the management council.

Functions Served by Groups in Organizations

As is clear from the examples above, groups serve many purposes simultaneously, some of which are generally acknowledged and some of which are subtle and implicit. To begin to make sense of groups and their effects, we need to understand all their major functions. They are summarized in Table 6.1.

The manager who understands these functions will be able to lead a group more knowledgeably than someone who assumes that the publicly stated purpose of the group is the only thing that counts. Moreover, the knowledgeable manager will be less likely to act in ways that accidentally subvert hidden but important group functions, thereby generating unexpected negative consequences.

FUNCTIONS FOR THE ORGANIZATION

Groups exist in organizations — whether by design or by unplanned evolution of managerial practice — because they serve important functions for the organization. What, then, are the functions that groups serve in meeting organizational needs for managerial efficiency and effectiveness?

1. Groups provide a means for accomplishing tasks that cannot be performed by individuals. An individual cannot perform a symphony or launch a rocket. Groups can. How *well* a group performs such tasks is affected by many factors, as we will see in Chapter 8. But the fact remains that for numerous organiza-

Table 6.1 *Functions Served by Groups in Organizations*

For the organization	For the individual
1. Accomplish tasks that could not be done by individuals working alone.	1. Aid in learning about the organization and its environment.
2. Bring multiple skills and talents to bear on complex tasks.	2. Aid in learning about one's self.
3. Provide a vehicle for decision-making that permits multiple and conflicting views to be aired and considered.	3. Provide help in gaining new skills.
4. Provide an efficient means for organizational control of individual behavior.	4. Obtain valued rewards that are not accessible through individual initiative.
5. Facilitate changes in organizational policies or procedures.	5. Directly satisfy important personal needs, especially needs for social acceptance.
6. Increase organizational stability by transmitting shared beliefs and values to new members.	

tionally important tasks, we are forced by the nature of the task itself to rely on a group to carry it out.

2. Groups provide the opportunity for multiple skills and talents to be applied to a task. For excellent performance, some tasks require a greater diversity of skill and talent than any single individual possesses. Examples include designing a multimedia advertising campaign, developing a computer-based management control system, or solving a complex technical or scientific problem. Groups have greater *total* resources than individuals, and they also have a greater *diversity* of resources.

3. Groups provide a vehicle for decision making that permits multiple (and potentially conflicting) views to be publicly aired and considered. Examples include a union meeting to establish priorities for contract negotiations, a session of a legislative committee, or an ad hoc meeting of the production, marketing, and financial managers of a company to allocate resources and plan production schedules. The potential for conflict among group members is present in all these cases — as is the possibility that the eventual decision will be more satisfactory and better accepted because of the diversity of viewpoints brought by group members.

4. Groups help control individual behavior within a large

social system. As the size of an organization grows, it becomes increasingly difficult to manage the behavior of organization members on an individual basis. When groups rather than individuals are treated as the "units" of the organization, some of the inefficiencies are avoided. Moreover, because individuals tend to be very responsive to the social rewards and sanctions provided by their co-workers, groups often can influence the behavior of individuals more directly and powerfully than formal organizational rules and policies. Even reward systems like those reviewed in Chapter 4 sometimes are less powerful in controlling individual work behavior than is direct pressure from a person's work group.

5. Groups are useful in implementing organizational change. Precisely because groups have strong effects on the behavior and attitudes of members, a group can help gain acceptance of change. By the same token, even the best-designed change will flounder if the groups that are affected by it develop a stance of skepticism and resistance.

6. Groups enhance the stability of organizations by transmitting to new members the beliefs and values that characterize the organization. Probably the most vivid illustration of this process is the family, where parents' religious, cultural, and political beliefs are transmitted to their children. Much the same process takes place in organizations. Work groups make sure that new employees develop the "right" beliefs and attitudes about management. Individuals promoted to management are provided by their new managerial colleagues with extensive (and sometimes intensive) instruction about "the way things are" in the organization from a managerial perspective. Even rather loose and informal groups in an organization (such as employees who happen to take breaks at the same time) can serve as vehicles for transmitting and enforcing shared beliefs and values about the organization.

It should be noted that while such socialization activities do provide stability across people and across time, they also can increase the inertia in an organization and thereby make it harder to carry out major changes in organizational purposes or work practices. For this reason, the stabilizing function of groups in organizations can be a double-edged sword: helpful for maintaining continuity but a problem when quick and major changes are required.

FUNCTIONS FOR THE INDIVIDUAL

Groups also are of great importance to the personal well-being of individual organization members in a number of ways. The most significant functions of groups for individuals are summarized below.

1. Groups help individuals learn about the organizational environment. When we can personally test our environment, we are inclined to do so. We try new behaviors to determine "what

would happen if . . ." Yet when the potential consequences of the test are very negative, or when the test is hard to do, we turn to our peers for advice and information about our environments. If we want to know how good a cup of coffee is, we simply taste it and find out. But we are much less likely to determine whether the windows are glass or break-proof plexiglass by testing them with a hammer, or to test behaviorally how much we can get away with in the organization before getting fired, because of the potentially negative consequences of such actions. In these and similar cases, we usually turn to members of our work groups for guidance. We also look to groups when it would take a long time to obtain information on our own (for example, "What's the best way to behave around here if you want to get promoted early?").

Because most groups value stability and uniformity of member views, our peers usually are quite willing to provide us with answers to our questions. The result is that groups turn out to be very useful to individuals who want to learn how their organizational environments work, especially regarding important and difficult questions about the rewards and sanctions present in the environment.

2. Groups help members learn about themselves. Individuals use groups for information not only about external reality, but to increase their self-understanding as well. When a person behaves in a certain way and then observes the reactions of others to that behavior, he or she can make some inferences about "how I am seen" or "what my impact is." These data are incorporated into the person's overall self-image. Moreover, groups provide standards of reference or comparison to assess how well we are doing, how acceptable our attitudes are, and so on. Without significant group memberships, it is difficult for a person to develop and maintain an accurate self-perception.

3. Groups help individuals learn new skills. Some groups are explicitly formed to help individuals improve their skills (for example, supervisory training designed to increase interpersonal competence and courses to improve technical skills). Also, groups created for other purposes often serve as an informal resource for members in honing their skills, as when one member obtains instruction from another about how to solve a specific work-related problem. Such sharing of skills and expertise is particularly characteristic of autonomous work groups (see Chapters 5 and 8). Members of such groups often find it advantageous to share with one another their special knowledge about work procedures and to train each other in task-relevant skills (Walton, 1972).

4. Groups help people obtain valued rewards that are not directly accessible to them as individuals. In many cases, individuals who speak with one voice can obtain rewards that otherwise

would not be available. Sometimes the goals of such collective activity are personal, as when employees unionize to seek from management improvements in individual compensation and working conditions. Other times the goals may be shared, with benefits that extend far beyond the people in the group, as when town residents form a volunteer ambulance company or street patrol. In both cases, the group serves to increase the leverage of individuals to obtain desired outcomes.

5. Groups provide for the direct satisfaction of important personal needs of their members. As stressed in Chapter 2, people are social beings and have needs for social relationships with other people. Simply being accepted and cared about by other people is important, especially in turbulent times when one's peers can provide the kind of reassurance that is needed to maintain a sense of self-worth and personal competence. We often underestimate the importance of having a comfortable "social home," simply because our social needs are satisfied most of the time. But in those circumstances when we feel alone and not cared about by our peers, the significance of this function of groups becomes very striking indeed.

INDIVIDUAL VS. ORGANIZATIONAL GOALS

Most groups in organizations serve personal and organizational functions simultaneously. The cross-departmental task force of which Arnold is a member, for example, was formed to perform an organizational task, namely, the redesign of data-processing procedures to improve the speed and accuracy of stock transfers. Yet because his membership in that group provided Arnold with exposure to technological issues and procedures that were new to him, the group also served an important function for him personally, namely, improving his technical skills and increasing his knowledge of the stock transfer operation as a whole.

Some groups are oriented primarily to organizational needs (such as work groups), while others mainly serve the needs of individuals (such as informal support groups of like-minded employees). Such differences in emphasis are to be expected when one examines the diversity of groups that exists in organizations. Yet when one set of functions becomes *too* dominant, problems can emerge: Individuals balk when they are asked to submerge most of their personal needs in the service of organizational goals, and organizational effectiveness suffers when organizational goals are ignored by a group that is wholly intent on meeting personal needs. To effectively manage groups in organizations, then, requires a *balance* between the functions that a group is serving for the organization and those it serves for the individual members. At times, it may be necessary for the manager to remind a group that is meeting the needs of its members that there is, in fact, a task to be done. Or, other times, it may be necessary for the manager to buffer the group from organizational pressures, in order to provide time for the group to work on relationships problems that are preventing members from experiencing social satisfactions within the group.

The Social Intensity of Groups

Some groups are hotbeds of important activities, with members intensely involved in their relations with one another or their work on the group task. Other groups are mere aggregations of individuals who have only superficial relationships with one another, and are not an important part of organizational life. These two types of groups differ in *social intensity.* And as will be seen below, how socially intense a group is may be one of its most important properties. Social intensity determines, for example, how much of an effect the group is likely to have on its members and on the functioning of the broader organization.

In Figure 6.1, we have drawn a continuum of social intensity ranging from very low to very high. The nuclear family is extremely high in social intensity. What goes on in the group is of great importance to its members, and shapes their personal identities and values. Lowest in intensity are statistical aggregations, such as field representatives in the midwest region of an insurance company. Such groups are hardly groups at all, since membership is determined simply by who happens to be considered together for statistical purposes.

We have selected three types of groups to illustrate the continuum of social intensity, one toward the high end of the scale (traditional groups), one toward the middle (coacting groups), and one toward the low end (reference groups).

TRADITIONAL GROUPS A traditional group is one that has developed its own history and set of traditions over time that are accepted and valued by all members. Members of traditional groups spend a great deal of time together, work interdependently, and view the group as an

Figure 6.1 *A Continuum of Social Intensity*

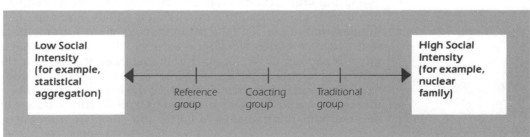

important part of their lives. Relationships among members of traditional groups are clear: People know their place in the group and act accordingly. While the group can have a strong influence on member beliefs, attitudes, and behaviors about group-related matters, this influence does *not* extend throughout the whole of members' lives and experiences. Instead, the impact of the group is mostly limited to the context in which the group exists. Attempts by a work group to influence member views about religious, political, or family matters might be considered out of bounds, and ignored. Members rarely are rejected from traditional groups (instead, the group is likely to apply strong pressure to bring deviant members back into line), but all members realize that staying in the good graces of the group is dependent on behaving in accord with group standards. Many work groups in organizations are traditional groups, such as aircraft cockpit crew members who fly together regularly, a management team, or an assembly crew in industry.

COACTING GROUPS

While members of coacting groups have face-to-face contact and informal interaction, they do not work together on a common group task. Instead, they have individual tasks that they perform in the presence of co-workers. It is unlikely that very elaborate social structures will develop in coacting groups, since members do not have to coordinate their activities. People tend to flow in and out of coacting groups easily, without other group members taking much notice. For this reason, members are rarely rejected from coacting groups, but neither are they likely to feel well accepted by other members or that the group is a very important part of their life at work. Coacting groups can develop into traditional groups if members decide to work together to achieve some goal. For instance, a coacting group of production workers assembling electrical components in the same room might decide to band together to obtain better working conditions or to oppose a change in work procedures, whereupon they would become interdependent and no longer mere coactors.

REFERENCE GROUPS

As used here, the term *reference groups* refers to some identifiable set of people that individuals use as a benchmark to assess the validity of their beliefs or attitudes, or to gauge their own level of ability or performance. Members of a reference group need not work together on a shared group task. Indeed, it is not even necessary for them to have direct contact with one another. All that is required is that the person using the group as a point of reference have some means of identifying who is (and who is not) a member of the group. While reference group members *may* develop some shared traditions or generate norms about appropriate behavior, this is not necessary for the group to be useful to individuals as a point of reference. Membership in reference groups tends to be determined by one's personal attributes: age, gender, race, ethnic or religious heritage, organizational affiliation, and so on. Rarely are individuals rejected from such groups (although it happens: "He's the whitest black man I know — don't have anything to do with him!"). Yet even when such rejection is attempted by the group, an individual may still choose to use the group as a point of comparison for his or her own beliefs, attitudes, and behaviors.

Consequences of Social Intensity

As should be apparent from the above descriptions, what happens in a group depends a great deal on its social intensity. If managers are to behave in ways that increase the effectiveness of groups in organizations, it is important that they understand both the benefits and the risks of high social intensity.

GROUP CONTROL OF MEMBERS

The more intense a group, the greater its impact on individual members, and therefore, the more the group can control member behavior. There are two reasons for this: (1) groups with high intensity generate more pressures toward conformity and uniformity and, at the same time, (2) members of such groups *care* more about interpersonal rewards and sanctions from their peers than do members of low-intensity groups. Thus, members of a high intensity group receive relatively more pressures to comply with the wishes of their peers, and tend to comply more with those pressures because of a fear of losing the positive regard (or gaining the disfavor) of those peers (Hackman, 1976).

While it is clear that group control over members is more powerful in high- than in low-intensity groups, what is uncertain is the *direction* of that control: toward (vs. against) organizational goals, or to enhance (vs. impair) the personal well-being of group members. One study, for example, showed that in work groups that were more cohesive or intense, there was less *variation* in the productivity of group members than was the case for looser and less cohesive groups (Seashore, 1954). But sometimes the performance of these groups was excellent (and congruent with organizational goals) and other times it was poor; all that the high level of member cohesiveness did was to give the group means to *enforce* whatever the standards of the group were.

ASSEMBLY EFFECTS

Social intensity also affects the likelihood that an *assembly effect* will develop as the group works on its task. By *assembly effect* we mean an outcome that is synergistic; that is, the unique product of the group members acting *together* (Collins and Guetzkow, 1964). Sometimes assembly effects are very much in the best interest of the organization (for example, when an interdisciplinary scientific team "clicks" and comes up with a new and original idea that is qualitatively more creative than the simple combined ideas of individual team members). Other times, the assembly effect results in an outcome that is qualitatively *worse* than the combined ideas of individual members. An example is the "groupthink" phenomenon, in which group members provide support and reassurance to one another about a planned course of action that is objectively disastrous, such as the planning for the Bay of Pigs invasion by members of the Kennedy administration (Janis, 1972).

A socially intense group "looks good" to most who observe it: Members are heavily involved in the group, they personally care about it, and lots of energy is expended on group-related matters. For this reason, managers often engage in "group building" activities to help a less intense group become more so, such as providing opportunities for members to spend more time together, exhibiting a leadership style that encourages high commitment to the group, and so on.

Such activities may indeed enhance the social intensity of the group. And as a result, the amount of control the group has over its members will increase, as will the likelihood that the group will generate synergistic outcomes. The problem is that such outcomes may or may not be beneficial. In Chapter 7, we will explore some of the factors that affect whether the activities of socially intense groups are more likely to contribute to organizational effectiveness and the personal well-being of group members, or detract from them.

A Summary Framework for Describing Groups in Organizations

In this chapter, we have suggested two dimensions on which groups in organizations can be differentiated: (1) their functions (relative emphasis on organizational vs. individual goals), and (2) their social intensity (high vs. low). These dimensions can be placed together, as depicted in Figure 6.2, to classify any group that exists in an organization.

What kinds of groups might characterize the four quadrants in the figure? Quadrant A is typified by a group of workers on a machine-paced production line. The group is strongly oriented toward organizational goals, and the fact that members are spread out along a noisy production line makes it unlikely that group interaction can become very socially intense. An autonomous work team, in which members share responsibility for a whole and meaningful piece of work, falls in Quadrant B. In this case, the emphasis still is on organizational goals, but members work together extensively and intensively in doing the work.

A personal growth group or encounter group in which members work together intensely to gain personal learning is an example of a group in Quadrant C. And, finally, an office party

Figure 6.2 *A Summary Framework for Describing Groups in Organizations*

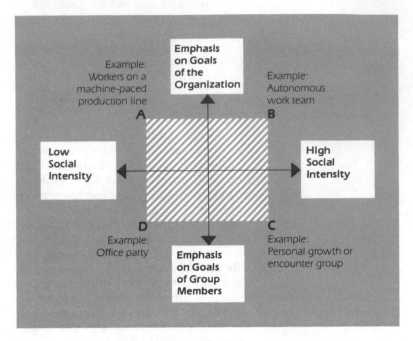

would be an example of a Quadrant D group. The emphasis in such gatherings is on personal needs and goals, and the transitory nature of the group insures that it is low in social intensity.

Most significant groups in organizations lie somewhere within the shaded area of the framework, that is, a group of moderate to high social intensity that must serve simultaneously the goals of individual group members and those of the employing organization. For high overall effectiveness, members of such groups must deal constructively with the conflict that sometimes occurs between these two sets of goals. At the same time, members must chart a course that capitalizes on the social intensity of the group to enhance group effectiveness, and avoids the real possibility that a socially intense group will turn sour.

A manager who is aware of the risks and benefits of high social intensity, and who understands the inevitability of occasional conflict between personal and organizational goals within a group, can help group members work together to achieve favorable outcomes. If the manager also has a good grasp of the ways that groups influence the attitudes and behaviors of their members, he or she will be able to help even more. It is to this question that we turn in the next chapter.

Suggested Readings

Cartwright, D., and Zander, A. *Group Dynamics: Research and Theory*. 3rd ed. New York: Harper and Row, 1968.

Davis, J. H. *Group Performance*. Reading, Mass.: Addison-Wesley, 1969.

Leavitt, H. J. "Suppose We Took Groups Seriously . . ." In *Man and Work in Society*, edited by E. L. Cass and F. G. Zimmer. New York: Van Nostrand Reinhold, 1975.

Chapter **7**

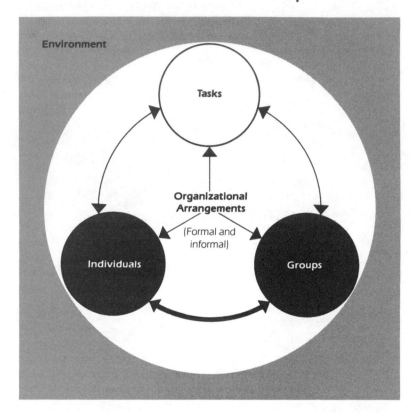

Group Influences on Organization Members

The mechanics in the vehicle maintenance department of a large midwestern retailing organization are a frequent topic of conversation among managers at the warehouse where the garage is located. This is not because the group is a problem. On the contrary, managers speculate about what makes members of that group so productive and so constructive in their attitude toward the work and the store.

Everybody seems to work very hard and without being pushed. It is almost as if the mechanics see it as a sign of personal failure if, at the end of any evening, any one of the store's automobiles or trucks is not ready to go on the road in the morning. Mechanics also exhibit a willingness to help one another. Each mechanic has a specialty (such as transmissions, brakes, or electrical systems), and each also does general repair work and preventative maintenance. If a transmission man runs into an electrical problem as part of his regular repair work, he will invariably call over the electrical specialist for help. Not only does the repair get done right, but the person who asked for help winds up learning something in the bargain.

The garage manager lets mechanics make most of their own decisions about how to do the work. He steps in only when asked to or when special circumstances arise, such as helping a new employee get settled in, or going to higher management to argue for new equipment or for a change in organizational policy to benefit the group. The manager reports that the friendly and cooperative spirit observed on the garage floor seems to extend to off-duty hours as well: Mechanics frequently stop off together after work for a beer or coffee or get together socially over the weekend. Sometimes work is a topic of conversation at these after-hours gatherings, and sometimes a mechanic comes to the garage on Monday morning with a new idea for doing some part of the work. The new rotational system for preventative mainte-

nance, for example, was suggested by a mechanic and seems to be working much better than the old fixed date system. That innovation reduced substantially the number of back-up vehicles needed, and resulted in a bonus for the mechanic who suggested it.

What could be done, the warehouse managers ask themselves, to make the shipping department function even half as effectively as the vehicle maintenance department? To describe the shipping department, one could simply describe the way things are in the mechanics group — in reverse. Nobody works very hard in the shipping group, not even when a long weekend is coming up and it is essential to clear the docks before closing up — not even when a truck is waiting outside, the driver impatient to get going so he can finish rounds before closing time.

The men in the shipping department seem to get on with one another perfectly well. At least there is a lot of friendly talk back and forth and apparently many private jokes and understandings among them. But the talk is rarely about work, other than to bring back into line someone who seems to be pushing too hard to get a shipment out in a rush. The men do help one another, but when a worker gets someone else to help him with a particularly bulky shipment, the work seems to move more slowly than it would had the first man done it alone.

The shipping foreman constantly gets complaints about delays and errors in shipments, and he always lets his men know of such problems. But they simply do not seem to care. Indeed, the foreman feels as if he is in a contest, with himself and the store and the customers and the truckers all on one side and the men in the shipping department on the other — and the men are winning!

The managers at the warehouse do not talk much about the inventory clerks. In fact, there is not much to talk about. The clerks come in, collect their data, make their reports, answer questions when someone calls, and go home. Each clerk has his or her own section of stock to keep track of, and people pretty much tend to their own business. Although all the clerks work in the same large room, there is not much informal talk among them. Indeed, the clerks are as likely to sit and talk with people from different departments at coffee or lunch as they are with other inventory clerks.

Some of the clerks work very hard, and others do not; some are almost perfectly accurate, and the work of others is riddled with errors. Nobody, save the supervisor, seems to notice these differences among the clerks. For her part, the supervisor tends those that need tending to, and leaves alone those who can get along without much help or supervision. She reports that she does not feel she is managing a "group" but rather a loose collection of individuals, some of whom are better workers than others. And that, the supervisor reports, is perfectly all right with her.

HOW ARE WE to understand the dramatic differences in the behavior of the people in these three groups? Why is it that each of the mechanics pitches in and works hard, while the men on the loading dock seem to work as hard at *not* working, and the inventory clerks differ widely on almost every performance measure?

The answer has to do with the effects of groups on their members, and in this chapter we will set forth the nature and extent of these effects. We will start by examining how groups affect members' *beliefs* and *attitudes*. Then we will turn to group *norms*, which are the shared views of group members about the desirability of various overt behaviors.

The chapter ends with a discussion of the key attributes of "good" groups in organizations (such as the group of mechanics described above), and with some suggestions of what managers can do to foster group-individual relationships that benefit both the organization and individual group members.

Group Influences on Member Beliefs and Attitudes

Our beliefs and our attitudes are continuously shaped by the social relationships we have and the groups of which we are members. This process starts in early childhood and continues throughout our lives. Other people affect not only what we think and feel about the world we live in, but also what we think of ourselves: how competent we are, how happy we are, how good a friend we are to others, and so on.

DISCRETIONARY STIMULI To understand how these effects develop and what can be done to manage them, we need a new concept — the *discretionary stimuli* that are exchanged among members of a group. A discretionary stimulus can be almost anything — a smile, a reprimand, money, information, expressions of caring or disdain, advice, or whatever. What is critical is that the stimulus is *given to a group member by his or her peers at their discretion,* depending on what the person says or does.

In the group of mechanics, discretionary stimuli might include congratulations for someone who solves a particularly tough repair problem, a disapproving glance for someone who is loafing, or some "confidential" negative information about a manager who is disliked by the group. These responses are all discretionary stimuli because they are transmitted to the individual contingent on the person's behavior in the group (Hackman, 1976).

Discretionary stimuli provide a convenient and direct means for group members to maintain order and predictability within the group about such matters as who is to do what, how the external environment of the group is to be dealt with, and what the bounds of acceptable individual behavior are. Thus, discretionary stimuli serve the group by helping it avoid the chaos that can develop when all members are behaving only to meet their own individual needs.

Why do discretionary stimuli work in controlling member behavior? Think back to Chapter 2, where the expectancy model of motivated behavior in organizations was presented. It showed that a person's motivation is affected jointly by (1) the person's expectancies (or beliefs) about the consequences of a contemplated behavior and (2) the valence or value the person attaches to those consequences.

Most people value the approval of their peers, and have needs for information from other group members. So if it becomes clear that a certain behavior will elicit approval from others (or prompt them to provide some needed information), then people are likely to engage in that behavior. If, on the other hand, the behavior will result in nothing but grief, then it is unlikely to be exhibited. People learn quickly which behaviors earn the esteem of their colleagues, which behaviors are risky, and therefore how to act so that the group experience is as satisfying as possible.

Discretionary stimuli affect far more than minute-to-minute behavior. They also shape what a person believes about the group and its environment, and even what the person likes and dislikes. We will look first at how groups shape member beliefs, and then turn to group influences on member attitudes.

EFFECTS ON MEMBER BELIEFS

There are two circumstances under which group members are likely to take a special interest in shaping the beliefs of other members. The first is when the group itself is new, and members are struggling together to develop a shared sense of the nature of organizational "reality." Unless some level of consensus is achieved in the group about what kinds of behavior pay off and what kinds do not, it is difficult for the group to develop into a mature social unit capable of coordinated action to achieve its goals. For this reason, there usually is a great deal of checking and testing in a newly formed group about what leads to what in the group and the organization.

A second time when discretionary stimuli are actively exchanged to shape the beliefs of group members is when the stability of the group is threatened. Such a threat may occur because of turbulence in the external environment of the group (for example, a new manager, new work procedures, or the possibility of layoffs) or turbulence internal to the group itself (for example, a change in group membership or disagreement and conflict among members about how people should behave).

How about the other side of the coin? When are individuals most likely to accept information about reality from their peers? In general, data from the group are mostly likely to be accepted:

1. When the nature of reality is objectively unclear. If "the way things are" is unsettled, vague, or confusing, then individuals are unable to obtain reliable, trustworthy information on their own and they turn to the group for help. This means that the group will have especially strong effects on member beliefs about the *social* aspects of the workplace (such as who is and is not powerful or the personality of a significant manager). These matters usually are harder to pin down on one's own than are more objective aspects of the organization.

2. When the individual feels poorly qualified to assess and judge reality. A low level of confidence can be a relatively enduring characteristic of the individual, in which case we would say that the person has low self-esteem. Or low confidence can be a more transitory state of affairs, perhaps induced by a recent failure to size things up correctly. In either case, the individual is likely to turn to the group for help in getting an accurate fix on reality.

3. When the group is viewed as an especially trustworthy and credible source of information. Obviously, an individual who needs help in developing accurate beliefs about the organizational environment is more likely to accept data from the group if that group appears to have trustworthy information than if it does not. Both the previous success of group members in discerning how things operate in the organization and the degree of unanimity among group members make the group believable. On the other hand, the attractiveness of the group itself will have little effect on the credibility of the group as a source of information.

To summarize, consider someone who joins a work group that has, over time, come to be a very high intensity social unit. Because the new member potentially could disrupt the comfortable, well-established group process, it is in the interest of veteran members to help that individual see things as the group sees them as quickly as possible. And because the new member is likely to be rather unsure in his or her perceptions of reality, the person is quite likely to turn to the group for information. As a result, a great deal of information is supplied by the group to the individual, who accepts most or all of it.

For the group and the organization, this has the advantage of maintaining control and keeping things running as they usually run even as new members are absorbed into the system. The disadvantage, of course, is that any fresh and innovative perceptions that the new member brings to the group are likely to be swamped as the person is socialized to see things "the way they are in this organization." The task of the manager, then, is to monitor the strength and extent of group influences on member beliefs — and to take action when necessary to help the group remain open to new ideas and perspectives while simultaneously maintaining appropriate internal stability and control.

EFFECTS ON MEMBER ATTITUDES

Attitudes refer to the liking or disliking an individual has for some person, thing, or idea. The difference between a belief and an attitude, in essence, is the difference between thinking and feeling. In general, attitudes tend to be more personal and resistant to change than are beliefs. Indeed, when groups do influence the attitudes of their members, it usually happens indirectly. That is, rather than attempting to directly change how much someone likes something, the attempt is to change what the person *believes* about it, or how the person *behaves* with respect to it. As discussed below, attitude change usually follows significant changes in beliefs or behavior.

Change via Beliefs. A person's attitudes are closely tied to the beliefs that he or she holds about the object of the attitude (Fishbein, 1967). For example, an employee's positive attitude toward labor unions (that is, "unions are good") might be based on beliefs that unions help workers earn more money, that unions keep managements from exploiting employees, and that unions contribute to a healthy national economy. If the employee is promoted to a management job, then he or she may be subjected to discretionary stimuli from new peers that tend to weaken those beliefs, change them, or add new beliefs (for example, unions hinder industrial progress, union officials often are corrupt, and so on). To the extent that the employee's new group succeeds in changing the content or the strength of his or her *beliefs* about unions, then the person's overall *attitude* toward labor unions is likely to change as well (Lieberman, 1956). It is hard to maintain an attitude about something when one receives and accepts information that is inconsistent with that attitude. And, as we have seen, groups often turn out to be among the most important sources of information about the work setting that are available to individuals.

Change via Behavior. Attitudes also are affected by how a person behaves. If the group can get a member to change his or her behavior (for example, through the use of discretionary stimuli), then the person's attitude often gradually falls into line with the new behavior.

Consider, for example, the group of men in the shipping department of the retail organization described at the beginning of this chapter. The group uses discretionary stimuli to enforce low effort on the job. When somebody seems to be working too hard, one of his colleagues is likely to let him know that he should "take it easy." What would happen to a new group member, who arrived with an attitude that "productivity is a good thing"? First, the person will learn that he receives more disapproval than approval from his peers when he works especially hard at getting shipments out. As a result, he probably will work less hard. Eventually his attitude about high productivity will become consistent with his behavior. At minimum, he will conclude that productivity is not necessarily desirable for its own sake, and he may even come to feel that high productivity is bad, something to be avoided whenever possible.

It is important to note that the more a group coerces a person to engage in behavior through powerful rewards or punishments, the *less* substantial the attitude change will be (Festinger, 1957; Bem, 1965). If the group gets a member to do something that the person would slightly prefer not to do through the offer of an enormous reward, then the person will experience little pressure to bring his or her attitudes into consistency with that behavior. The large reward suffices as an explanation for the behavior. If, on the other hand, the group elicits the behavior subtly (for example, "Come on, everybody else is doing it, and what's so wrong anyhow?"), then a large attitude change may result.

SUMMARY: DIRECT AND INDIRECT INFLUENCES ON BEHAVIOR

Drawing once again on the expectancy model (see Chapter 2), we can now specify two different ways that groups influence the work behavior of their members. These are summarized in Figure 7.1.

The *direct* way that groups influence member behavior is to use discretionary stimuli to shape member behavior on a continuous basis. When the individual values the discretionary stimuli used by a group, these effects can be quite strong, even to the extent of getting a person to behave in ways contrary to his or her preferences. The problem, when there is a problem, has to do with *persistence* of the behavior. That is, if a person feels that he or she is doing something only because of coercion by other group members, the behavior may disappear as soon as the persons who are administering the discretionary stimuli are no longer in the picture. In effect, the group has obtained behavioral compliance from its members, but without personal commitment to those behaviors.

Such difficulties are avoided when the group influences individual behavior *indirectly*, by altering what people in the group

Figure 7.1 *Direct and Indirect Group Influences on Member Behavior*

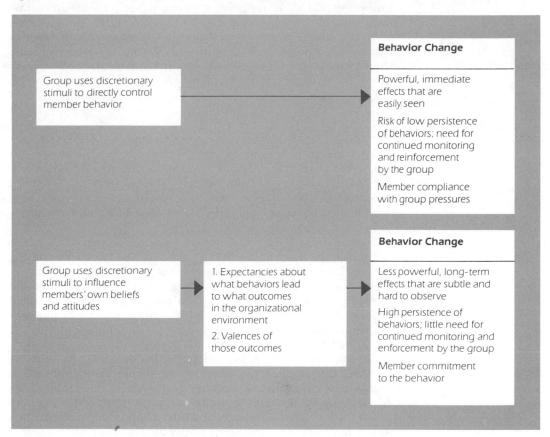

want to do. If the group can change an individual's private beliefs about the outcomes of behavior, or the attitudes of that person about the desirability of those outcomes, then motivated behavior will follow without any direct group pressure. The individual is simply behaving in ways that he or she finds personally advantageous. Such indirect influences on behavior also can be powerful but are relatively difficult and time consuming to establish.

In different ways, both the direct and indirect strategies for group influence consume a good deal of the group's energy. The continuous use of discretionary stimuli requires constant reinforcement of "correct" behaviors to avoid the persistence problem. And shaping behavior via changes in beliefs and attitudes tends to be a slow, long-term process.

Over time, groups develop *norms* that guide member behavior and shortcut the need for continuous social influence within the group. As will be seen below, norms provide a means of behavioral control in groups that can be both powerful and efficient. In many cases, managers will find it advantageous to manage behavior in groups by dealing directly with group norms, rather than by involving themselves in the internal influence processes that take place among group members.

Group Norms

Norms are so pervasive in groups that one commentator has suggested that "it is only in imagination that we can talk about a human group apart from norms" (Davis, 1950, p. 53). They summarize the agreements that members have reached, whether explicitly or implicitly, about what behaviors are appropriate and inappropriate in the group.

Norms make it easy to describe a group. We can speak of the norm that the mechanics (in the case described at the beginning of this chapter) have about helping one another in repairing vehicles. Or we can describe the norm of shipping department workers not to work very hard. In each case, knowing about norms tells us a great deal about the group and what happens within it, and allows us to make some predictions about how the group will respond to various kinds of managerial actions.

Group norms are important for efficient group functioning because they reduce the need to use discretionary stimuli to regulate and regularize member behavior in the group. Only when someone deviates from an accepted norm are discretionary stimuli needed to reestablish desired behavior. And only then may the existence of the norm become apparent to an outside observer.

A MODEL OF NORMS Norms apply only to the overt *behavior* of group members — what people do and what they say, including what they say about their attitudes and beliefs. We can characterize norms by two properties: (1) the *amount* of a given behavior that is exhibited by a group member, and (2) the degree to which other group members *approve or disapprove* of that behavior. Any norm can be depicted graphically in terms of these two properties, as is shown in Figure 7.2. The norm in Figure 7.2 has to do with the number of times a member initiates a "leadership attempt" in a group meeting. The norm in Figure 7.3 deals with the time group members arrive at work in the morning. For both norms, the vertical axis of the graph shows the amount of approval or disapproval associated with various behaviors, ranging from strongly negative (-3), through neutral (0), to strongly positive ($+3$). The horizontal axis is the amount of the behavior in ques-

Figure 7.2 *An Illustrative Norm for Leadership Acts*

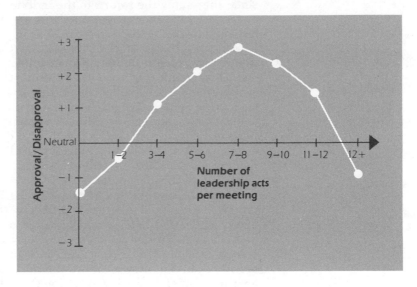

Figure 7.3 *An Illustrative Norm for Punctuality*

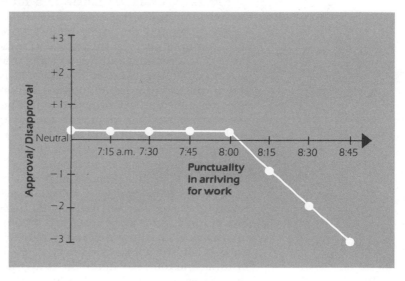

tion. The curves themselves are called "return potential curves," since they show the return to the individual (in the approval or disapproval of other group members) for any amount of the behavior (Jackson, 1965).

We can tell a number of things about a norm by examining the return potential curve. For example, we see that seven to eight leadership acts per meeting is most approved by members of the group. This peak of the norm curve is called the *point of maximum return*. We also see that one must be fairly extreme to obtain disapproval regarding leadership behavior: only if one initiates almost no leadership acts, or a dozen or more of them, does the curve fall into the disapproval range, and then only moderately so. Thus, the group shows a wide *range of tolerable behavior* for this particular norm.

As can be seen by comparing Figures 7.2 and 7.3 return potential curves can take quite different shapes. For the norm about leadership acts, a middle-range of behavior is most approved, and extreme behavior (at either end of the behavioral continuum) is disapproved. This is a fairly typical shape of a group norm. But now examine the norm about getting to work on time. Official starting time for the job is 8:00 A.M. sharp. Members do not much care if people arrive earlier than that: the curve is flat and near neutral from 7:00 A.M. until 8:00 A.M. But from 8:00 A.M. on, the curve heads rapidly down. After that, the later you are, the more your behavior is disapproved. The group member who arrives at 8:15 may be greeted with a few raised eyebrows; the one who arrives at 8:45 might find that he or she has to provide, to a skeptical audience, an explanation for clearly unacceptable behavior.

Figures 7.4 and 7.5 illustrate a different property of group norms, the *intensity* of a norm. Both norms refer to the same behavior, namely the number of work units produced by individual group members in the course of a day. For both norms, the point of maximum return is 90 units and the range of tolerable behavior is from just over 70 units to just under 110 units. But the norm in Figure 7.4 has a great deal more punch. By comparing the shaded areas of the two return potential curves, you can see that substantial approval and disapproval are associated with behavior for the norm in Figure 7.4; for the norm in Figure 7.5, only mild approval or disapproval can accrue to a group member.

A final important property of norms not shown in the figures is the *crystallization* of a norm. A norm is well-crystallized when group members agree on what behaviors are approved and disapproved, and how strongly so. When members' views about appropriate and inappropriate behavior are in substantial disagreement, the norm is said to be poorly crystallized — a state of affairs common early in the life of a group when members are in the process of "feeling each other out" about standards and as-

Figure 7.4 *A High Intensity Norm about Productivity*

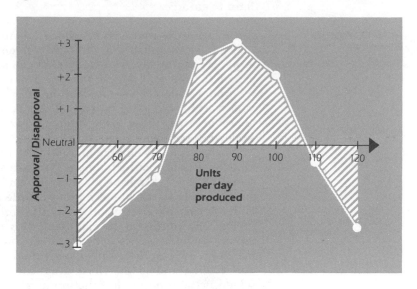

Figure 7.5 *A Low Intensity Norm about Productivity*

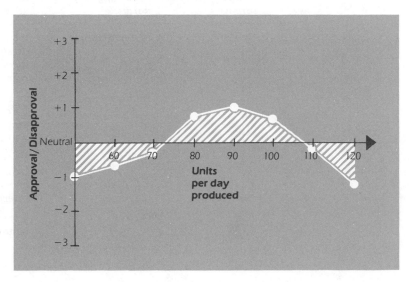

pirations for behavior in the group. Poorly crystallized norms are hard to enforce.

HOW DO NORMS DEVELOP?

Because norms are under the shared control of group members, they can be established or changed whenever members agree to do so. We might say, for example, "Let's not talk until the other person is finished," and if all agreed that this was a good idea, we would have created a norm on the spot. Thereafter, people who wait for others to finish before talking would receive mild approval, and those who interrupt would receive (probably somewhat stronger) disapproval.

Norms typically emerge gradually, as members achieve informal consensus about what behaviors are and are not valued. As seen in Table 7.1, norms about some kinds of behaviors tend to emerge early in the life of a group, while other behaviors come under normative control only after the group has matured.

The first norms to develop deal with the boundaries of the group — who is and is not a member, how much commitment members have to the group, expectations about attendance and punctuality, and so on. These are basic issues that must be resolved if the group is to function at all effectively. Early in its life, a good deal of a group's time and energy are spent on questions of membership and commitment.

Next come questions of influence: Who is going to have how

Table 7.1 *Typical Sequence of Norm Development in Work Groups*

Stage of the group	Focus of group norms	Illustrative behaviors addressed
Early	Membership	Who is and is not a member, attendance at group meetings, punctuality, commitment
	Influence	Leadership roles, strategies for doing the work of the group, status, and dominance relations among members
	Affection	Patterns of intermember liking and disliking, balance between task work and interpersonal relationships
Late	Growth	Experimentation with new behaviors, adaptation of group norms and processes to a changing environment

much "say" in what the group does, and how will group members organize themselves to carry out the task? Intermember conflict usually develops at this stage, and it must be resolved before the group can get on with efficient task work. One outcome of negotiations about member influence is the creation of special *roles* for certain group members. One person may be given the role of "task specialist," and thereafter the approval of that member's behavior is contingent on the person making sure that the details of the task are organized so that the group can deal with them efficiently. Another member may have the role of "tension reliever," and be the person the group looks to for comic relief when things get too tense for comfort. The specific roles that a group creates depend on many factors, including the personal styles of the members involved. But all groups develop special roles for some of their members. Once formed, the approval of other group members is contingent on the member behaving in accordance with the role. For example, if someone in a leadership role inexplicably quits leading, there is great pressure for that person to get back "into role" so the group can proceed with business as usual. Thus, roles are enforced for individual group members just as norms are enforced for the group as a whole.

When (and if) the group succeeds in generating shared norms and roles to deal with influence and task processes, issues having to do with affection among members (liking and disliking) often come to the surface. Norms about these questions usually specify who has a special (and often protected) relationship with whom, just what the limits are for affection in relationships among members, and how the group will balance its energy between interpersonal and task concerns. As might be expected, norms about affection are especially significant (and often difficult for members to deal with) in groups that have members of both sexes.

If a group has developed relatively clear and acceptable norms about membership, influence, and affection, it should be mature enough to proceed with its work without wasting much time on internal process issues. Yet there is a fourth developmental stage that groups sometimes reach. We can characterize this as the growth stage. It involves active experimentation with new and different ways of behaving in the group, and a more adaptive and responsive stance toward changes in the task or organizational environment. Because the group is a "success," members are able to take some risks in attempting to discover even more effective ways of behaving. Sometimes these risks involve questioning or changing the norms and interpersonal processes that were established earlier in the life of the group.

Groups do not march inexorably through the four stages shown in Table 7.1, tidying up process issues relevant to one stage and then moving into a rational discussion of its norms for the next stage. Behavior in groups is far too ad hoc and seren-dipitous for that to happen. Instead, there is a *general* tendency for movement from questions of membership to those of influ-ence, affection, and (sometimes) growth. Inevitably, a good deal of recycling occurs as that happens, often because work on one issue reveals some new perspectives on an issue dealt with ear-lier. For example, if events that transpire at the affection stage lead a member to feel personally rejected by others in the group, then the group inevitably will find itself once again dealing with issues of membership and commitment that had been settled earlier in the life of the group.

Yet when the energy of a group *is* focused on one of the stages specified in Table 7.1, members are unlikely to be very receptive to matters that have to do with other stages. A manager who attempts to push a new group into discussions about who will do what in getting the task done, when the group members are more concerned with questions of membership and commit-ment, is not likely to find the group very responsive to his or her initiatives.

The implication, then, is that a manager should be aware of the general stages through which a group passes in achieving maturity as a social system, and should tailor managerial ac-tions to help group members deal with, and develop appropriate norms about, the issues that are of greatest significance to the group at each stage. The manager should not attempt to force the group to deal prematurely with issues that may be of great organizational significance, but that are not yet "alive" for the group itself.

WHEN DO MEMBERS COMPLY WITH GROUP NORMS?

What determines when people will and will not comply with group norms? The answer has to do with (1) properties of the norm itself, (2) properties of the individual group members, and (3) properties of the group as a social unit.

Properties of the Norm. Norms that group members *care about* (that is, those with high intensity) and *agree about* (that is, those with high crystallization) are likely to elicit more member com-pliance than less intense or poorly crystallized norms. Such norms are characterized by Jackson (1975) as being high in "normative power." Members who deviate from them do so at considerable personal risk.

When crystallization is high but intensity is low, the group is in a state of "vacuous consensus." Everybody agrees about what should be done, but nobody cares much about it. Deviance from the norm is not likely to be very costly to a group member, but neither will compliance with the norm be particularly advan-tageous.

Finally, when intensity is high but crystallization is low, the group has high potential for internal conflict. People have strong individual views about what are good and bad behaviors within the group, but there is substantial disagreement among members about these views. If the norm in question is central to the purpose of the group, such a situation is highly unstable. Unless members somehow resolve their disagreements about the group norm, a great deal of energy is likely to be expended rather inefficiently attempting to regulate the behavior of individual members. It is unlikely that the group will be able to get its work done through a coordinated, concerted effort.

Properties of Group Members. Individuals often are described as conformers or rebels based on the assumption that people are predisposed either to conform or not to conform to group pressure. Such characterizations do not have a great deal of validity. On some occasions each of us conforms to group norms; other times we resist normative pressures. There simply is not enough consistency from time to time and group to group to validly attribute one's compliance with group norms (or deviance from them) as a stable personality trait. We can predict conformity to norms much better if we know (1) how much the person needs or values the rewards provided by the group, and (2) the particular status of the person in the group.

The first factor simply documents the fact that people are more likely to comply with group norms if they need or want what the group has to offer than if they do not. One of the writers of this text was called to task by his neighbors for the condition of his lawn. It was clear that disapproval would be received if the weeds were not pulled and the lawn mowed more regularly. The hope of great positive regard was even held out should beds of flowers somehow appear. Did your author conform to this well-crystallized (if low intensity) norm? No. Does this mean that he is self assured, that he has an independent personality, or, even better, that he is a rebel? Also no. He simply does not value the approval of his neighbors because he gets his social approval elsewhere.

Elsewhere, for your author, prominently includes his professional colleagues, among whom are the other two authors of this book. And when members of *this* group let it be known that the chapter you are now reading was late in arriving (about six months so), and that disapproval for tardiness was just around the corner, the author placed himself at the typewriter to attempt to reduce somewhat his deviance from the specified norm of one chapter every two months. Has his personality changed from that of a rebel to that of a conformer? Of course not. He merely cares a great deal more about maintaining the esteem of his colleagues than that of his neighbors and, therefore, is spending this fall evening writing a chapter instead of raking the leaves.

The second factor that affects member compliance concerns

the status of the individual in the group. People can earn "idiosyncrasy credits" in groups that permit them to exhibit some deviant behaviors without incurring the sanctions that might otherwise be applied (Hollander, 1958). Idiosyncrasy credits can be generated by being a good citizen in the group (for example, generally conforming to group expectations and contributing to the accomplishment of the task) or by having particularly high status or prestige (such as might derive from holding high office or from having great wisdom relevant to the task at hand). A new group member, just off the street, has few idiosyncrasy credits: he or she has no special prestige and has not had time to earn credits by exhibiting good citizenship within the group. If that individual cares about the rewards of the group, high conformity to group norms would be expected. By contrast, an esteemed veteran member of the group should have a positive balance of idiosyncrasy credits, and, therefore, more freedom to deviate from established group norms. Group leaders often have precisely this kind of freedom and use it to introduce innovations that violate existing group norms about how people should behave.

Properties of the Group. In Chapter 6, we pointed out that the amount of control a group has over its members is a direct function of the social intensity of the group, sometimes called *group cohesiveness*. What actually transpires in a cohesive group when someone deviates from a group norm? If the violated norm is reasonably intense and well-crystallized, action is usually taken at once to bring the deviant member back into line. Communication to the deviant member increases, and discretionary stimuli are used to help the member see the advantages of behaving in accord with the group norm.

While swift stamping out of deviance effectively eliminates the appearance of problems in the group in the short-term, it can be argued that the long-term effectiveness of the group may be harmed in the process. If members comply to norms primarily because of pressure from their peers (whether real or anticipated), the result may be public compliance *at the expense of* private commitment to the behavior in question (Kelman, 1961). And when a group is populated by individuals who are saying and doing one thing, but thinking and feeling another, serious problems eventually emerge.

Moreover, when deviance is extinguished very quickly, the group may lose the opportunity to explore the validity of the norms it is enforcing. That is, if compliance to a norm is enforced so well that no one ever deviates from it, the group will be unable to test whether or not that norm actually helps the group achieve its goals. Behavior will continue to be guided by traditional standards, and the kind of innovation that sometimes arises from deviant perspectives and behaviors will be precluded.

For these reasons, highly cohesive groups that have intense and well-crystallized norms, and that show few signs of behavioral deviance, may not be particularly task-effective or innovative. As will be discussed below, group effectiveness requires a good deal more than orderly internal processes.

Fostering Healthy Group–Individual Relationships

In this chapter, we have seen just how pervasive and powerful group influences on individual group members can be. Although managers often assume that what happens in an informal work group is out of their control, in fact there are many ways that managerial actions affect how groups influence individuals. In the concluding pages of this chapter, we present some guidelines for creating groups that are more like the mechanics than like the shippers introduced at the beginning of this chapter.

1. *Help the group achieve a moderately high level of social intensity.* If social intensity is very low, then a group can have little impact on its members, either for better or for worse. This is the state of affairs for the group of clerks described earlier: the beliefs, attitudes, and behavior of individual clerks are mostly unaffected by others in the group. If we were to measure the norms of that group about attendance or productivity, we would find that the norms are low in both crystallization and intensity. Neither the individual clerks nor their employing organization benefit from the fact that these people work in close proximity; things would be little different if the clerks were located in physically separate rooms.

On the other hand, groups that are very high in social intensity can develop and enforce restrictive norms about productivity (for example, those that characterize the crew in the shipping department), and sometimes generate pressures for conformity that are so strong that the individuality of members is compromised in unhealthy ways. Such problems do not, of course, develop in all socially intense groups, but are especially likely in groups that for some reason become *extremely* close-knit and cohesive. So the optimum probably is a moderately high level of social intensity, which allows for substantial group influence on individual members but does not seriously risk the rigidities that can develop when a group becomes excessively intense.

Achieving this optimum level of intensity is something of a balancing act for a manager. For it to happen, the group should be composed of people who are moderately homogeneous, since excessive differences among group members can lead to conflict and to failure of communication. Yet too much homogeneity can rob the group of task-relevant expertise — and lessen the chance that effectiveness-enhancing "creative tensions" will emerge within the group.

In addition, the manager must make sure that the group has enough, but not too much, togetherness. If group members are physically distant from one another most of the time (or working in such a noisy environment that communication is all but impossible), they cannot develop into a socially intense unit. In such conditions, the manager might wish to provide some *protected* time for group members to use in coordinating their activities and dealing with interpersonal matters. On the other hand, a group that is together all the time may develop boundaries that are so rigid and impermeable that broader organizational concerns are forgotten, and the group begins to operate as if it exists only to serve the needs of its own members. When this is a risk, if often is helpful to arrange things so that regular interchanges with nonmembers are required to get the work done.

Finally, to manage the tension between too little and too much social intensity, the manager must be sensitive and responsive to the social dynamics that take place among group members. Sometimes this will involve intervention to help members deal with interpersonal conflicts and "process problems" to increase the cohesiveness of the group; other times, when members become a bit too engrossed in the group itself, it may involve bringing the task of the group more to the forefront of members' attention.

2. *Help the group achieve a balance between the use of indirect social influence and norm enforcement in controlling member behavior.* Problems arise when a group relies excessively either on indirect social influence (such as persuasion to change member beliefs and attitudes) or on direct normative control of behavior. Indirect social influence, while useful for fostering long-term commitment to the ideas and aspirations that are most central to the group, are too time consuming to be used for the hour-by-hour management of routine group behavior. And direct normative influence, while efficient for routine behavioral control, risks compromising the commitment of individuals and extinguishing innovation if applied to too broad a spectrum of behavior. So a *balance* between direct and indirect influence strategies is called for.

Early in the life of a group, the problem is likely to be insufficient normative control over what group members do. For "young" groups, a manager can be helpful by providing members with the time and guidance they need to develop appropriate group norms and to evolve special roles for group members. In doing this, the manager must be sensitive to the group's developmental stage (that is, whether issues of membership, influence, or affection are paramount), taking care to focus on the problems that are particularly salient for the group at this time.

As the group matures, an increasing proportion of member behavior comes under normative control. As this happens, the manager should be watchful to ensure that the group does not become rigid in enforcing its norms, swamping the individuality of its members and the unique contributions that they might make to the work of the group. How the group handles deviance can be very informative in this regard. If there is *no* deviance (or if occasional deviance is immediately extinguished by other members), then the manager might help the group explore the potential usefulness of minority views. This sometimes can be done by directly fostering and supporting alternative views. Alternatively, the manager can help group members "check out" the validity of their norms. It often turns out that the norms are not as appropriate as members thought they were.

It is easy for a group, especially one high in social intensity, to become an efficient norm-enforcement machine. An important role for the manager is to make sure that the norms being enforced are functional for the group and the organization, and that they are loose enough to allow innovative ideas to be expressed and considered.

3. *Create an environment for the group that actively supports productive work behavior.* Both the mechanics and the shippers are groups of moderately high social intensity. And both groups seem to be reasonably balanced in their use of direct and indirect means of influencing their members. What, then, accounts for the striking difference in the character of these two groups and in the behavior of their members? Why are the mechanics so motivated to perform well, while the shippers use social influence to restrict productivity?

The answer, we believe, largely has to do with the environment of the work group; specifically (1) the tasks that are being done, (2) the rewards that employees obtain at work, and (3) the quality of the relationship between the group and the manager.

The nature of the group task strongly influences the set of people toward their work. As was discussed in Chapter 5, if the task is boring or frustrating, employees are likely to be oriented *away from* the work itself and toward more pleasant aspects of the work environment; if, on the other hand, the task is challenging and involving, employees are likely to be oriented *toward* the work and motivated to do it well. These tendencies grow out of the relationships between individuals and the tasks they do, and the group reinforces and amplifies them. If, as is the case for the shippers, the work is nonchallenging and tiring, group members may develop norms that restrict production, thereby maintaining equity among members and ensuring that nobody has to experience an excess of task-based frustration. Or they may generate alternative activities that are more interesting than the task, such as finding ways to "beat the system" or "fool the foreman." In either case, the cohesiveness of the group is maintained or even enhanced but at the expense of productive work. When, on the other hand, the work is challenging and involving (as is the case for the mechanics), then the opposite state of affairs often develops. Group members generate norms that actively encourage hard and committed work on the task, and an attitude of helpfulness toward each other and toward the organization.

The second factor has to do with the reward system. If it pays off in valued coin for excellent performance, and if group members perceive this, then proproduction work norms are likely to emerge (see Chapter 4). For the mechanics, there are at least two favorable outcomes of good performance. First, when the work is done well and swiftly, mechanics can spend more time learning from one another — something that most of the mechanics value. And, occasionally, a financial bonus can be earned when (as with the rotational system for preventative maintenance) the work activities of the mechanics save the company money. This is not the case for the shippers: the more they work, the more boring work they get. Moreover, financial rewards for especially good work are unknown in the shipping department. So, with little external incentive for high productivity, the workers settle into a comfortable and congenial pattern of working as little as possible.

The third factor that influences the direction of group norms is the quality of the relationship between the group and those who manage it. The manager of the mechanics appears to be well-aware that his "client" is as much an intact group as it is a collection of individuals. He speaks for the group when something is needed from higher management, he involves himself in the affairs of the group only when he can be helpful (for example, in times of internal turbulence), and he does whatever he can to facilitate cooperation and helpfulness among group members. This type of managerial behavior serves to build trust between group members and management, to strengthen the group itself, and to increase the chances that the increased potency of the group will be used to facilitate rather than impair the achievement of organizational goals.

There are at least two ways that poor management can turn a group sour. One is to violate the boundaries of the group by pretending that the group does not exist. This, in essence, is the strategy of the clerks' manager: she manages group members as if they were autonomous individuals. It is not surprising that the group of clerks is quite low in social intensity. Another faulty management strategy is to get into a tug-of-war with the group. This is the route taken by the manager of the shippers. He is management, they are workers, and he never lets them forget who is who. The result, over the years, has been the development of an "us vs. him" attitude on the part of the shippers, and a "me vs. them" mentality on his own part. We know that one of the best ways to increase the internal cohesiveness of a group is to provide it with an external enemy. The manager serves that function nicely for the shippers. Because member attitudes and behavioral norms usually become congruent with the *basis* of the group cohesiveness, it is not surprising that the shippers have developed an antiorganization attitude and well-enforced norms of low productivity.

Summary

No group is a sure bet for high productivity and internal health. If a group is low in social intensity, then it is unlikely to create major problems for the organization, but neither will it develop and enforce favorable group norms or positive member attitudes. Groups high in social intensity are sure to have substantial effects on the beliefs, attitudes, and behaviors of their members. The manager who understands the extent and dynamics of social influences on organization members will be better able to manage those influences constructively than one who does not. And he or she will realize that the *direction* of social effects on member behavior — toward or against high work productivity — depends not only on what happens within the group but also on how the manager chooses to design the work of group members, to reward their performance, and to relate to the group as a social unit.

Suggested Readings

Bem, D. J. *Beliefs, Attitudes and Human Affairs*. Belmont, Cal.: Brooks/Cole, 1970.

Hackman, J. R. "Group Influences on Individuals in Organizations." In *Handbook of Industrial and Organizational Psychology*, edited by M. D. Dunnette. Chicago: Rand McNally, 1976.

Lawler, E. E., and Cammann, C. "What Makes a Work Group Successful?" In *The Failure of Success*, edited by A. J. Marrow. New York: Amacom, 1972.

Chapter **8**

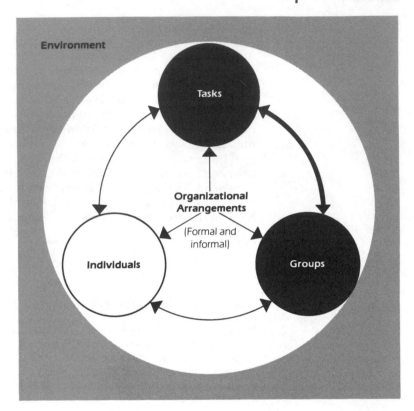

Designing Effective
Work Teams

Assembly of grain driers at Butler Manufacturing Company in Story City, Iowa, is a complicated operation.[1] The grain driers are two stories high, contain as many as three thousand parts, and sell for about $25,000. Rather than set up a traditional production line operation to assemble the driers, Butler decided that it would give *teams* of workers responsibility for constructing them. Using the language of Chapter 5, we could say that autonomous work groups were formed in the Butler plant.

Members of the Butler teams can work together pretty much as they wish in getting the driers assembled. Employees change their job assignments frequently within the teams, both as part of a formal rotational program and informally with the approval of other work team members. Typically, operators in their first eighteen months on the job master three of five basic tasks: assembly, fabricating, machining, painting, and shipping. In addition, they gain some experience with the other two types of work. At the end of eighteen months, most employees are competent to build an entire grain drier by themselves.

As part of their work, employees participate in the design and development of new products and tools. In some areas, they purchase tools and materials on their own, obtaining supervisory approval only for purchases over $200.

Work is not restricted to the plant itself. Employees are also sent out on service calls throughout the region. According to plant manager Larry Hayes, "It teaches them the impact on a farmer's business if a machine isn't working. They also learn more about the technical aspects: how the product is used in the field. And they become more in tune with our customers, our bread and butter."

There are no quality inspectors at Butler, only two engineers, and very few foremen. As

[1] This description is adapted from the *World of Work Report*, published by Work in America Institute, Inc., November 1977, pp. 124–126.

a result, there is substantial team involvement in supervisory functions, including hiring and promotion. Workers help select new team members, and two supervisors were picked by other staff from among the employees. One supervisor described how his functions are different from those of traditional first-line managers: "It's not the traditional scheduling, pushing people, and taking names. My job is heavily counseling people and behavior modification, and that's more interesting. Meanwhile, every night the conference room is filled with people having their team meetings during working hours and carrying on joint supervision."

There are many kinds of meetings. Probably most important are the weekly team meetings, in which production, quality, tooling, maintenance, and behavioral problems are considered. Leadership of the meetings rotates weekly. A monthly plant-wide meeting is held to discuss financial results and economic trends (productivity data are provided daily to each team). And a plant-wide advisory group of six production workers meets every two weeks with the plant manager, a meeting Mr. Hayes characterizes as the "pop-off valve." A summary of the questions and answers exchanged at this meeting is posted on the plant bulletin board.

With all the teamwork and meetings, it is not surprising that interpersonal skills are seen as critical to the successful operation of the plant. To facilitate development of these skills, a training program involving a thirty-hour taped seminar has been initiated.

How is it all working? Most employees seem pleased. Sue Loder reports, "Basically, you are your own boss. We are presented with a challenge: how to get an order out. It is up to us how long it takes. We get satisfaction out of doing better than standard. The team finds out a few days later how we did on any job order. We try to beat the previous month's record."

Absenteeism and turnover data also suggest that employees are, for the most part, responding positively to the team concepts. Absenteeism averages only 1.2 percent, compared to a typical rate of 5 percent or higher for factory employment. Turnover is 10 percent to 12 percent on an annual basis, compared to an average of about 35 percent for U.S. production workers. Of those who have left, less than 4 percent have been terminated; the rest have resigned, mostly to attend school.[2]

Management also is pleased with the way the plant is operating. According to the plant manager, total plant expenses are considerably lower than they were projected to be when production began. Cost reductions are especially marked in overhead expenses such as tooling and supplies, and in indirect labor costs such as salaries for office, staff, and supervi-

[2] In interpreting the absenteeism and turnover data, it should be recognized that the workforce is young and that the plant is located in a rural community where people traditionally have been hard-working and affluent.

sory functions. In addition, Mr. Hayes likes the way equipment and materials are used by employees. "We have a proprietary feeling about our equipment," he says. "People make it work."

Profits also are excellent. Before the plant opened, Butler projected what its short-term profitability would be. It turned out that profits have run 20 percent higher than projected for the first two years. "In effect," Mr. Hayes says, "we didn't lose what we expected in 1976, and this year we have made more than we expected." Mr. Hayes estimates that "we are probably 10 percent higher in profitability than comparable operations elsewhere which have been in business for 10 years or more."

"If we weren't," he adds, "the Story City plant might be in trouble. After all, there has to be a reason for doing something differently. Butler wants to see if this system, which people here call 'self-managed work teams,' truly affects productivity. We aren't in it for the fun and games; we have lots of competing companies in our marketplace."

What Are the Ingredients of Work Team Effectiveness?

What differentiates the drier assembly teams from less effective teams? What factors are most responsible for their effectiveness — and what mere window dressing? To answer such questions we must agree on what we mean by "team effectiveness." We believe that team effectiveness can be gauged by the following three criteria.

1. The productive output of the group meets or exceeds organizational standards of quantity and quality. If the group product is not acceptable to management, then the team cannot be considered a "success." Problems may develop that have to do with the quality of the product (such as a grain drier that does not work), or with the quantity of work produced (such as one grain drier every month, when one is supposed to be produced every week).
2. The group experience serves more to satisfy than to frustrate the personal needs of group members. Sometimes groups develop patterns of interpersonal behavior that are destruc-

tive to the well-being of group members. If most members find that their experiences in the group serve to frustrate their own needs and to block them from achieving personal goals, then it would be hard to argue that the group is a successful social unit.

3. The social process used in carrying out the work maintains or enhances the capability of members to work together on subsequent team tasks. Some groups operate in such a way that the integrity of the group itself is destroyed; that is, the group "burns itself up" in the process of performing the task. Even if the product of such a group is acceptable, we would not define as successful a group that generates so much divisiveness and conflict among members that they are unwilling or unable to work together in the future.

How can a work group be designed and managed so it meets or exceeds these three criteria? It would be lovely if there were simple and straightforward answers to that question, but unfortunately there are not. Nor is there any single set of managerial rules or principles that, if used, guarantees improvements in group effectiveness.

It is necessary, therefore, to work backwards from the three criteria to understand what group conditions are most closely associated with effectiveness, and then to determine how groups can be set up consistent with those conditions. In effect, we must build a model of team effectiveness that can guide a manager in identifying the actions that will enhance team effectiveness in various kinds of task and organizational circumstances.[3]

Intermediate Criteria of Team Effectiveness

The first step in building the model is illustrated in Figure 8.1. There we specify three intermediate criteria of team effectiveness; that is, criteria that are not a final measure of group effectiveness but that relate closely to how well a group performs.

The intermediate criteria are (1) the level of *effort* that group members bring to bear on the task, (2) the amount of *knowledge and skill* available within the group for task work, and (3) the appropriateness of the *task performance strategies* used by the group in carrying out its work.

If by some magic we could set all three of these intermediate criteria at an appropriate level, we would be able to help almost any group, working on virtually any task, become effective. We could, for example, ensure that members worked hard enough to complete the task correctly and on time. We could tinker with

[3] The material to follow is adapted from chapters by Hackman (1978) and Hackman and Oldham (1979).

Figure 8.1 *The Intermediate Criteria of Work Group Effectiveness*

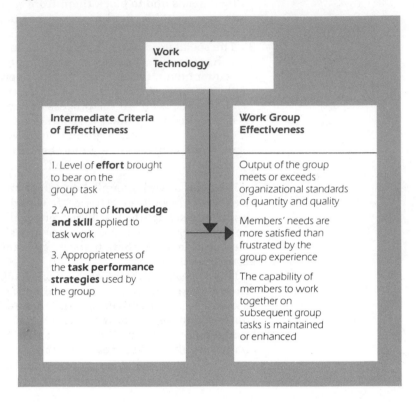

Work Technology

Intermediate Criteria of Effectiveness

1. Level of **effort** brought to bear on the group task

2. Amount of **knowledge and skill** applied to task work

3. Appropriateness of the **task performance strategies** used by the group

Work Group Effectiveness

Output of the group meets or exceeds organizational standards of quantity and quality

Members' needs are more satisfied than frustrated by the group experience

The capability of members to work together on subsequent group tasks is maintained or enhanced

the amount of talent in the group, including the mix of skills held by different group members, to make sure that there was plenty of talent available to meet the demands of the task. And we could adjust the performance strategies used by the group in its work — the ways members go about working together on the task — to make sure that these strategies were fully appropriate for the kind of work being done as well as being consistent with the personal needs of group members.

For some tasks, such as the assembly of the grain driers at Butler, all three of the intermediate criteria, as described in Figure 8.1, need to be at a high level. Producing large quantities of high quality driers requires a high level of effort, a good deal of knowledge and skill, and a relatively sophisticated performance strategy that sequences and coordinates the work of members for maximum efficiency.

For other kinds of tasks, only one or two of the intermediate criteria needs to be high. Consider, for example, a simple group assembly task, in which no complex knowledge or skill is required for satisfactory performance and for which assembly procedures (that is, the performance strategy) is fully preprogrammed. In this case, only the effort that the group members apply to the task is likely to affect how well the group performs.

What determines how important each of the intermediate criteria is for a given task? The nature of the technology with which the group works (that is, equipment, materials, and prescribed work procedures) has a strong effect, as illustrated in Figure 8.1. It usually is possible to determine which of the intermediate criteria are important in affecting group performance for a given technology simply by asking, If greater effort (or different levels of knowledge and skills, or different performance strategies) were brought to bear on this task, would group performance effectiveness change markedly? If the answer is yes for the intermediate criterion being considered, then it is significant in influencing group effectiveness.

Consider a surgical team carrying out a complex operation. Will team effectiveness (defined here as the well-being of a patient after surgery) be influenced by the knowledge and skill brought to bear on the task by team members? Yes, knowledge and skill are salient for this task. Will effort make a difference? Yes, but only moderately so; it's much more a matter of skill. How about strategy? Yes, but also only moderately; the procedures that can be used to carry out the operation are mostly prescribed by the technology, so the latitude the group has to alter its effectiveness by changing how it goes about the work is limited. Thus, we would conclude that all three intermediate criteria help determine surgical team effectiveness, but that knowledge and skill is of greatest importance.

The implication, then, is that to create an effective work team, we should first inspect the technology to determine which of the intermediate criteria are most important, and then turn our attention to ways of increasing the group's standing on those criteria. The problem, of course, is *how* to manipulate the amount of effort the group brings to bear on the task, or the knowledge and skill it has for task work, or the appropriateness of its performance strategies. We turn to that question now.

Key Features in the Design of Work Teams

Three aspects of the design of a group are key in affecting the standing of the group on the intermediate criteria. They are (1) the design of the group task, (2) the composition of the group, and (3) group norms about performance process. As illustrated in Figure 8.2, each of these design factors is closely related to one of the three intermediate criteria.

Figure 8.2 *Relationship between the Design Factors and the Intermediate Criteria of Group Effectiveness*

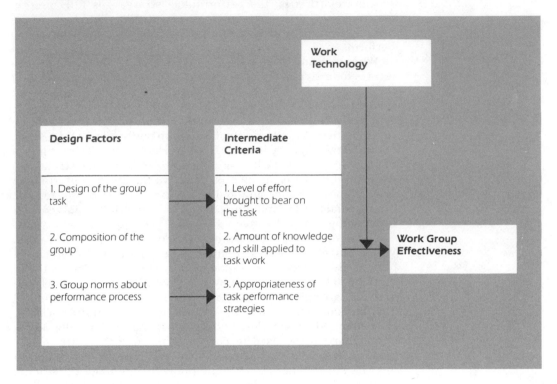

DESIGN OF THE GROUP TASK

How a group task is structured directly affects the amount of effort group members put into their work. When a manager discusses the effort (or lack of effort) that rank-and-file employees exhibit at work, the conversation often centers around the personalities of the employees or the norms of the work group. So we hear that Ann is "really a hard worker," or that Janice is "just lazy," or that the shippers discussed in Chapter 7 have an "antimanagement" group norm.

While it is true that people differ in their needs and energy levels, management cannot do a great deal about employees' personalities. Similarly, while norms clearly do develop in groups that encourage especially high or low member effort, attempts to *directly* alter group norms about effort are probably doomed to failure. The reason is that such norms do not develop accidentally. Instead, they emerge as devices *for dealing with particular problems or opportunities that confront the group.*

One important influence on norms about effort is the way the group task is designed. If a task is very low in motivating potential (see Chapter 5), group members will find work on the task boring, frustrating, and generally unpleasant. As they share their private reactions to the work with one another, eventually they may develop an informal agreement that the best way to minimize their shared negative feelings is simply not to work so hard. When members begin to enforce such an agreement, we would say that a group norm has developed that restricts work effort. Any attempt to alter that norm that does not also deal with the *reason* the norm developed would probably be futile and might even backfire.

On the other hand, if a task is high in motivating potential, so that members find the work exciting, fulfilling, or in other ways rewarding, these experiences also are likely to be shared among group members. A norm encouraging high effort on the group task may develop. The implication, then, is that altering the design of the group task is usually a better way to influence the effort expended by group members than are direct attacks on the productivity norms themselves. To do the latter, in many cases, would be to address the outcropping of the problem rather than the problem itself.

Thus, group tasks should be designed so they prompt a shared commitment among group members to work hard and perform well. We can be guided here by the properties of motivating individual tasks as described in Chapter 5. Group members should be motivated to expend high effort on the group task when most of the following conditions are met:

1. The task requires use of a variety of group member skills for successful completion.
2. The task is a whole and meaningful piece of work; that is, it has high task identity.
3. The task is significant, in the sense that the outcomes of the group's work "make a difference" to other people within or outside the organization.
4. The group has substantial autonomy to make decisions about how the work will be carried out, including the methods to be used, the assignment of individuals to subtasks, the pace of the work, and so on.
5. The group as a whole receives feedback, preferably from doing the work itself, about the adequacy of its performance.

If a group task has these properties, then the chances are increased that members will develop commitment to excellent group performance and will expend as much effort as is needed to accomplish the task. The Butler grain drier teams are a good case in point. Assembling driers is a complex and challenging undertaking, and the motivational attributes listed above are all present. Many different skills are required to assemble the drier; the group has responsibility for the whole task; the work is significant, in that how well a drier works is critical to the business of the farmer customers; the group has substantial autonomy for determining who does what when and how in carrying out the assembly; and feedback about quantity and quality of performance is either generated directly by group members (such as through their own inspection of completed driers) or provided to the group by clients (such as farmers who find that their driers do not work as they are supposed to).

COMPOSITION OF THE GROUP

How the group is composed directly affects the amount of knowledge and skill that can be applied to task work. To borrow from the Marine Corps, what is needed is a few good people. *Good* people, because far and away the most efficient device for increasing the complement of knowledge and skill available for work on a group task is to put very talented people in the group. As we saw in Chapter 3, procedures are available for use in assessing the skill requirements of various tasks and for measuring the capabilities of people to meet those requirements.

A *few* good people because member motivation tends to drop, and intermember coordination becomes increasingly difficult, as team size increases. Moreover, the unique, additional contribution made by each incremental member of a group is less and less as size increases. Adding a third person to a dyad may provide the group with substantial new resources; but adding one more person to a twenty-person group is unlikely to add much to the resource base of the group (Steiner, 1972).

In general, the risks of making groups too large are more substantial than are those associated with undermanned work groups. Yet large work groups and committees are widely used in organizations. The reasons, we believe, have less to do with considerations of group effectiveness than with emotional issues (such as using large numbers to share responsibility and spread accountability) or political considerations (such as ensuring that all relevant specialties and functions are represented in the group so they will accept its work). In many cases, managers would be well-advised to make work groups and committees smaller, and to use alternative means for dealing with worries about accountability and acceptance.

Two factors complicate attempts to compose small groups consisting of members who have high task-relevant knowledge and skill. The first has to do with the *heterogeneity* of members' skills. On the one hand, if members' skills are too homogeneous, some of the advantages of having a team are lost — including the special expertise held by different individuals for different parts of the task, and opportunities for individuals in the group to learn new skills from their co-workers. Too much heterogeneity, however, can impair group effectiveness, because insufficient common ground among members makes communication difficult or provides less-than-needed interchangeability among members. Even when the heterogeneity of member skills is at about the right level, problems can develop, particularly around the reluctance of members to share their own special skills with one another. Often individuals in a work group have a vested interest in keeping to themselves expertise they have developed, for therein lies their own distinctiveness and status.

The second complicating factor derives from the fact that an effective work group requires members to have (and to use) *interpersonal* skills as well as task-relevant skills. Interpersonal skills are needed simply to bring the task skills of members effectively to bear on the work of the group. As was pointed out in Chapter 2, people in organizations possess such skills in varying degrees, and they are not easily learned in a short period of time.

The managers who designed the assembly teams at Butler Manufacturing appear to have been sensitive to both of these complicating factors. Initial training involved mastery of three of five basic jobs, and teams were composed of individuals who had different "mixes" of skills. This provided some common and redundant skills within the group, which increased internal flexibility in assigning different individuals to different tasks as needs and circumstances changed. A moderate level of heterogeneity also was achieved, allowing (and perhaps even fostering) sharing of expertise among team members who had experienced different initial training. Moreover, management has instituted training programs specifically oriented to the interpersonal skills of the workforce, employees and managers alike. These programs have increased team members' skills in working together and their competence in managing communications between groups and across hierarchical levels in the organization.

GROUP NORMS ABOUT PERFORMANCE PROCESSES

The norms of a group affect the appropriateness of the performance strategies used by the group in carrying out the task (see Figure 8.2). Performance strategies are the choices members make about how they go about performing a task. For example, a group might decide to focus its energy on checking and rechecking for errors in the interest of a high quality product. Or members might choose to free-associate about ideas for proceeding with work on a new task before starting to perform it. Or the group might decide to divide itself into two subgroups, each of which would do part of the overall task.

All of these are choices about performance strategy, and those choices can be very important in determining how well a group actually performs. If, for example, successful completion of a certain task requires close coordination among members, with the contributions of each member made in a specific order at a specific time, then a group that has developed an explicit strategy for queuing and coordinating member inputs probably will perform better than a group that proceeds with the task using procedures that happen to emerge "naturally." What specific strategy will work best for a given group task, of course, depends heavily on the requirements of that task.

Unfortunately, group members rarely take the time and trouble to check how appropriate their strategies are for their task, even when they are told that it is to their advantage to do so, or when strategies presently in use are not working. Instead, members typically share a set of expectations about the "proper" way to carry out the work, and to some extent enforce those expectations as norms of the group.

Norms about strategy can be advantageous in that they short-cut the need to manage and coordinate group member behavior on a continuous basis: everyone knows how things should be done, and everyone does them that way with minimum fuss and bother. More time becomes available for actual task work, and the effectiveness of the group should benefit. This advantage accrues to a group, however, *only* if the norms that guide the use of task performance strategies are task-appropriate. If existing norms about strategy are not appropriate, then performance will suffer unless the norms are changed, despite their time-saving advantages.

Norms about strategy (in contrast to norms about effort) are relatively amenable to change, since they are more likely to be present out of habit than as a reflection of some basic structural feature of the task or environment. Yet, because such norms are rarely examined or tested by the group, the impetus for change often must come from outside the group.

One way to alter group norms about performance processes is for an outside agent to independently diagnose the requirements of the group task, and then to generate a strategy for the group that is objectively more task-appropriate than the one currently in use. The problem is that such an intervention is unlikely to help group members increase their *own* capability to consider and reformulate their performance processes when effectiveness is poor or when task demands change. Therefore, it usually is better to involve group members in interventions intended to improve the task-appropriateness of group performance strategies. Such an approach also can help work groups and their members become adept at handling their own task and interpersonal processes.

SUMMARY

Three design factors have been proposed as useful points of intervention for fostering work team effectiveness. Specifically, as shown in Figure 8.2:

1. The level of *effort* members bring to bear on the group task is affected primarily by the design of the group task.
2. The amount of *knowledge and skill* available for task work is affected primarily by the composition of the group.
3. The task-appropriateness of the *performance strategies* used by the group in carrying out its work is affected primarily by group norms about performance processes.

The design factors may, of course, affect the intermediate criteria in ways other than those specified above. The point is simply that these are the most potent effects of the design factors and, therefore, the most useful points of intervention.

Fostering and Supporting Work Group Effectiveness

The three aspects of work group design discussed in the previous section have strong effects on team performance, and they are things a manager can influence directly. However, they are not the whole story. The intermediate criteria — and therefore the eventual effectiveness of a work team — also are affected by the organizational context in which the group operates, and by the interpersonal processes that develop within the group itself. In this section, we review ways a manager can create a supportive context for a work team and foster task-effective internal processes among team members.

CREATING A SUPPORTIVE ENVIRONMENT

Hundreds of aspects of the environment can affect how well a group performs, ranging from mundane items such as the temperature of the workplace to more socially significant features such as the other groups with which a team relates in carrying out its work. Managers should monitor the environment of their work teams and take corrective action whenever blocks to good team performance are noted.

We have selected three aspects of the environmental context for special mention, because they are especially powerful in affecting a group's standing on the intermediate criteria of effectiveness. These are shown in Figure 8.3. First are the *rewards and objectives* for team performance. If a team is given more or less autonomous responsibility for accomplishing a given task, it is important that compensation be arranged so that rewards are contingent on group or organizational performance, rather than on the relative level of individual team member performance. As noted in Chapter 5, a group-based incentive system leads to increased individual effort and to members working together to obtain the group-level rewards. Dysfunctional group interaction that grows from the fear (or the fact) of pay inequities among members is reduced because compensation is tied directly to the output of the group as a whole (Lawler, 1977).[4]

[4] Nevertheless, a group-based reward system will not automatically solve all problems of pay equity among members, especially for groups whose members were differentially skilled and paid when the group was formed. In such cases, it may be necessary both to tie overall rewards to the performance of the group as a whole and to help the group devise an equitable internal mechanism for distributing those rewards among members.

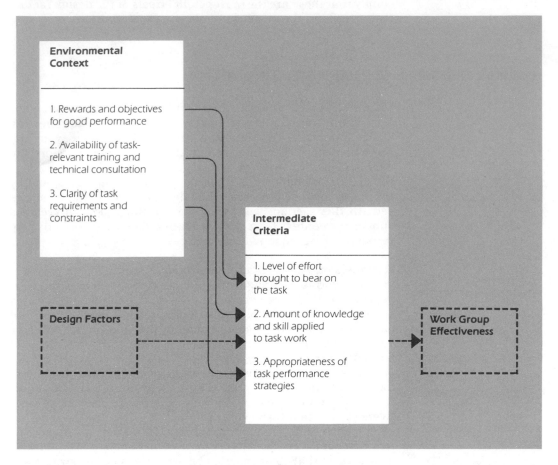

The same line of reasoning applies to performance objectives that are set for self-managing work groups, and to organizational feedback and control systems that are used to monitor performance. In general, when a group accepts a moderately difficult performance objective and has available to it feedback regarding its progress toward achieving that objective, group performance is enhanced (Zander, 1971).

Second, *training and technical consultation* relevant to the work of the group must be made available, especially when knowledge and skill are important for group effectiveness. Often autonomous work groups are formed, given a complex and challenging task, and then left to work it out on their own. If the knowledge and skill required for effective work is not already available within the group, this can be both frustrating to group members and counterproductive. So it is important that resources be made available to the group (but not forced on the group) to help members gain and share the knowledge and skill needed to perform well. In practice, this often means that a direct link is needed between the work team and a staff group that has special information or expertise about the team task. Since staff groups (such as an engineering service group in industry or a tariffs group in a regulated service organization) typically deal only with managers, the team manager often must help members of both the staff group and the work team learn that transactions between the two groups are not only appropriate but desirable. Similarly, it may be necessary for the manager to work with the organization's training department to gain acceptance of the work team as a legitimate client of training services.

Finally, the manager must take pains to clarify the objective *requirements of the group task* and any constraints that may limit how the group can carry out its work. As noted in the previous section, a well-designed work group has norms that permit active consideration of various performance strategies. The success a group has in exploring possible performance strategies depends in part on how well group members understand just what are and are not firm task requirements, and what the operating constraints are. Unfortunately, these matters are often obscure, either because nobody has taken the trouble to analyze them, or because the manager has neglected to share information about task requirements and constraints with the group. Unless such information is made available to the group, members risk developing a set of performance strategies that are nicely suited to a set of incorrect perceptions about what the task requires or what the constraints are under which the group must operate.

INTERPERSONAL PROCESSES

The quality of the interpersonal relationships among group members often leaves much to be desired. People fall too readily into patterns of competitiveness, conflict, and hostility; only rarely do group members support and help one another as difficult ideas and issues are worked through.

It would seem, therefore, that improving the quality of interpersonal relationships among members should directly increase group effectiveness. A number of approaches to improving intermember relationships in groups are based on this assumption and have been applied to work teams in organizations (see, for example, Argyris, 1962; Blake and Mouton, 1975). Such approaches often involve experiential sensitivity training or team building with intact groups, and they focus directly on relationships among members rather than on the interface between the group and its task. The goal is to help individual members gain the interpersonal skills required for high task effectiveness, or to help the group as a whole understand and improve its norms. Ideally, the group develops interpersonal skills and group norms that foster interpersonal openness about ideas and facilitate individual and group risk-taking.

Interpersonal training techniques can be powerful in changing the patterns of behavior that occur during the training itself and in altering member beliefs and attitudes about behavior in groups. The problem is that such new learnings do not transfer readily from the training setting to "back home" work groups. Nor, as was stressed in Chapter 4, do newly learned behaviors persist for long in the absence of on-going support and reinforcement. Moreover, the actual *task effectiveness* of groups whose members have received interpersonal training is rarely enhanced (and sometimes is impaired) as a result of that training (Hackman and Morris, 1975). Apparently the link between the interpersonal competence of group members and the task effectiveness of the group as a whole is neither as direct nor as straightforward as one might wish.

We believe that a manager should take a more focused approach to interpersonal processes in work teams, as summarized in Figure 8.4. As is shown in the figure, three aspects of the interpersonal process seem to be especially important in affecting the three intermediate criteria of effectiveness.

Coordinating Efforts and Fostering Commitment. When effort is salient in determining group effectiveness, it is important that members coordinate their activities in such a way that the amount of wasted effort is minimized. There is always some slippage in the coordination process that prevents a group from achieving its maximum productivity. Moreover, the larger the group, the greater this loss, simply because the job of getting members functioning together in a coordinated fashion becomes increasingly difficult as size increases. When effort is important to group effectiveness, then, the manager can help the group find ways to minimize wasted effort and to coordinate member activities so that the greatest possible "leverage" is achieved on the energy expended by each member.

The effort applied by group members also is affected by how committed members are to the group. When members value their membership in the group and find working collaboratively with other group members rewarding, the overall level of effort expended by group members working on the task usually is enhanced. Managers often can foster such commitment by helping group members understand the importance of the group's work or by encouraging the development of a positive group identity that is valued by members and consistent with their own needs and goals.

Figure 8.4 *How Interpersonal Processes Affect the Intermediate Criteria*

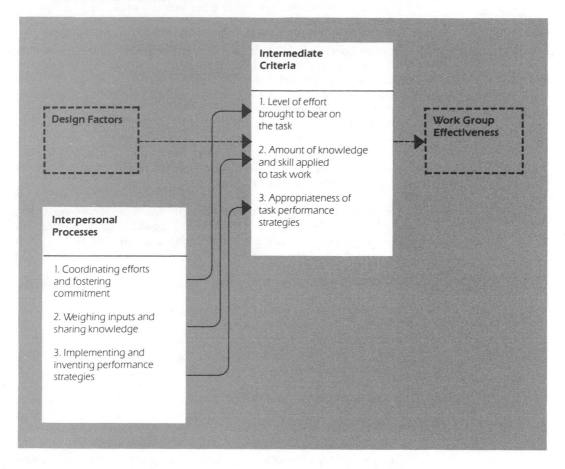

Weighting Inputs and Sharing Knowledge. Consider now tasks for which member knowledge and skills are important in affecting how well the group performs. Most groups turn out to perform less well than they "should" have performed, given the expertise of their members. Apparently, the group interaction process, through which the talents of members are assessed, weighted, and brought to bear on the task, is usually less than optimal.

Managers often can help group members improve how they assess and weight each other's contributions to the task. How this can be done is shown in a study which used the following task (Maier and Solem, 1952):

A man bought a horse for $60 and sold it for $70. Then he bought it back for $80 and again sold it for $90. How much money did he make in the horse business?

Individuals were given one minute to solve the problem by themselves and to write down their answers. They then discussed the problem and their answers in groups of five or six. Each group selected one person as its representative. Half of the groups were told that the representative would be an observer and would refrain from expressing any views about the problem. The other half were told that the representative was to function as a discussion leader, encouraging all members to participate and asking questions to help the group think together rather than as individuals. Discussion leaders were prohibited from expressing views about the task itself.

After eight minutes of group discussion, each individual again wrote a solution. Of the original (prediscussion) answers, 45 percent were correct. After the discussion, significantly more answers were correct for people who had been in groups with discussion leaders than for people in groups with an observer (83 percent vs. 72 percent).

Why did the groups with discussion leaders do better? Almost all people given this task quickly conclude that the answer is either $0, $10, or $20. Once a person has settled on either of the incorrect answers, it is possible to generate a reasonable-sounding defense of that answer. In some groups, the individual (or individuals) who had the correct answer were in the minority. These individuals may have been hesitant to argue for an answer that was at variance with the majority view, or they may have found that the other members united to convince them of the error in their thinking. The net result, in some groups, was that at least one individual had the right answer — but was unsuccessful in convincing other members of that fact. The presence of an observer had no impact on this state of affairs. But the discussion leader (who was charged with assuring that everyone had the chance to speak and be heard) apparently facilitated group consideration of minority views. In some cases, this resulted in the majority considering and accepting an initially discredited (but correct) minority view. Managers often can perform similar functions in working with task-oriented teams in organizations.

Managers also can help members of work teams learn how to share with one another special task-relevant skills, and even to work together to gain knowledge or generate skills that previously did not exist within the group. Employees who are accustomed to working more or less on their own, turning to the supervisor when help or information is needed, tend not to be practiced or skilled at sharing task-relevant knowledge with one another. Thus, managerial assistance that helps members gain this capability can be very helpful when the task requires substantial knowledge and skill for effective performance.

Implementing and Inventing Performance Strategies. The kinds of process problems that are likely to develop in groups working on various tasks are, to some extent, predictable. A knowledgeable manager often can anticipate these problems, and help group members locate or invent performance strategies that lessen the chance that members will go about the task in wrong or grossly inefficient ways.

The particular performance strategy that will work in a given instance, of course, depends on the requirements of the task at hand. That is why it is important that those requirements be as clear as possible, so the group will have as much information as possible to use in charting its own strategy for carrying out the task.

A number of standard or "off the shelf" performance strategies do exist, and often can be adapted for use by a work group. Indeed, standard parliamentary procedure can be viewed as one such device that is useful for social decision-making tasks. For tasks requiring group judgments, procedures such as the Nominal Group Technique (NGT) and the Delphi method can be helpful in combining member opinions with minimum distortion (Delbecq, Van de Ven, and Gustafson, 1975). When NGT is used, members first generate their individual ideas about the task (which has been carefully formulated and phrased beforehand), and then use a structured round-robin technique to record each idea for later consideration by the group. Each idea is then clarified so that all members understand it before evaluative discussion takes place. Actual decision making involves a structured and iterative voting procedure, which gradually narrows the number of ideas being considered and eventually leads to a group consensus.

The Delphi technique structures the group process to an even greater extent. Members make private estimates about the question that has been posed, then are provided with summaries of the views of the group as a whole. After studying this feedback, members make a new set of estimates, and the process continues until an acceptable level of consensus is reached. There is no need for face-to-face interaction at all using Delphi. A group decision can be reached with each member communicating only with a central staff by mail.

Other commonly used strategies, such as brainstorming, synectics, and creative problem-solving techniques, are oriented toward creating synergy among group members that can make the group product especially creative (Stein, 1975). In brainstorming, for example, a group follows three general rules: (1) ideas are expressed as they come to group members, no matter how silly they may seem, (2) members are encouraged to elaborate on one another's ideas, and to use a preceding idea expressed by one member as a stimulus for a new idea by someone else, and (3) no ideas can be evaluated until all ideas have been stated. These rules separate the process of idea generation from the evaluation process, so that new ideas can emerge in a storm of free-thinking without the dampening effect of comments such as, "Yeah, but that won't work. . . ."

Research on the effects of brainstorming has yielded mixed results. There are numerous case reports of enhanced creativity under brainstorming rules, and it appears that brainstorming instructions do prompt higher creativity when brainstorming groups are compared to groups in which no special instructions are given. On the other hand, there is reason to question whether gains in creativity obtained using brainstorming are attributable to special features of the *group interaction process* itself. Some studies have shown that "nominal" groups (in which individuals operate alone under brainstorming instructions with their ideas pooled later by the experimenter) show as much or more creativity as do "real" groups in which members work together interactively under brainstorming instructions (Dunnette, Campbell, and Jaastad, 1963).

Thus, while it is clear that group members often feel more creative when working under special task instructions such as brainstorming, it remains an open question just how much of a process gain, if any, actually results from the use of such techniques. For this reason, it may be advantageous for a manager to first make sure that the task requirements are clearly understood by group members, and then help group members invent and test their *own* strategies for going about the task. As members become practiced at assessing task requirements and developing strategic plans to deal with them, they may come up with ways for proceeding that are considerably more effective (and better tuned to their own group and its work) than are any of the "off the shelf" strategies that are available.

Summary: The Role of the Manager

We now have a full model of work team effectiveness, summarized in Figure 8.5. This model identifies those factors that are especially critical to group effectiveness, and it has a number of implications for how a manager should proceed to design and manage a work team.

The first thing the manager needs to know is which of the intermediate criteria are of special importance in determining group effectiveness. To determine this, the manager should look to the *technology* and ask if team effectiveness is affected by how hard the group works, by how well it applies the knowledge

Figure 8.5 *A Summary Model of Work Group Effectiveness*

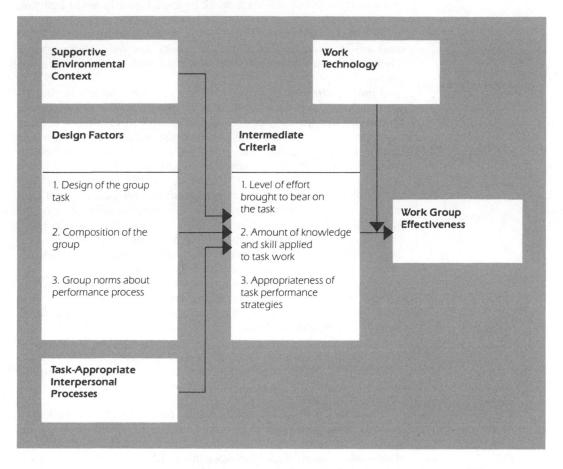

and skills of group members to the task, and by the appropriateness of the group's performance strategy. In many cases, two or all three of the intermediate criteria will turn out to be of importance.

The second step is to consider the *design* of the group. Is the group designed so that it can achieve the salient intermediate criteria? Is the task well constucted from a motivational point of view? Is the group about the right size, and does it have the right mix of members? Do the norms of the group foster open and inventive formulation of task-appropriate performance strategies?

If the design of the group is satisfactory or can be made so, then the manager's attention should turn to the *environmental context* in which the group works. Are rewards and objectives supportive of hard, effective work by group members? Is training or consultative help available, if needed, to aid group members in honing their task-relevant skills or in obtaining knowledge and information needed to do the work? Are task requirements clear, so the group will be able to devise performance strategies uniquely appropriate to the task?

Finally, after assessing both the design of the group and its environment, the manager should examine the internal processes of the group itself to determine if interactions among members are helping or impairing group effectiveness. If effort is important for group effectiveness, how are members coordinating their work on the task? Is commitment to the group and its work sufficiently high? If knowledge and skill are important, how are the talents of different group members weighted and brought to bear on the task? Are the contributions of certain talented or knowledgeable members not getting the attention they deserve? Are the views of high status individuals being taken too seriously? Are members sharing uniquely held knowledge and skills with one another? And, even better, are they working together to improve the overall level of talent of the group? Finally, if performance strategies are important, how well are members executing their chosen strategies? Is there slippage or apparent disagreement among members about how the group should proceed? Are the strategies in use fully appropriate to the task, or should the group be encouraged to reconsider how it is going about its work? Are there any "off the shelf" performance strategies that might usefully be brought to the attention of group members?

The order in which various parts of our model of work group effectiveness have been discussed — that is, technology, group design, environmental context, and interpersonal process — is deliberate. Too often a manager or consultant attempts to fix a faulty work team by going directly to work on obvious problems that exist in the interpersonal process that occurs among group members. And, too often, these problems turn out to be not readily fixable because they are only symptoms of more basic difficulties in the design of the group or its organizational environment.

The manager of a work team has a difficult job. He or she must give up traditional directive approaches to management, concentrating instead on matters of group and environmental design, and sometimes even on difficult interpersonal issues that arise among group members. As we will see in the next chapter, these activities are not likely to be familiar to managers accustomed to dealing with individuals and coaching groups in organizations. They require some special skills if they are to be carried out effectively.

Suggested Readings

Cummings, T. G. "Self-regulating Work Groups: A Socio-technical Synthesis," *Academy of Management Review*, 1978, *3*, 625–634.

Hackman, J. R. "The Design of Self-managing Work Groups." In *Managerial Control and Organizational Democracy*, edited by B. T. King, S. S. Streufert, and F. E. Fiedler. Washington, D.C.: Winston and Sons, 1978.

Schein, E. H. *Process Consultation*. Reading, Mass.: Addison-Wesley, 1969.

Steiner, I. D. *Group Process and Productivity*. New York: Academic Press, 1972.

Chapter 9

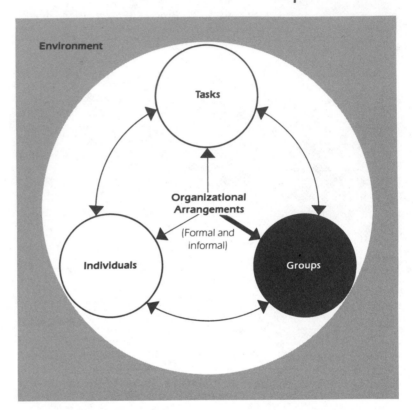

Managing
Individuals
and Groups

Joan Szczarba is a regular customer of Soup 'n Burger restaurants. There are about half a dozen Soup 'n Burger locations in the large city where Joan lives, but she frequents only two of them — the Eastside Soup 'n Burger, located near Joan's suburban home, and the Central Soup 'n Burger, located in another suburb near her office.

The two restaurants are very similar. They were built within a year of each other from the same plans and are decorated in nearly identical "fast food modern" furnishings. They serve about the same number of customers each day and, by management directive, follow exactly the same procedures in preparing and serving the food. Eastside and Central are so much alike, in fact, that it would be nearly impossible for Joan to tell which one she was in if she were to observe only the restaurant's physical layout.

But it is always *very* clear to Joan where she is eating. She is not sure why, but there is a special "feel" to each restaurant, a kind of social atmosphere that pervades the place. At Eastside, everyone seems happy. The waiters and waitresses go out of their way to be helpful, and Joan has never had trouble catching the eye of someone when she needed something. During the noon hour, when business is especially heavy, the staff seem determined to provide especially efficient and friendly service.

The atmosphere at the Central Soup 'n Burger, on the other hand, is decidedly gloomy. Everyone on the staff seems angry or impa-tient at something or somebody. Occasionally, a waiter or waitress has brought Joan food she did not order (something that has never happened to her at Eastside), and then glowered at her when she pointed out the mistake. Once Joan waited twenty-five minutes to have her order taken, while people who arrived after her were already eating. When she complained to a waiter, he informed her that it was her problem, not his, that she was in such a hurry. Joan was sufficiently upset by the event that she sought out the manager to complain. He was apologetic and promised to talk to the entire staff about the importance of prompt service and a pleasant attitude. But nothing seemed much different on future visits.

Joan, a manager herself, is puzzled by the differences between the two restaurants and has tried to figure out the reasons for them. At first, she thought that the people were somehow different, but she could not figure out in what ways. There seemed to be about the same numbers of males and females, blacks and whites, and young and old workers. The nature of the work itself, order-taking and service procedures, and physical arrangements were all very similar.

Maybe, Joan has concluded, the differences have something to do with the two managers. Maybe one is a better, more inspiring leader than the other. But what, Joan wonders, might be the specific differences between the managers that account for such large differences in the climate and work behavior of employees in the two restaurants?

EVERYONE KNOWS that leadership makes an enormous difference in the attitudes, motivation, and performance of people in organizations. But how? What is it about some leaders that inspires commitment and enthusiasm among their subordinates, and what is it about others that engenders subordinate apathy — and that only because overt rebellion is not worth the bother?

Early researchers guessed that the key had to do with the leader's personality. Surely, they thought, some personality traits — perhaps extroversion or perseverance — could be used to separate effective from ineffective leaders. A long line of investigations by researchers attempted to identify such traits. And while some individual differences were found that related to leader effectiveness, the size of the relationships were so small that they were not very meaningful or useful.

More recently, researchers have tried to identify effective leadership *behaviors*. It may be that effective leaders typically behave in certain ways, and ineffective leaders tend to behave in other ways, regardless of their personality makeup. If such behaviors could be identified, then it might be possible to train leaders to behave effectively. Maybe virtually anyone can be an effective leader, if he or she can be taught the right way to relate to subordinates.

How has the idea worked out? Sadly, not as well as once was hoped. There are several reasons why. For one, it turns out that it is not altogether clear *what* behaviors should be taught to leaders. Should they be trained to give subordinates as much autonomy as they can? Or to be very closely involved with them, but only to help them develop their own approach to doing the work? Or to be closely involved and highly directive about what to do when? Or to be very democratic or participative? All of these behavioral strategies work sometimes; other times they do not.

Perhaps, then, we should train leaders to be *responsive* to their subordinates, to the imperatives of the task and technology, and to the organizational context in which the work is done, adapting their leadership behaviors and styles to the situations in which they must carry out their leadership activities. This seems somehow more realistic, but what aspects of the people, the work, and the workplace are most critical, and what behaviors are best under which circumstances?

Unfortunately we do not yet know for sure. There has been a great deal of research on "consideration" and "initiation of structure" as leadership styles, for example.[1] However, it is not yet clear exactly how these important behavioral dimensions affect the productivity of subordinates (although there does

[1] Consideration reflects the degree to which the leader relates warmly to subordinates, shows trust in them and listens to them, is willing to explain his or her actions, and so on. Initiation of structure is the degree to which the leader actively organizes and structures the work, and specifies who is to do what under various task and organizational circumstances. The two dimensions of style are independent: it is possible to be high on one and low on the other, high on both, or low on both.

seem to be a reasonably stable finding that subordinates are more *satisfied* when the supervisor behaves considerately than when he or she does not). Research presently is exploring the contingencies that determine when "structuring" and "considerate" styles will be best for productivity and satisfaction. But at present we do not know a great deal about the circumstances under which one or another supervisory style is optimal, and it is starting to look as if the answer that eventually emerges is going to be a complex one.

Indeed, the findings that are emerging from research on leadership style suggest that the complications are such that it may never be realistic to fully "program" someone in how to behave in different leadership situations. And even if such a program could be developed and taught to a leader, real questions remain about whether leaders would be willing and able to behave in accord with the program.

Until recently, most research and theory on leadership have been based on the assumption that the behaviors of the leader *caused* changes in the work behavior and satisfaction of subordinates. It now appears, however, that the leader's style may in many circumstances be as much a consequence of subordinate behavior as it is a cause of that behavior (for example, Lowin and Craig, 1968; Farris and Lim, 1969). Specifically, if a supervisor is charged with managing a group of subordinates who are competent in carrying out their work and pleasantly cooperative with the supervisor, then the supervisor may "naturally" behave in ways that are considerate of the employees, and be very participative with them in making work-related decisions. But if the subordinates are clearly incompetent in their jobs, and moreover behave with active hostility to the supervisor, the natural course of action may be a much more structuring, directive, and autocratic style.

In sum, many leadership training experiences appear to be based on assumptions that (1) leaders are substantially in control of their own behavior vis-à-vis subordinates, and (2) leader behavior influences subordinate attitudes and work behavior much more than vice versa. There now is reason to be suspicious of both assumptions and, therefore, to be skeptical about the degree to which substantial improvements in employee work behavior and satisfaction can be wrought simply by training supervisors to behave differently.

Where does this leave us? The findings summarized above require us to view leadership basically as an *influence process* in which people attempt to get other people to behave in certain ways. And we must view that process as two-directional, with both leaders and subordinates on both the sending and the receiving ends of influence attempts (cf. Graen, 1976).

In the next section, we will provide a basic model of leadership as social influence to help us understand how it is that influence attempts by leaders affect, and are affected by, the behaviors of followers. Then, in the sections to follow, we will discuss in turn special leadership issues in managing individuals, managing coacting groups, and managing intact work teams. This chapter will conclude with a discussion of the different kinds of *roles* leaders have in organizations. Defining those roles appropriately is as important to leadership effectiveness as picking "good people" to fill them.

Leadership as Social Influence

When we talk about influence processes, we are necessarily talking about power; that is, the capability a person has to get others to behave in a desired way. There are five *bases* of power that leaders can have (French and Raven, 1958):

Reward power: The leader's control of rewards that are valued by the subordinate.

Coercive power: The leader's control over punishments or sanctions that the subordinate wishes to avoid.

Legitimate power: The leader's occupancy of a formal position within a social system that gives him or her the right to request compliance, and that obligates the subordinate to comply.

Expert power: The leader's special knowledge or expertise relevant to an organizational situation or task.

Referent power: The leader's attractiveness to the subordinates, which leads subordinates to want to identify with and be like the leader; this often involves behaving as the leader does or as he or she wishes.

LEADER POWER BASES The managers of the Eastside and Central Soup 'n Burger restaurants, like most organizational managers, have an overall power base that is a mix of these five types. First, of course, is legitimate power. They are the bosses, their employees are the subordinates, and many routine instructions and requests are accepted simply because everyone agrees that subordinates should do what managers say. The managers also have reward power; they control merit increases in pay (awarded every six months), promotional opportunities, and various day-to-day rewards (such as assignment to a more attractive task for a day or permission to leave work early for personal reasons). They have some coercive power; they can recommend that an employee be fired, and they can dock pay for excessive tardiness. The managers also probably have expert power (that is, they know a great deal about food service operations that can be helpful to employees in carrying out their work). They may or may not have referent power, depending on whether or not their subordinates like, respect and identify with them.

If the power base of a leader is limited, then he or she may have great difficulty in wielding enough influence to get the work done. This sometimes is the case for first-line supervisors in hierarchical, structured organizations with strong labor unions. These individuals often have very little reward or coercive power and highly restricted legitimate power (that is, the negotiated rules about what the supervisor can and cannot do reduce the number of issues for which his or her requests are viewed as legitimate). This forces the supervisor to rely on expert and referent power. Yet for some complex or highly technical tasks, subordinates may have more task-relevant expertise than the supervisor, which leaves the supervisor with only referent power to use in influencing the subordinates.

For a respected and admired supervisor, referent power may suffice: subordinates may comply because they like and identify with their boss. But if the supervisor in such circumstances is *not* respected, he or she may have virtually no clout to use in getting the work done. This is an untenable management situation, and one to which most supervisors do not respond well. Some yell and get angry and find that it makes no difference, only to yell louder and get even angrier, but still to no avail. Others try to be liked far too hard, earning the ridicule rather than the respect of their subordinates, and become less rather than more powerful in the process. Still others abdicate their role and no longer attempt to influence. Not to have a base of power is not to be a leader.

Having a solid power base is, however, far from the whole story. The leader must also be willing and able to *use* the power he or she has; that is, to administer rewards and punishments when needed, to share expertise, and to issue requests and commands with the full expectation that they will be followed. Moreover, subordinates must understand the consequences of complying with (or resisting) the leader's influence attempts, and they must be motivated to obtain (or avoid) those consequences.

INFLUENCE PROCESSES The influence process is illustrated in Figure 9.1. The leader makes an influence attempt, and subordinates either are or are not motivated to comply with what the leader wants. Motivation to comply can be understood in the expectancy theory framework as set forth in Chapter 2 and used throughout this book. The subordinates have perceptions of what the outcomes will be of complying or not complying. These perceptions are influenced both by the nature of the influence attempt itself and by subordinate perceptions of the leader's bases of power. If the perceived consequences are significant to the individual (that is, strongly valued or highly aversive), then they will affect the subordinate's decision about whether to comply; if the perceived consequences are trivial, then compliance may depend more on

Figure 9.1 *Model of Subordinate Compliance to Leader Influence*

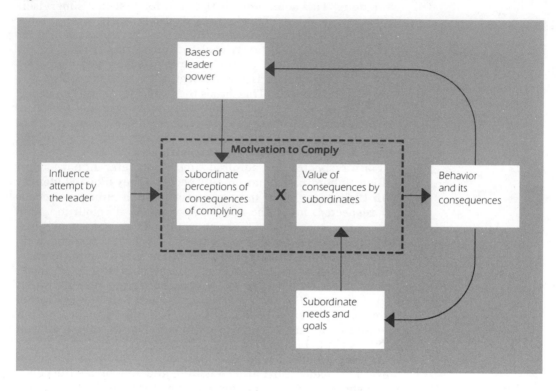

whether or not the individual personally *wants* to engage in the behavior than on the power of the leader.⟩

As shown in the figure, the value subordinates place on various consequences is affected by their own needs and goals. If the primary base of leader power is expertise, but a subordinate feels expert enough to do the work without help, then compliance will be limited. The same is true if compliance holds the promise of monetary reward, but the subordinate is not much interested in more money, or if noncompliance risks being fired but the subordinate has been thinking of quitting anyway.

Finally, some behavior — whether compliance or noncompliance — is exhibited, and that behavior has consequences for the leader, the subordinate, and the work of the organizational unit. Among the consequences may be a change in the power of the leader (for example, when the leader has "used up" his or her rewards, or when the behavior is so effective that the leader gains in subordinate esteem for having suggested it), or a change in subordinate needs and goals (for example, when the consequences serve to frustrate or to satisfy important personal needs). Each time that power is used to gain compliance, therefore, the nature of the leader-subordinate relationship is affected. Sometimes that relationship is improved and strengthened; other times it is worsened. But it always is changed.

The need to examine *both* leader power and subordinate needs in understanding leader influence processes is hard to overemphasize. Indeed, some writers (such as Emerson, 1962) have defined the *power* of one person in terms of the *dependence* of someone else on that person. If you are dependent on me for something you care about, then I have power over you and vice versa. According to this way of looking at things, power and dependence are two sides of the same coin.

This raises a new issue, namely, the power of subordinates over their leaders. While subordinate dependency on leaders for important outcomes creates conditions for the exercise of influence by leaders, it also is true that leaders are dependent on their subordinates for many things. If subordinates fail to comply with leader requests, refuse to do the work, or visibly show their disdain for the leader, then life at work for the leader is made difficult and unpleasant. Most leaders are dependent on their subordinates for energetic and cooperative behavior, and for positive affect and esteem. Such dependency means that the subordinates have *power* over the leader. This is why, at the beginning of this chapter, we took care to speak of leadership as a two-way influence process.

THE POWER BALANCE

The balance between leader and subordinate power is illustrated in Figure 9.2. The box on the left side of the balance represents the dependency of the subordinates on the leader, and thus the leader's power; the box on the right side represents the leader's dependency on the subordinates, and thus the subordinates' power. In the figure, the two boxes of power are of about the same size, indicating that the balance is even. This is probably both an unstable and an undesirable state of affairs in an organization (Emerson, 1962). It is unstable because, when power is high and equal, struggles between the two parties tend to develop over who is dominant in the relationship. That may be undesirable because power struggles siphon off energy from the work of the organization. Organizations usually operate better if managers do have somewhat more power than the individuals they manage. Managers are, after all, expected to take initiatives in influencing and changing what goes on in the organization.

Yet, if the power balance shown in Figure 9.2 gets tilted *too* much in favor of the leader (that is, subordinates are excessively dependent on the manager, but the manager is only minimally dependent on the subordinates), then the relationship may also be unstable. This is because a decidedly imbalanced power rela-

Figure 9.2 *Balancing Leader and Subordinate Power*

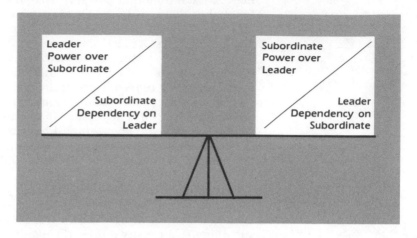

tionship encourages the use of unilateral power by the more powerful party, which can set in motion balancing operations on the part of the less powerful party. Balancing operations take many different forms (Emerson, 1962). The subordinate can withdraw from the relationship entirely (such as resign), thereby removing all dependency on the leader. Or the subordinate can cultivate relationships with other people to obtain a greater proportion of one's satisfactions from them, also reducing dependency. Or the subordinate can engage in behaviors to make the leader more dependent on him or her (such as negatively evaluating the leader in public), thereby increasing subordinate power and moving toward a more balanced relationship. Or, finally, a group of subordinates can form a coalition, as in unionization, to make the leader highly dependent on the *group* of subordinates (even though dependence on any one of them is very slight).

In every case, time and energy are taken from the work of the organization to achieve a more acceptable balance of power and dependency. Our conclusion, therefore, is that while a leader *must* have some power to be able to do his or her job effectively, and while an imbalanced power relationship in the leader's favor facilitates organizational functioning, excessive use of leader power usually is unstable and dysfunctional for the effectiveness of the leader and the work unit.

Leader Behavior and the Work Performance of Individuals

Now that we have analyzed the bases of leader power and how that power is used in leader-subordinate relationships, we are in a position to understand how leader influence can be used to improve work performance. In this section, we will examine the use of leader power in managing the performance of individuals. Then, in subsequent sections, we will turn to the management of coacting groups and interacting work teams.

USING POWER

The most direct way for a leader to influence subordinate work behavior is through the raw use of reward and coercive power. Instructions and directions are given to individuals, and it is made clear to them that significant outcomes are contingent on compliant behavior. This strategy follows directly from our discussion of rewards in Chapter 4, and is the same kind of process used when groups shape the behavior of their members through the direct use of discretionary stimuli (see Chapter 7).

Such power tactics can be efficient when compliance is needed in a hurry: "If you don't get that machine shut down before the gears are ruined, I'll have your job!" But, as was suggested previously, excessive reliance on reward and coercive power can deplete these bases of leader power, and can set in motion balancing operations by subordinates that compromise the leader's legitimate power as well. Few people who have a choice in the matter willingly work for a dictator, even if he or she is a very powerful dictator.

The implication is that using coercive influence strategies for the ongoing management of individual work performance is not a good idea. A better approach is to help subordinates understand what is expected of them at work, to provide them with information about how to meet those expectations and with support as they are doing so, and to supply feedback and reinforcement when the expectations are met.

Operationally, this first involves discussing performance goals with subordinates and helping them set realistic but challenging goals and objectives. Goals can be powerful in energizing and directing the work performance of individuals. Working with a subordinate to set clear, difficult, and well-accepted goals may be one of the most efficient ways for leaders to influence individual work performance.

When goals are set, leaders can further aid performance by specifying good paths to the goals that have been established. The leader can provide information about efficient work procedures, can point out blind alleys and shortcuts, and can provide technical assistance and consultation along the way. Especially important is making sure that the subordinate receives feedback about how well he or she is doing and soliciting from the subordinate information about any difficulties that are encountered.

The leader also can provide social and emotional support for subordinates as they work toward their goals. Such support is especially needed when a subordinate is trying new ways of going about the work that have some chance of failing. And the leader can serve as a source of reinforcement when goals and objectives are achieved. It is a good feeling when someone you admire compliments you for achieving an objective that you previously had agreed was a tough one. Indeed, by demonstrating commitment to excellent performance (and by modeling it in his or her own work), the leader can increase a subordinate's own aspiration to excellence, thereby further energizing and directing subordinate effort on the job.

PATH-GOAL THEORY

The guidelines specified above have much in common with the "path-goal" theory of leadership (see House and Mitchell, 1975). This theory suggests that leaders facilitate subordinate performance to the extent that they (1) increase the number and kinds of positive outcomes associated with good performance, and (2) make the paths to these outcomes clear and easy to travel (such as by eliminating barriers to good performance or by coaching and directing subordinates about good work procedures).

The theory emphasizes that not all leader behaviors are desirable in all situations. Sometimes information and expertise will be critical (for example, for an unstructured task with an eager but inexperienced employee); other times support and reinforcement will be more important (for example, for an "old hand" who is about to try a new way of doing the job); still other times the leader will need to attend carefully both to the informational and interpersonal aspects of his or her role.

Appropriate leader behavior, then, is contingent on the needs and skills of the subordinates, on the nature of the task, and on the constraints of the organizational context where the work is done. Even though we cannot provide a detailed program that specifies exactly how the leader should behave under all contingencies, it is important to reemphasize that there is no single best way for the leader to relate to subordinates. Leaders who have relatively fixed styles of managing will find that their effectiveness waxes and wanes as the situation changes. More flexible leaders will attend carefully to the constraints and opportunities in the situation and adapt their styles to those situations. Or, in some cases, they will attempt to change the situations to make them more amenable to leader influence (Fiedler, 1971).

ORGANIZATIONAL SYSTEMS AND LEADERSHIP

Throughout this discussion of managing the work performance of individuals, we have emphasized the relationship between the leader and the subordinate. It has been as if the major influences on individual performance derived directly from the leader-subordinate relationship. This is not the case. The organizational systems discussed in Section II of this book also have a strong impact on individual work performance. If the selection system has placed an individual on the job who is fully qualified to do the work (but not overqualified), if the compensation and performance appraisal systems support good performance, if the job itself is motivating, then the leader may have little to do other than "fine tune" a well-designed person-job relationship.

If, however, the operating systems of the organization have resulted in a poor person-job fit and a nonsupportive organizational context, then the leader may find that he or she is swimming upstream against a strong current in attempting to use leader power to achieve excellent subordinate performance. Indeed, in many such situations, the leader may be better advised to try to alter the operating systems of the organization than to attempt to counter the impact of those systems via the leader-subordinate relationship. The problem, for many first-level managers, is that they are expected to manage for high individual performance within faulty organizational systems, and they have neither the mandate nor the authority to alter those systems. This circumstance is virtually a recipe for leadership failure, a kind of failure about which the leader can do little.

Leadership of Coacting Groups

The discussion in the preceding section presumed that leaders are dealing with subordinates on a one-to-one basis; that is, one leader and one subordinate. In fact, such circumstances are relatively rare in organizational life. More typically leaders deal with coacting groups in which there are a number of individuals, each with his or her own task, all of whom report to the same supervisor (Chapter 6).

In such circumstances, the leader must continue to be an excellent manager of individual performance. All that was said in the last section continues to hold. But in planning his or her behavior, the leader must also take into account the fact that the subordinates are not working in social isolation, that an informal *group* of workers exists. As discussed in Chapter 7, coacting groups can powerfully affect the beliefs, attitudes, and work behavior of their members. Therefore, the leader must attempt to manage the group so that the group experience is fulfilling (rather than frustrating) to group members, and so that work performance is facilitated (rather than impaired) by the presence of the coactors.

GUIDELINES FOR MANAGING GROUPS

Three guidelines were suggested at the end of Chapter 7 for creating healthy group-individual relationships and are repeated here.

□ Helping the group achieve moderately high social intensity, so the group can serve as a source of social and emotional support for members, and so the group has the capability to enforce norms supportive of work effectiveness.
□ Fostering in the group a balance between the use of direct and indirect tactics of social influence, so that deviance from

group norms can be controlled, without swamping the individuality of members or their unique ideas and contributions.
□ Creating an environment for the group that supports productive work behavior, to increase the chances that group norms will encourage high individual performance rather than protective restrictions of productivity.

The third guideline deserves special emphasis because of the additional leverage on individual work behavior that a group provides. If a leader is dealing one-on-one with individuals, how things develop are largely dependent on how that *individual* is managed. But groups create and enforce their own views of social reality. If organizational systems are faulty (for example, demeaning jobs, exploitative control systems, capricious compensation arrangements), then there is an excellent chance that group members will share with each other their views of such matters, and group norms will develop that protect members against perceived exploitative or aversive organizational experiences. Managerial action may be insufficient to alter these views of social reality and the ensuing group norms, unless such actions result in changes of the organizational systems that gave rise to those perceptions.

Two special issues arise in leading coacting groups. The first has to do with perceptions of equity among group members. When a group of people are doing the same work in the same setting supervised by the same manager, those people are sure to compare perceptions on most aspects of their work experiences. That is one reason why it is important the work environment be objectively supportive of good performance. Beyond that, individuals look to other group members for information about how well they are performing and, importantly, about the rewards and satisfactions they are receiving. If certain people in the group are viewed as being treated more favorably than others (for example, in pay or in esteem received from management) for no legitimate reason, feelings of inequity are likely to arise and tensions will develop among members as well as between members and the manager. Because such feelings can compromise the health of the coacting group and the work performance of group members, the manager of a coacting group should be especially attentive to questions of equity and fairness within the group. In particular, the manager should make sure that his or her behaviors do not give the appearance of playing favorites.

The second special issue has to do with the involvement of group members in decision making about work policies, procedures, and practices. While leaders generally are charged with making decisions about how the work will be done, what courses of action to take, and what objectives to seek, they may choose to involve their subordinates in such decision making, or even delegate decision making to them. Involving a group of subordinates in decision making has some advantages: the subordinates may have information that improves the quality of the decision that is made, they may be more accepting of the decision because they understand the reasoning behind it, and they may be more committed to implementing the decision because they feel they "own" it. On the other hand, group participation in decision making takes time and effort, and may not always result in a high quality decision. When should managers involve their group of subordinates in making work-related decisions, and when should the managers do it themselves?

A DECISION-MAKING MODEL

A model that deals with this question has been developed and is presented in Figure 9.3 (Vroom and Yetton, 1973). Five decision-making strategies are identified in the model.

AI. The leader solves the problem or makes the decision himself, using information available to him at the time.

AII. The leader obtains necessary information from subordinates, and then decides on the solution to the problem himself. Subordinates are not involved in generating or evaluating alternative solutions.

CI. The leader shares the problem with relevant subordinates individually, getting their ideas and suggestions without bringing them together as a group. Then the leader makes the decision, which may or may not reflect the influence of subordinates.

CII. The leader shares the problem with the subordinates as a group, collectively obtaining their ideas and suggestions. Then he or she makes the decision, which again may or may not reflect their influence.

GII. The leader shares the problem with the subordinates as a group. Together the leader and the subordinates generate and evaluate alternatives and attempt to reach agreement on a solution.

The model identifies three general criteria of effective decision making in organizations (the objective quality of the decision, the time required to make it, and the degree to which the decision will be acceptable to subordinates) as well as various attributes of the decision-making situation (Do subordinates have the information necessary to generate a high-quality decision? Are subordinates likely to be in disagreement about preferred solutions? and so on). The problem attributes are combined with the decision-making criteria in a flow chart that specifies the best decision-making style for a leader to follow in any specified situation.

Consider, for example, a decision about whether or not to introduce flexible work scheduling at one of the Soup 'n Burger restaurants described earlier. The manager would ask, sequentially, the questions at the top of Figure 9.3, and eventually would reach a strategy for proceeding with the decision-making process. This might go as follows:

9.3   *The Vroom-Yetton Model of Leader Decision-making*

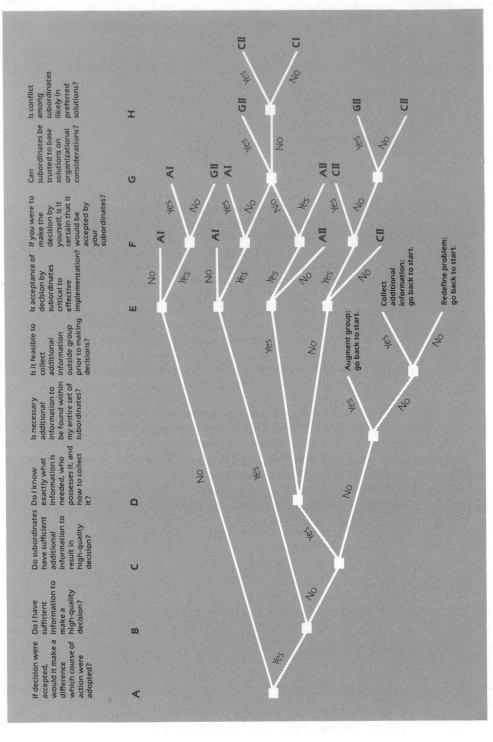

Adapted from Vroom and Yetton, 1973.

A If the decision were accepted, would it make a difference which course of action were adopted? (Yes)

B Do I have sufficient information to make a high-quality decision? (No. I need to know subordinate preferences about schedules.)

C Do subordinates have sufficient additional information to result in high quality decision? (Yes)

D Do I know exactly what information is needed, who possesses it, and how to collect it? (Yes)

E Is acceptance of the decision by subordinates critical to effective implementation? (Yes. People care very much about their schedules.)

F If you were to make the decision by yourself, is it certain that it would be accepted by your subordinates? (No. Much resistance and hostility might develop if I attempted to impose a decision on this matter.)

G Can subordinates be trusted to base solutions on organizational considerations? (No. They are more likely to base their views on the perceived impact of the decision on their personal lives.)

H Is conflict among subordinates likely in preferred solutions? (Yes. I anticipate that subordinates will have widely varying and strongly held views about the desirability of flexible work hours.)

Following the flow chart, given these answers, results in a CII decision strategy, sharing the problem with the group of subordinates and obtaining their collective ideas and suggestions but making the final decision myself.

While the Vroom-Yetton model has not yet been fully tested (and therefore some of its predictions may not be complete or correct), it serves to emphasize the *contingent* nature of leadership decision making regarding when the leader should (and should not) share responsibility for making decisions with the group being managed.

Leadership of Intact Work Teams

Work teams, in which members work interdependently and with substantial autonomy to generate a group product, are very different from coacting groups; they require a different type of leadership. The manager does not assume responsibility for the work behavior and productivity of individual group members, as was the case for coacting groups. Instead, he or she must deal with the group as a *unit,* and help that unit become a productive and healthy part of a larger organizational system.

As suggested in the last chapter, this involves three basic managerial activities:

□ Making sure that the group is designed right in the first place (that is, that the group has an appropriate number and mix of members, that the group task is a whole and meaningful piece of work, and that group norms support the development of task-appropriate strategies for performing the task).

□ Creating a supportive work environment for the group, including providing group-level rewards and objectives, creating opportunities for training and technical consultation as needed, and clarifying task and technological requirements and constraints.

□ Consulting as needed with group members in developing task-appropriate and socially healthy interpersonal processes.

Managing an intact work team is neither an easy undertaking nor one that is familiar to most managers. Worse, the skills required to manage groups effectively are not well practiced by most managers. Especially problematic is the need for the manager to exercise real authority in dealing with the group and simultaneously to serve as a process consultant to it.

In many cases, when managers who are experienced in traditional management techniques assume leadership of an intact work team, they feel that their own status has somehow been compromised and that the meaningfulness of the managerial job has been stripped away. This is understandable, since many traditional managerial activities are now the responsibility of the group itself. Moreover, if the manager has limited power to adjust the design of the group or to alter the group's working environment, he or she may feel that there is not much to do, other than help the group with its internal processes. Because the manager often is inexperienced in the strategy and tactics of process consultation, such help with internal processes may wind up being viewed by group members as managerial meddling. This, in turn, may compromise the effectiveness of the group as a performing unit and further distress the manager as he or she searches for an acceptable and effective way to lead the group.

These problems are critical to the effective management of intact work teams, and there are no easy solutions to them. For this reason, it is essential that higher management give special attention both to the role and the person of the first-line manager when work is designed for teams, and that these managers be provided with the opportunity to learn and practice the *new* managerial skills they will need in their new leadership role.

The Many Faces of Leadership in Organizations

It should be clear by now that there is no single route to leadership effectiveness in organizations. Indeed, the very *focus* of leadership activities changes, depending on who and what are

Figure 9.4 *How the Focus of Managerial Activities Changes Depending on What Is Being Managed*

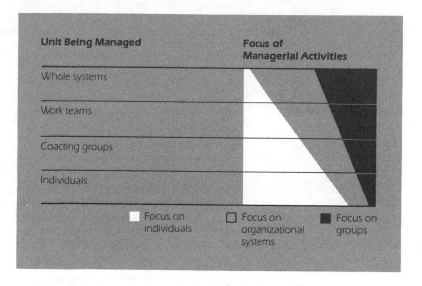

being managed. Often the emphasis is on directly influencing individual subordinates. Other times, building a cohesive and healthy group is more important. And sometimes the focus must be on the design and management of organizational systems and environments. Figure 9.4 shows how the managerial role changes as the unit being managed changes from individuals to coacting groups to work teams to entire work systems.

When, for example, a leader is charged with managing *individuals* who work more or less independently, he or she must be expert in managing one-on-one relationships. The power bases of the leader are especially important, as they affect the leader's capacity to wield interpersonal influence, to share information and expertise with subordinates, and to guide and direct individuals with confidence and a sense of personal legitimacy. Also important is the capability to modify those organizational systems (such as job design and compensation) that affect the fit between the employee and the organization. This sometimes can be done directly by the leader but more frequently is carried out using *upwards* influence, convincing more senior managers that the alteration of organizational systems or practices is called for. For managing individuals, group relations skills are relatively unimportant.

When a manager is dealing with *coacting groups*, the skills and resources needed to manage individuals continue to be required. But now the leader must also address issues of group process and group development. The leader must be skilled in diagnosing and dealing with interpersonal issues that arise within the group. Group and interpersonal skills are even more important when the units being managed are *intact work teams*. In this case, the skills needed to deal one-on-one with individuals are less salient and less critical to leadership effectiveness. Much more critical are capabilities to influence the basic design of the work group, to create a supportive organizational environment for the group, and to deal constructively with interpersonal process issues that emerge within the work team. One of the reasons why managing intact teams is such a significant managerial challenge is the requirement for the manager to keep constantly in mind (and to balance among) issues that arise at the individual level, within the group itself, and in the technical and organizational environment.

Finally, when a leader is given responsibility for managing *entire work systems* — that is, a top management position — the skills required for effectiveness once again change. At this level, one-on-one relationships with individuals diminish considerably in importance. (Indeed, the top manager who spends most of his or her time dealing with particular problems of particular people is almost sure to be ineffective in increasing the performance of the system as a whole.) Instead, top management activities need to involve, in about equal proportions, the design and functioning of organization-level systems (including systems that relate the organization to its environment) and the management of group and intergroup relationships. These matters will be explored in detail in Section IV of this book.

Summary

We have taken the position in this chapter that there is no such thing as a "best" leadership style or strategy. How the leader should behave, what kinds of power he or she needs to perform effectively, the skills that are required, and the very design of the leadership role, we believe, strongly depend on who and what is being managed. Thus, the question, How much power should the leader have? is not a useful one. The reason is that the kind of power needed to manage individuals (that is, power for interpersonal influence) is quite different from the kind of power needed to manage intact work teams or total organizational systems (that is, power to alter group or organizational design and the operating systems of an organization). The same is true when we ask about specific kinds of leadership skills or useful leader behaviors.

Too often we turn to questions of leader personality, interpersonal style, or managerial technique in trying to understand leadership effectiveness or in designing selection or training programs aimed at improving it. The message of this chapter is that we are better advised to focus on the way the leader's *role* is defined and, especially, on the kinds of power and authority that are given to the leader to use in enacting that role.

Suggested Readings

Fiedler, F. E. "The Leadership Game: Matching the Man to the Situation." In *Perspectives on Behavior in Organizations*, edited by J. R. Hackman, E. E. Lawler, and L. W. Porter. New York: McGraw-Hill, 1977.

McCall, M. W. "Leaders and Leadership: Of Substance and Shadow." In *Perspectives on Behavior in Organizations*, edited by J. R. Hackman, E. E. Lawler, and L. W. Porter. New York: McGraw-Hill, 1977.

McGregor, D. *The Professional Manager*. New York: McGraw-Hill, 1967.

Vroom, V. H., and Yetton, P. W. *Leadership and Decision-making*. Pittsburgh: University of Pittsburgh Press, 1973.

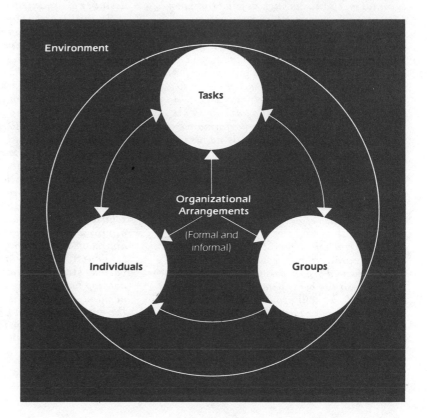

The Design and
Management of
Organizations

OVERVIEW / Section IV builds on the concepts of individual and group behavior and places them within the context of the larger organization. Up to this point, we have focused on how individuals and groups perform tasks within organizations. While some mention has been made of the role of organizational mechanisms such as selection, performance measurement, or pay systems, in many ways individuals and groups performing tasks have been considered in a vacuum.

In fact, organizations are made up of many individuals and many groups performing many different tasks. Looking even further, organizations themselves exist within dynamic and ever-changing environments which place demands on the performance of those tasks. One of the critical demands is for coordinated behavior. In order to meet the challenges of the environment, the behavior of all the different individuals and groups that make up the organization somehow needs to be integrated or made to fit together to create effective organizational performance.

Organizations attempt to achieve this needed coordination through the development of formal organizational structures (see the figure at the beginning of this section). In Chapter 10, we will provide an introduction to the design of organizational structures. The role of organization design in influencing behavior will be discussed and specific design leverage points presented. A model for thinking about organization design, based on concepts of information processing, will be set forth. In Chapter 11, this model will be extended and used to discuss the various mechanisms for coordination and control that are available to the manager and designer of organizations.

In the first two chapters in this section, emphasis is placed on the explicit, planned, formal arrangements that organizations develop. In addition, informal organizational arrangements develop over time. One of the most pervasive patterns of these informal arrangements is seen in the conflict that frequently arises among groups or coalitions of groups. In Chapter 12, we will focus on power and conflict in organizations and suggest how conflict can be managed so that it does not reduce organizational effectiveness.

As mentioned earlier, organizations exist within a larger environment. As a system, the organization needs to maintain favorable relations with the various institutions and groups within that environment. One approach to the management of organization-environment relations is to think of the various strategies that organizations can develop for matching their resources to the demands, constraints, and opportunities of the environment. In Chapter 13, we will discuss strategy and the relationship of strategy to organizational behavior.

Chapter **10**

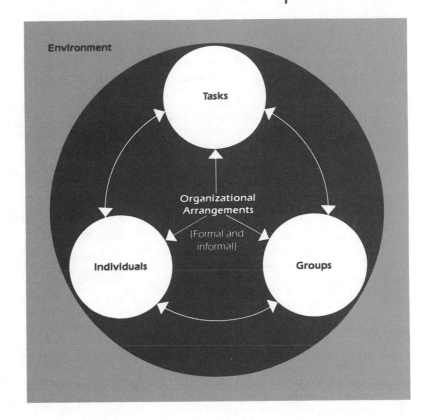

Organization
Design

John B. Green, Senior Vice President for Branch Operations of the Columbia National Bank (CNB), is considering a change in the design of his part of the CNB organizational structure. CNB is the largest of three major banks in a midwestern city of about one million people. Green is responsible for the retail banking operations. Retail services are delivered through a system of bank branches located throughout the metropolitan area. Two basic functions are performed through the branches. First, customers are provided with facilities to conduct financial transactions such as changing balances in accounts, cashing checks, maintaining savings, and so on. These transactions are done by bank tellers or, more recently, by banking machines. Second, the bank offers customers a range of more complex financial services such as consumer or commercial loans, mortgage loans, and such. Both transactions and financial services are delivered through the branches. Each branch is treated as a profit center; its expenses and revenues are monitored as if it were an independent business, and the branch manager is compensated based on the performance of his branch.

Green manages the total branch system. He has a small staff consisting mainly of three assistant vice presidents in the areas of planning, control, and personnel. All of the twenty-one branch managers (ten more are planned in the next two years) report directly to Green (see Figure 10.1 for an organization chart of the branch system). All branches are directed by a branch manager. The various operations concerning customer transactions are directed by a teller supervisor who manages a group of tellers, while an assistant manager is responsible for the performance of the various desk personnel who provide financial services. (See Figure 10.2 for an organization chart of a typical branch.)

Recently, Green has become concerned about the management of the branch system.

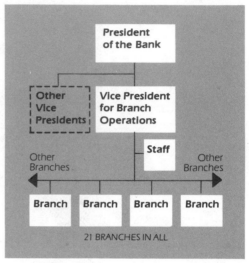

Figure 10.1 *Current Organizational Design of Branch System at CNB*

Figure 10.2 *Organization Design of a Typical Branch at CNB*

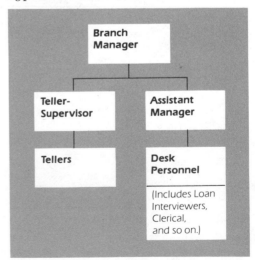

The system is continuing to grow in size, and the environment in which CNB operates is becoming increasingly competitive. At the same time, problems of coordination and effective management seem to be increasing. Green thinks that many of these problems stem from the fact that it is hard for him to provide direct support and coordination for the twenty-one managers who report to him. He feels he just has too many people working for him. Green is considering some changes in the structure of the branch system, such as grouping branches together and creating some kind of area director or "super manager" to be responsible for sets of branches. Another alternative is to break out the lending activity from the basic operations (teller transactions) as is done in some banks in other parts of the country and manage these segments of the business separately. Right now, Green is not sure which direction he will take.

ORGANIZATION DESIGN is a major influence on how organizations function. The design of organizational structures is a critical tool that managers can make use of in efforts to improve how organizations operate. Frequently, for example, when a new manager takes over an organization, a reorganization soon follows, involving changes in how the organization is structured. John Green, at CNB, feels the need to make changes in the design of his organization. His assumption is that if he somehow changes the arrangements of the branch system by grouping different people together, adding levels of hierarchy, or splitting groups apart, the result will be a branch system that can perform more effectively.

Underlying most efforts at organizational design is the basic assumption that how individuals and work units are grouped and linked together makes a difference in how an organization performs. Both managerial experience and organizational research indicate that, to a large degree, this assumption is true. Organizations operating in the same environments with the same types of resources may be more or less effective depending on the appropriateness of their structures. An important question, then, is what types of organization structures are appropriate for different situations.

In this chapter, we will focus on a number of key issues in structures. First, we will consider what are the elements of design. In other words, what exactly is organizational structure? Second, we will consider how the structure of an organization influences the behavior of individuals and groups. Third, we will identify some critical leverage points in organizational design; these leverage points constitute key structural variables. Finally, we will present a model that should aid both in analyzing organizational structures and in designing new ones. In Chapter 11, this model will be used to examine the question of how to design organizations to achieve coordination and control.

The Nature of Organizational Structure

What is organizational structure? When asked that question, people usually think about the formal organization chart or table of organization that shows specific relationships, work units, and levels of hierarchy. For example, if asked about the structure of CNB, most people would quickly point to the organization charts provided in Figures 10.1 and 10.2. However, organizational structure is much more than the boxes and lines that appear on a chart. It involves a number of different elements that delineate how individuals, groups, and units function. At the most basic level, structure can be thought of as how organizations are segmented into units and patterns of relationship among units (Thompson, 1967). Structure refers to the relatively stable relationships that exist among different elements of the organization over time.

While the concept of stable relationships is helpful, it does not capture the full range of issues involved in designing organizations. When we think about an organization, we also need to think about the various systems that exist to help get the work done and maintain the organization. We also need to consider the various procedures or processes that have been developed and the special mechanisms that have been designed to coordinate work. For example, in CNB, to understand how the organization functions, we need to know how people are hired and placed in jobs, how they get rewarded for their work, how jobs are grouped together into units, what reporting relationships exist, how information moves between people, how the organization determines if it is doing well or poorly, and so on. Given the range of elements involved, the term *organization structure* will be used to indicate all of those features of the organization itself, including structures, processes, systems, and mechanisms. A number of critical elements of structure are identified in Table 10.1, which presents a list that illustrates the range of dimensions of structure. (Hall, 1972; Porter, Lawler, and Hackman, 1975, provide a more detailed discussion of the specific elements of organizational structure.)

Finally, the process of *organization design* is that of determining or developing the most effective structure for a set of units or an organization as a whole. Our concern here will be, therefore, on how structure affects behavior, what are the most critical elements of structure that managers can manipulate, and how to make choices about the most effective structures.

How Does Organization Structure Affect Behavior?

In our discussions of group and individual behavior, a model was presented of how behavior occurs. This model depicted a series of events over time. People form *expectancies* about the conse-

Table 10.1 *Some Major Elements of Organization Structure*

Composition of units	What roles or positions are grouped together into work units; what units are grouped together into larger units.
Reporting relationships	What individuals or units are accountable and report to other individuals or groups.
Design of tasks and roles	How different positions in the organization are designated, including the content of the work, the demands of the position, the decision-making authority, and so on.
Communication patterns	The patterns of movement of information between and within different units of the organization.
Measurement and information systems	Formal systems to collect and distribute information about organizational functioning.
Reward systems	Formal mechanisms to provide rewards or sanctions for different kinds of behavior.
Selection, placement, and development systems	Procedures for attracting and hiring new organization members, placing them in positions, and developing capabilities over time.

quences of their behavior. The existence of these expectancies combined with individual needs leads to the individual putting forth *effort* aimed toward some kind of activity. The result of that effort, combined with ability and other constraints, leads to a certain level of *performance*.

Given this approach, it is possible to identify three distinct ways in which the structure of an organization affects the behavior (or performances) of individuals and groups (see Figure 10.3). First and perhaps most obvious, the organization's structure can affect the expectancies that individuals have, and thus influence behavior through a *motivational* effect. The nature of formal reward systems, the design of jobs and tasks, the nature of career paths, the types of measurement systems, and the like are all elements of structure which involve rewards that can be tied to behavior. As such, they have the potential of influencing expectancies and thus motivating individuals to behave in certain ways.

Second, the organization structure may make it difficult for individuals to translate intentions or effort into actual performance. Although an individual may want to perform in a certain way, that person may not have the necessary information,

Figure 10.3 *How Organization Structure Affects Behavior*

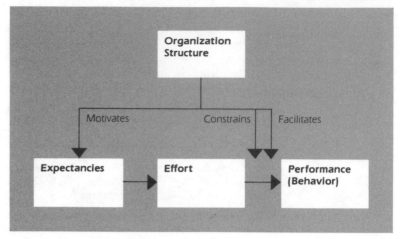

access to the appropriate individuals, or authority to do so. In such cases, the organization structure serves to *constrain* behavior. This constraining effect may be intentional or desirable, as when controls and similar procedures prevent action that might have negative consequences if those actions were to occur. On the other hand, constraints on action are frequently costs that organizations pay in order to obtain other benefits of design. For example, we might put all of the people doing a certain function (say, bank tellers) together in a unit because it is easier to manage them as a unit and so that their work can be coordinated. At the same time, we provide constraints on their action, since we make it harder for them to interact with and get information from people in other units (lending offices, financial consultants, and so forth). Thus, structure affects the kind of behavior that can occur through a constraining effect.

Third, the organization structure can aid people in translating intentions and effort into action. In such cases, the organization structure serves to *facilitate* the behavior that has been motivated. By providing information, access to individuals, authority, and resources, the organization helps individuals and groups perform their tasks effectively.

Almost any organization structure affects behavior in all three ways. Any design choice has the potential of influencing behavior through motivation, constraint, or facilitation.

Organization Design Leverage Points

If organization structure has the potential of affecting the behavior and performance of individuals and groups, what are the specific aspects of structure that are most critical? In earlier chapters, a number of aspects of organization structure were discussed in detail from the perspective of the individual. First, attention was given to the systems for assessing, recruiting, and developing individuals for organizational roles. Second, the various formal reward systems of the organization including compensation systems and measurement technologies were discussed. Clearly, such systems serve as powerful tools to influence behavior. Third, the design of work for individuals and groups was identified as another element of organization design of special importance. In addition to these, however, three elements of overall organization structure need to be mentioned. These are aspects of structure that are central from an organizational standpoint, in that together they define the total organization structure. They are leverage points for changing the functioning of the organization:

1. Aggregation. A basic element of organizations is that different roles or positions tend to be grouped together or aggregated into work groups, teams, or units. In turn, these units are aggregated into larger units, called divisions, departments, agencies, bureaus, and the like. One set of design choices then is how to aggregate positions and which positions to group with others.

A critical aggregation choice in CNB concerns placing tellers and loan officers in a unit called a branch. An alternative would be to put many loan people together under separate management and perhaps even in different locations. Originally, the aggregation rule employed at CNB was to put together those people serving the same market area as opposed to putting together those doing the same work regardless of market area.

Any choice to group roles or units together is two-sided. By grouping people or units together, communication between them is facilitated; if they are doing similar tasks, often economies can be gained by using centralized resources (that is, a single, bigger, and more efficient computer rather than numerous small computers). Similarly, any choice to group certain roles or units together also is implicitly a choice to separate other roles. By putting together all of the computer people into one unit, the computer people are separated from (and thus may find it harder to coordinate with) the units they have been servicing.

2. Intraunit Relationships. A second element of structure is the nature of relationships within work units. Relationships among roles within a larger work unit can be highly formalized with rigid specifications of jobs, procedures to be used, and communication patterns. On the other hand, roles can be less formally defined, with individuals doing different jobs at different times and with highly dispersed patterns of communication. Organizational theorists have labeled these two approaches to structuring the relationships within work units: the highly formalized and narrowly specified type is called a *mechanistic* form of organization, while the more informal and highly interconnected type of design is called an *organismic* form of organization (Burns and Stalker, 1961).

Thus, one of the design elements and choice points is how to structure the internal relationships within units along a continuum ranging from organismic to mechanistic.

3. *Interunit Relationships.* Given work units (as a result of aggregation decisions) that have different patterns of relationships within them (as a result of design choices along the organismic-mechanistic continuum), a final design issue is the manner in which the activities of groups are linked together, or the nature of the formally structured relationships that exist among different work units. This is the question of coordination and control. Mechanisms need to be developed to coordinate the activities of different units. These may range from fairly simple approaches (such as specifying rules and procedures or adding a level of supervision above the two units to be coordinated) to relatively complex ones (such as matrix organizations, product teams, and so on). The central question is how to pick the type of mechanism that will most effectively link together groups, particularly those likely to come into conflict).

The process of organization design involves manipulating these three primary factors — aggregation, intraunit relationships, and interunit relationships. Together with the related structured elements of work design and rewards systems, they are the central leverage points for changing and improving organization structures.

A Model for Choosing Organization Designs

So far, we have examined some of the dimensions of organization structure. We have considered how structure affects patterns of behavior and have identified some of the key leverage points in design. What still needs to be done is to provide a framework or model that will enable one to make design choices.

The basic approach to organization design used here can best be labeled *information processing theory* (Galbraith, 1973, 1977; Tushman, 1976; Tushman and Nadler, 1978). This approach considers the transmission of information (communication) as the most central function of organization structure. At the core of the model is the following concept:

> Organizations doing different kinds of work require different kinds of structures to perform effectively.

Again we see a contingency approach. There is no one best way to structure an organization. What the most effective structures are will depend or be contingent on the kind of work that the organization and the units making up the organization have to perform. In simpler terms, it is a design principle that says, much as certain approaches to architecture do, that form should follow function.

In order to understand how information processing theory can be applied to organization design, the basic propositions of the model need to be laid out. The model is built around three central propositions:

1. Different organizational tasks pose different levels of uncertainty and thus require different amounts of communication among task performing units.
2. Different combinations of organizational structures provide different capacities to process information among units.
3. Organizational effectiveness will be greatest where the information processing capacity of the structure matches or "fits" the information processing requirements of the work to be done.

After we discuss each of these in some detail, an integrative model will be presented, and an approach to using the model for the analysis of organization designs will be described.

DIFFERENT TASKS REQUIRE DIFFERENT INFORMATION PROCESSING

Referring again to CNB, the two work units that function within each branch provide an illustration of how different tasks present different information processing requirements. One of the work units in the branch is the teller unit. Tellers, under the supervision of a teller supervisor, carry out transactions using information provided to them by customers who walk into the branch. They cash checks, post deposits and withdrawals, obtain balances, and so forth. A second work unit is the lending unit. Made up of lending officers, this group is responsible for identifying potential lending customers, selling financial services, and evaluating and processing applications for consumer installment loans, mortgage loans, and commercial loans.

One way these two work tasks (teller task and lending task) differ is in the degree of uncertainty associated with them. Uncertainty is simply the lack of or absence of information about what will occur in the future. In the teller task, relatively little uncertainty exists; it is possible to predict ahead of time what kinds of work requirements and demands will be made on the tellers. A customer can approach the teller with one of a number of predictable transactions, each requiring a predictable type of operation by the teller.

On the other hand, the lending task has somewhat higher levels of uncertainty. While parts of the job are routine and predictable (such as processing and approving/disapproving loans), much of the work is not. The group needs to organize itself, develop a strategy for generating loan volume within the market area, identify methods of implementing strategy, and so on. It is less clear in this situation what steps to take next or what is to be done by each person. It takes much longer to find out whether the group or individuals are doing a good job. It is more difficult to predict the problems that may be encountered, such as competition from other banks, inroads from other lending sources, and changes in market conditions.

Given these two different types of work tasks, the next step is to think about the different kinds and amounts of information that have to flow among the different individuals within each of these two units if their jobs are to be done well. In the teller unit, there is relatively little need for large amounts of information to move between the different people. To perform a transaction, a teller does not need much information from the supervisor or other members of the work group (assuming the teller has been adequately trained and thus given the appropriate rules and procedures). Each transaction falls into a predictable category and, therefore, can be dealt with without getting more information. The types of information that the teller needs to obtain (for example, information on balances and such) are also predictable and do not require consultation and information exchange with others in the unit. Only when infrequent exceptions to the rules come up, does the teller consult the teller supervisor. Thus, very limited information flow is needed to perform the job well.

In the lending unit, the story is very different. The loan officers have varying amounts of information about the marketplace. To develop a strategy, that information needs to be exchanged among members of the group. While implementing the strategy, if individual loan officers encounter new information, it is critical that other members of the group have access to it. Thus, development and implementation of a marketing strategy for lending requires a high degree of information flowing between the members of the lending unit.

Because the tellers' task and the loan officers' task differ in certainty, the nature of the information flow needed to perform the tasks varies. As illustrated in Figure 10.4, the information that needs to be processed among the individuals performing the task in the administrative unit is much less than that needed to be processed among those in the lending unit. Most importantly, the pattern of information flow (rather than just the amount) is not the same, the lending task requiring people to be more highly

Figure 10.4 *An Illustration of Information Processing Requirements for Two Different Work Tasks*

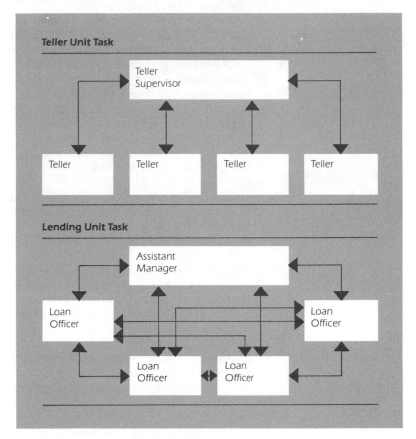

interconnected by information. Different tasks pose different degrees of uncertainty and thus create different information processing requirements.

While the example from CNB involves information processing requirements among individuals within specific work units, the concept also applies to information processing requirements among several units that are performing tasks. The basic principle is that as the amount of uncertainty associated with a work task increases, so do the requirements for information to be processed among the units (units could be individuals, work groups, or other work units) that are involved in performing the task. Research has indicated that a number of key factors affect the uncertainty associated with a task, and thus the information requirements that a task will have. These factors include the nature of the work, the environment in which the work is performed, and the interdependence of the different work elements (Tushman and Nadler, 1978).

Nature of the Work. A critical factor in the nature of the work is the degree to which the work is routine as opposed to nonroutine. Tasks differ in their degree of predictability (Galbraith, 1973). Tasks that are not well understood, that are unpredictable or nonroutine, pose greater uncertainty and require a greater amount of information to be processed among individuals or units, since they cannot be planned for in advance (Perrow, 1970; Van de Ven, Delbecq, and Koenig, 1976). In summary, as work becomes more unpredictable, the requirement for information processing increases.

Nature of the Work Environment. Another source of uncertainty is the larger environment in which the work must be performed, including the environment that exists outside of the organization (Lawrence and Lorsch, 1967a). Here the critical issue appears to be how stable (as opposed to changing) the environment is as well as the speed or rate of change (Duncan, 1972). As the environment in which the task is performed becomes more dynamic (as opposed to static), uncertainty increases, and there are needs to respond quickly to opportunities, to change in response to demands, and so on. Again, preplanned approaches may not be adequate, and there is a need for individuals or units to exchange information rapidly in order to act. In summary, as the environment becomes more dynamic, the information processing requirements increase.

Interdependence of Work Elements. A final factor is the degree to which the different elements that make up the larger task (for example, making transactions or providing financial services) are connected to each other. Where the components of the larger task are minimally connected — where one part of the task can be done independently of other parts — then the task is considered to have low interdependence. However, when the performance of one element of the task requires other parts of the task to be done, the task has high interdependence. As the interdependence of tasks increases, uncertainty increases, and the amount of information that must flow between the individuals and units performing the different tasks also has to increase (Thompson, 1967). In summary, as task interdependence becomes greater, so do the information processing requirements.

For any organization or part of an organization, we can get some idea of the nature of the task-related uncertainty and, therefore, information processing requirements, by examining the nature of the work to be done. Specifically, we need to consider the predictability of the work, the stability of the work

Figure 10.5 *Factors Determining the Information Processing Requirements Facing Work Units or Sets of Work Units*

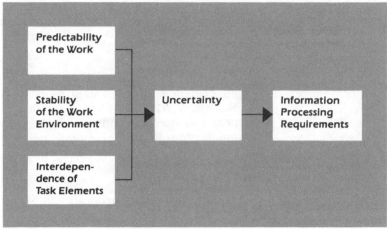

Adapted from Tushman and Nadler, 1978.

environment, and the degree of task interdependence (see Figure 10.5).

DIFFERENT ORGANIZATIONAL STRUCTURES PROVIDE DIFFERENT INFORMATION PROCESSING CAPACITIES

Putting the issue of information processing requirements aside for a moment, let us now turn our attention to the organizational structure. The organizational structure can reduce the amount of uncertainty faced by individuals or work units through providing information. In the simplest form, this occurs by providing instructions, rules, procedures, and such. In a more complex way, the structure helps the units to exchange information and coordinate activities.

Different organizational structures vary in their capabilities to process information quickly and accurately, and thus reduce the uncertainty faced by individuals and units. Again, three factors seem to be important in determining the capacity of any organization structure to process information: the composition of work units, the structuring of relationships within the work units, and the mechanisms for coordinating and controlling multiple work units. (These correspond to the design leverage points mentioned on pp. 185–186)

Unit Composition. Organizations group individuals, and subsequently work groups, into work units to gain economies from specialization. Other things being equal, it is easier to process information among individuals (or units) within the same work unit than it is among those outside the work unit. Obviously, where those in the same unit are physically adjacent, information processing is easier. In addition, as pointed out in the discussion of conflict, different work units tend to develop problems in communicating as a result of specialization and the development of perceived group differences (Lawrence and Lorsch, 1967a). Thus, the information processing capacity between two individuals is increased by grouping them together into the same work unit.

Intraunit Relationships. As mentioned earlier, work units can be designed to be organismic or mechanistic. (Burns and Stalker, 1961). The communication patterns in these two approaches vary. The individual roles in the organismic system are much more highly interconnected (see Figure 10.6). Research

Figure 10.6 *Two Approaches to Structuring Work Units*

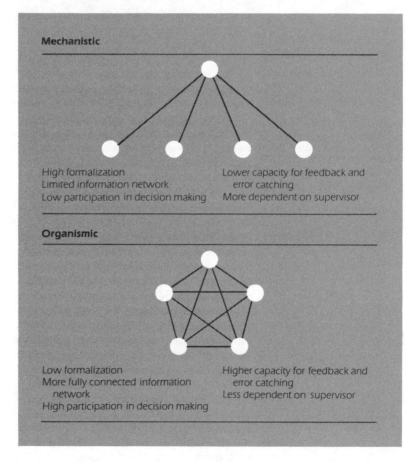

Mechanistic

High formalization
Limited information network
Low participation in decision making

Lower capacity for feedback and
  error catching
More dependent on supervisor

Organismic

Low formalization
More fully connected information
  network
High participation in decision making

Higher capacity for feedback and
  error catching
Less dependent on supervisor

indicates that the organismic structure, while more costly in some ways, is able to deal with greater amounts of uncertainty than mechanistic structures (Duncan, 1973; Van de Ven, Delbecq, and Koenig, 1976). Thus, organismic units provide greater information processing capacity than mechanistic units.

Coordination and Control Mechanisms. Organizations develop methods for dealing with uncertainty. These methods involve the movement of information between and among a number of work units. They range from fairly limited and simple approaches, such as rules, plans, and hierarchy, to fairly extensive and complex mechanisms such as formal control systems (budgets, accounting systems), special cross-functional groups, and matrix organizations. (These will be discussed in more detail in Chapter 11.) As the extensiveness and complexity of the coordination and control mechanisms increase, so does their capacity to process information among units. At the same time, so does their cost.

In summary, the way that organizations are structured can affect their capacity to process information and thus aid in reducing and coping with uncertainty. Three factors in particular (see Figure 10.7) are critical in determining the information processing capacity of an organization: the composition of work units, the internal structuring of those work units, and the mechanisms for coordination and control.

Figure 10.7 *Factors Determining the Information Processing Capacity of an Organizational Structure*

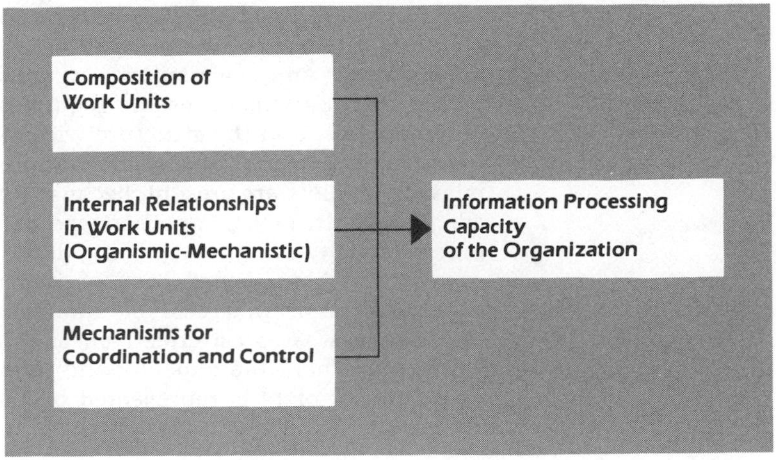

Figure 10.8 *Possible Combinations of Information Processing Capacity and Requirements*

Information Processing Requirements	Information Processing Capacity	
	High	Low
Extensive	**A** Match: Effective organization	**B** Mismatch: Ineffective organization
Minimal	**C** Mismatch: Ineffective organization	**D** Match: Effective organization

Adapted from Tushman and Nadler, 1978.

ORGANIZATIONAL EFFECTIVENESS AND INFORMATION PROCESSING FIT

So far, we have seen that different types of tasks provide different levels of uncertainty, and, therefore, have different information processing requirements. Similarly, organizational structures differ in their capacities to process information, although at a cost. As information processing capacity increases, so does the cost of coordination time, information processing mechanisms, and so forth.

The final element in the model should now be obvious; organizations will be effective to the degree that the information processing capacity of the structure matches or "fits" the information processing requirements posed by the tasks to be done. This is diagrammed in Figure 10.8. In cells A and D, the requirements facing the organization are matched by the capacity of the structure, and as a result the organization is effective. In cell B, the information processing requirements posed by the task are extensive, and the structure with low capacity is unable to function effectively. Coordination problems occur, deadlines are missed, conflicts are present, because information is not moving adequately. In cell C, another type of problem is present: too much capacity for the task being done. The organization is incurring much unneeded cost for information processing that is not required; that cost of unneeded coordination reduces effectiveness. Greatest effectiveness (other things being equal) will occur where the capacity and requirements are matched. This concept of fit is represented by the total model of Figure 10.9.

Figure 10.9 *The Information Processing Model for Organization Design*

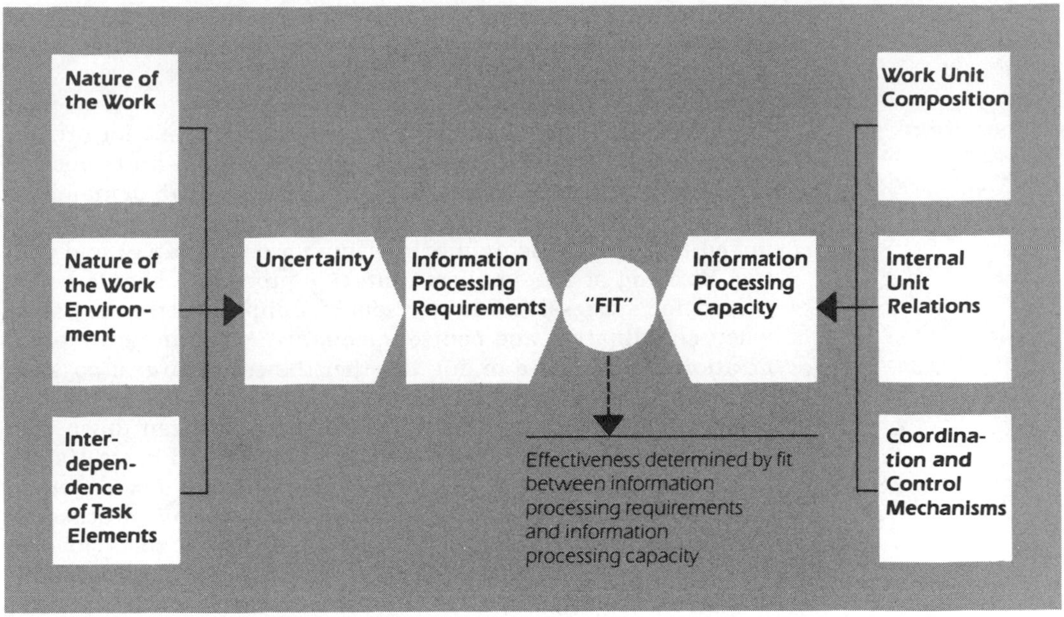

Adapted from Tushman and Nadler, 1978.

Using the Model to Design Organizations

The model presented here provides the tools to examine the appropriateness of a number of organizational structures. Specifically, the model can be used as a set of steps to analyze an organizational situation and develop an effective structure.

Before presenting these steps, two cautions should be noted. First, no one single design will necessarily be best. Given the possible combinations of group composition, mechanistic vs. organismic structure, and control and coordinating mechanisms, several different designs probably will be equally effective in most situations. These designs constitute what Galbraith (1977) calls the "feasible set" of designs — the varying designs that would feasibly meet the information processing requirements of the task. The job of the manager, having identified the feasible set, is to decide on those designs most appropriate, given the costs of changing structure, the individual and group issues involved, the relevant political factors in the informal organization, and so on.

A second caution is that the model has not yet been completely presented. A major element, coordination and control mechanisms, has not yet been discussed in any detail. This will be examined in Chapter 11. Consequently, the design steps presented below should be reexamined after a consideration of the mechanisms for coordination and control.

In general, the model suggests a two-stage process for organizational design. In the first stage, organizational units need to be formed and structured appropriately, given the demands of the task. In the second stage, these units need to be adequately linked together by using mechanisms for coordination and control. Starting at the smallest unit, this procedure should be repeated for successively larger sets of units until the last step, when coordination and control mechanisms for an entire organization are designed to link together the set of largest possible subunits.

This general approach to design can be broken down into seven steps of analysis and decision making (see Figure 10.10):

1. *Analyze the relative degree of interdependence among roles to identify the most critical information processing needs.* The first step is to look at tasks and specific roles (jobs) to determine where the highest or strategically most critical information processing needs are. These would be the roles that have the highest degree of interdependence among them; for example, loan officers in CNB serving a specific market area.

Figure 10.10 *The Design Process*

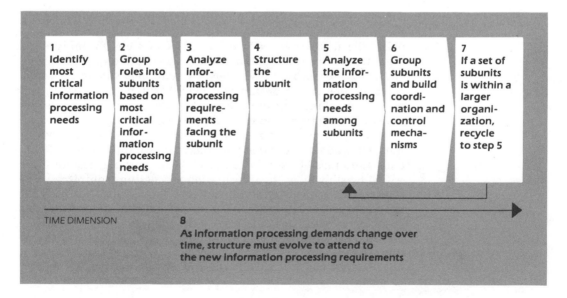

2. *Group roles together into units so that roles that have the highest information processing needs between them are together in the same unit.* The second step is to form units by grouping together those roles that have the highest information processing needs among them. Thus, units should be grouped around the critical tasks that are performed. Depending on the organization, however, the most critical information processing needs may differ. For example, in some cases it may be around a product or service (large commercial loans), while in others it may be around a function performed by people who need to consult each other (lending officers) or around a service delivery point (a bank branch).

3. *Analyze information processing requirements of each unit based on the degree of uncertainty posed by its task characteristics, environment, and interdependence.* Focusing now within the units that have been formed, the next step is to determine what the information processing requirements will be among the roles *within* the particular unit. This is done by examining the degree of task uncertainty, the task environment of the unit, and the degree of interdependence between the various roles performing the task within the unit.

4. *Based on the information processing requirements of each unit, determine appropriate unit structures.* Building on the analysis of the third step, the next step is to pick the appropriate structure for each individual subunit, based on its own information processing requirements. Units with high internal information processing requirements should generally have more organismic structures, while subunits with low internal requirements should have more mechanistic structures.

5. *Analyze information processing requirements among a set of units by determining the degree of differentiation and remaining interdependence.* Having structured individual units, the focus now switches to a set of comparable or related subunits. The information processing requirements among these units need to be determined. The primary factor to be examined is interdependence. The greater the interdependence among units, the greater the information processing requirements. Not all of the interdependence between roles will be accounted for by grouping them in subunits. A lot of interdependence between units will still be left over even in the best of structures. In addition, units should be analyzed for degree of differentiation—how different in structure and orientation are the units in the set. The greater the differences, the harder it may be to communicate information between them; thus, the greater the information processing requirements.

6. *Based on information processing requirements among the units, determine appropriate coordination and control mechanisms.* Given data about the information processing requirements among units, the next step is to link together those

subunits that require it with coordinating and control mechanisms. One of the basic mechanisms is hierarchy, to create a supervisory or managerial role over two or more subunits that need to be coordinated. Thus, one of the basic steps in coordination and control is the grouping of subunits into *sets*, thereby creating new and larger subunits (for example, bank branches in CNB might be put in a unit called Western division). In addition, other coordination and control mechanisms can be used to link together units (such as planning, goal setting, rules and procedures, control systems, cross-unit task forces, or special ad hoc groups). As the information processing requirements among the subunits increases, more complex and sophisticated coordination and control mechanisms are needed.

7. *If a set of subunits is part of the larger organization, consider it as a unit, and recycle to step 5.* The set of units, now linked together by coordinating and control mechanisms, may be just one of several sets within a larger organization. (For example, a hospital pavilion may be one of several; the Western division of CNB just one of several divisions.) If so, each of these should now be considered as a subunit and the design analysis should return to step 5 (analysis of information processing needs among the new subunits). Depending on the number of levels in the organization, this recycling may have to happen a number of times until the whole organization has been considered. Similarly, coordinating mechanisms may have to be altered to ensure consistency across levels.

8. *If information processing requirements change over time, organizational structure must adapt to those changes.* This final step simply suggests that the problem of design is never fully accomplished. Managers must reevaluate their unit's information processing requirements–information processing capacity fit. The need for structural change may be due to either environmental change or changes in the nature of the unit's work over time.

Summary

Organization structure and design is an important factor influencing the behavior of individuals and groups and thus has a major impact on the effectiveness of the total organization. We have identified the critical elements of design here, and have presented an approach to designing organizations based on the concept of information processing. Such an approach lends itself to a step-by-step process of design.

Organization design is largely a managerial function. It is the manager who usually makes decisions about what the organization will look like, although managers frequently get assistance from staff or consultants. While it is natural to think of organizational design as a top management function, in reality, it goes on continually at all levels of the organization. Much as in the case of job design (noted in Chapter 5), the manager designs the organization through day-by-day decisions. When faced with a task and a set of individuals to perform the task, the manager makes design decisions when determining how to group people and how to link them together. Thus, the design model presented here is one that is applicable at all management levels.

The emphasis in this chapter has been on the rationale for design and an approach to design decisions. Clearly, one element of design is still missing. Once roles have been grouped together into units and the patterns of internal communication have been established, the critical question arises of how to link together effectively the activities of those different units. This is the question of coordination and control, an important part of our design model, which will be discussed in Chapter 11.

Suggested Readings

Galbraith, J. R. *Designing Complex Organizations*. Reading, Mass.: Addison-Wesley, 1973.

Galbraith, J. R. *Organization Design*. Reading, Mass.: Addison-Wesley, 1977.

Lawrence, P. R., and Lorsch, J. *Organization and Environment: Managing Differentiation and Integration*. Boston: Harvard University Graduate School of Business Administration, 1967.

Lawrence, P. R., and Lorsch, J. W. *Developing Organizations: Diagnosis and Action*. Reading, Mass.: Addison-Wesley, 1969.

Tushman, M. L., and Nadler, D. A. "Information Processing as an Integrating Framework in Organization Design," *Academy of Management Review*, 1978, *3*, 613–621.

Chapter **11**

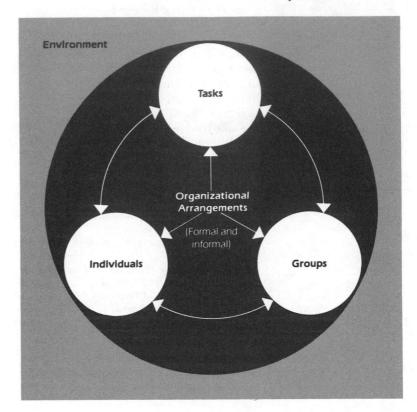

Design Mechanisms
for Coordination
and Control

Dr. Kathleen Seward is the Vice President for Technical Services of a large developer and producer of sophisticated medical instruments. Dr. Seward's job involves the management of all research and development activities for the firm. Since the technology of medical instrumentation changes quickly, effective research and development, aimed at the design of new and successful products, is particularly important to the firm. Dr. Seward's division is responsible for basic and applied research, developing new technologies and products, building prototypes of new products as well as developing production processes for new products.

Recently, Dr. Seward has become concerned about the problems that occur during the new product development process. In particular, she has become worried about two of her departments, applied research and systems development, as to whether they are working together effectively (see Figure 11.1 for the organization chart). She's wondering what kind of changes ought to be made to deal with the problems.

The applied research department is responsible for identifying and developing technologies that can be used in new products. The systems development department, on the other hand, is responsible for taking these technolo-

Figure 11.1 *Major Work Units in the Technical Division*

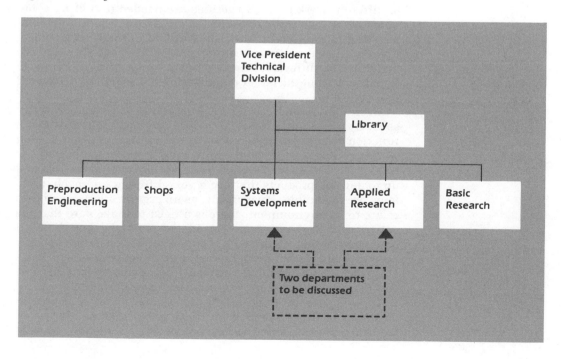

gies and developing specific products that can be produced and marketed. Typically, the applied research department works on refining a specific technology that might be applicable to the company's product line. At any time, this department might be working on as many as 10–15 different product-related technologies. When a technology is developed to the point where it looks promising, the project is passed on to systems development which develops specific products.

Usually, the project ends up being bounced back and forth between the two departments. Systems development people may identify bugs or problems in the core technology that require additional work by applied research. Similarly, applied research may continue to work with that technology and may come up with insights that require changes to be made in work that systems development is doing.

This is a normal and expected part of the development process.

Currently, the heads of each of these two departments report to Dr. Seward, along with three other department heads. Seward has a good technical background, but she also has major responsibilities at the corporate level, so she has little time to become involved in the day-to-day activities of the division.

Recently, Dr. Seward has noted that major problems have been experienced, particularly in these two departments. Excessive costs have been incurred, major delays have been experienced, and misunderstandings have occurred between the units, with each blaming the other for costs and delays. Some of the products that have been developed by these groups have subsequently encountered major technical problems in the field, necessitating costly and embarrassing recalls.

THE PROBLEMS DESCRIBED HERE, involving the systems development and applied research departments, are not unique. In fact, a basic concern in organization design is how to develop a structure that will bring about the integration of the activities of different work units. Structures are needed that bring about appropriate levels of control and coordination. Control involves assuring that different work units are performing as intended. Coordination goes beyond control and involves assuring that the activities of different interdependent units will fit or mesh together, so that the larger organizational task will be performed effectively.

Coordination and control are important for a number of reasons. At the simplest level, it is difficult for an organization to function effectively if the subunits of that organization are not working in concert. If applied research is trying to develop one type of technology while systems development is getting geared up to develop products that use a very different approach, problems are inevitable. Particularly, as an organization attempts to relate to its environment, there is a need to make sure that the activities of work units are coordinated. Going back to the CNB case described in Chapter 10, if one branch is pushing checking accounts while other branches are trying to get customers to use automatic bank machines instead, the customer may become confused and, ultimately, the organization may suffer.

Drawing on the information processing model presented in Chapter 10, every set of work units in an organization faces requirements for information processing. Somehow mechanisms need to be developed to ensure that needed information flows in a timely and undistorted manner among the work units. Thus, the model makes clear the need for the development of such mechanisms.

Finally, coordination and control is necessitated by something else — conflict. Groups within organizations frequently move into states of conflict. (We will discuss conflict and conflict resolution in Chapter 12.) One of the manifestations of conflict is that units fail to cooperate or coordinate effectively with one another; sometimes they even act to hinder the performance of other units. The negative consequences of conflict underscore the need to give the question of coordination and control explicit management attention.

In this chapter, we will build on the information processing framework developed in Chapter 10. In particular, we will discuss potential coordination and control devices. This set of devices (based on design alternatives identified by Galbraith, 1973, 1977) provides a useful tool for thinking about the organization design options available. First, the various mechanisms will be presented, with examples from Dr. Seward's Technical Division. The CNB case, introduced in Chapter 10, will also be used for illustrative purposes. Second, the question of choosing among design alternatives will be addressed.

Coordination and Control Mechanisms

Because organizational units have varying degrees of need to relate to each other, they have different information processing requirements. As mentioned earlier, these requirements depend on the nature of the tasks being performed, the environment, and the degree of interdependence involved in the task. Coordination and control mechanisms basically link together units by facilitating the processing of information among them. The nature of the information processing requirements between and among work units is the key determinant of the type of coordination and control mechanisms needed (Thompson, 1967; Galbraith, 1973). As information processing requirements increase, so does the need for more extensive and complex coordination and control mechanisms.

What are the various devices available to aid in the processing of information? Five major types of information processing mechanisms can be identified: (1) hierarchy of authority, (2) rules and procedures, (3) planning and goal setting, (4) vertical information systems, and (5) lateral relations. Each one of these mechanisms is capable of assisting the processing of information between and among groups. Thus, organizations can use combinations of mechanisms to achieve the degree of information processing capacity needed to effectively perform the tasks at hand. Next we will provide some sense of what these mechanisms are, how they get used, and how they fit into the larger model for the designing of information processing systems.

HIERARCHY OF
AUTHORITY

Returning to Dr. Seward's two departments, the task which faces them — developing new products — is relatively unpredictable. It needs to be done in a dynamic environment and requires the two units to work together: it is interdependent. Thus, the task has a high degree of uncertainty and requires a large amount of information processing between the two departments.

Perhaps the simplest way to cope with the uncertainty facing the groups and to help them coordinate their activities is to add another level of supervision. Instead of having the units report to a largely absent vice president, a new position, director of new product development, could be created. The two departments would report directly to this new manager (see Figure 11.2). Information that needs to move between the two groups goes up the hierarchy to the director and then over to the other department. The director serves as an information channel and can also exercise control over how much information moves between the groups. A similar approach might be used in CNB. Branches facing similar market areas might be put under the control of regional managers. They would coordinate the activities of the branches within a market.

While the addition of a level in the hierarchy of authority aids information processing and coordination, it has limits. In fairly stable or certain situations, such an approach may be enough, but in most cases the amount of information that needs to be processed is more than can be handled by one person. Thus, other mechanisms are needed in addition to hierarchy.

Figure 11.2 *Coordination and Control by Hierarchy*

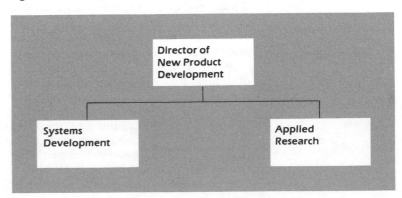

One way of coordinating and controlling activity is to specify
ahead of time how behavior should occur. By providing initial
information in the form of rules, procedures, and policies, it is
possible to ensure that certain desired types of behavior will
occur.

In the Technical Division, in addition to adding a new product
director, Dr. Seward might institute a series of policies that
would help to coordinate and control the work. For example,
management could specify a series of tests that must be passed
by a new technology before it is handed over from applied
research to systems development. This would prevent premature
movement of projects, and so forestall repeated reworking of
technologies with associated costs and delays.

Clearly, in CNB much coordination has already been
achieved through rules and procedures. Procedures for making
transactions, approving loans, and so on have been used to
ensure that branches will operate in a consistent manner.

For rules and procedures to be effective, individuals in the
organization must believe that rewards will accrue to them from
following the rules or that sanctions will be administered for
failing to adhere to the rules. Thus, the effectiveness of such
mechanisms depends on the reward system in the organization
and the nature of the expectancies that are developed around
the specific structural mechanism.

While rules together with hierarchy can aid in coordination
for relatively certain tasks, problems are encountered when
work is uncertain. In Dr. Seward's Technical Division we might
find many instances where it is impossible to specify ahead of
time what constitutes a completed or finished technology. Given
the demands of the environment, more and more exceptions to
the rules might come about for products that are in great
demand. Hence, as uncertainty increases, it becomes more difficult to specify behavior in advance through rules and procedures; the existing mechanisms become overloaded.

A third mechanism that can be used for coordination, in addition
to hierarchy and rules, is planning and goal setting. (See Newman and Warren, 1977, for a discussion of issues in planning.)
Through the setting of goals and the formulating of plans, different units' activities are coordinated, since they are all suppos-
edly heading in the same direction or toward the same targets.
The units, however, are frequently left with discretion about
how to reach those targets. What this does is to reduce the need
for information flowing up and down the hierarchy by moving
some of the decision points in the organization down to a lower
level. As long as effort is directed toward an agreed-upon goal
and is within general rules and procedures, decisions can be
made at lower levels of the organization. When decisions are
made at lower levels, information does not need to be transmit-

ted up and down the hierarchy. This is especially desirable when there is great uncertainty, resulting in the need for decisions to be made quickly by those who are close to the action.

Using goals and targets and allowing discretion at lower levels often provides an opportunity for designing tasks that have higher motivating potential, since those doing the work have greater discretion and more autonomy and variety. Planning, by itself, may have only a limited impact on behavior. It is important to remember that organizational rewards (see Chapter 5) are important in motivating individuals and groups to exert effort toward meeting goals or plans.

In the Technical Division, targets might be set for completion of each stage of development by the applied research and systems development departments. The individual product groups within each department might then plan to determine what they will have to do to achieve the targets that have been set. Thus, the activities of the two units will be coordinated, in that they will be consistent with a single plan or timetable for development.

Despite their appeal, plans, goals, and targets have only limited usefulness. The ability to develop targets requires enough certainty about events in the future that reasonable goals can be identified. When this is not true, goals tend to slip by, targets have to be reset, and coordination problems persist. As uncertainty increases, the devices of hierarchy, rules, and plans are frequently not sufficient to process enough information to enable effective coordination and control. In CNB, these devices are adequate because the task is relatively stable and has low levels of interdependence. On the other hand, in the Technical Division hierarchy, rules, and some general plans and goals are not sufficient to effectively coordinate the activities of the two departments.

Having made use of hierarchy, rules, and plans, organization designers face a choice of ways to cope with increased uncertainty and very demanding information processing requirements. One general approach is to change the organization to reduce the necessity for processing information. Another approach is to make use of more extensive, costly coordination devices to further increase the information processing capacity of the organization structure. Two types of mechanisms increase capacity. Vertical information systems increase the capacity of the structure to move information up and down the hierarchy in a timely and effective manner, while lateral relations move information processing between units down to lower levels. We will discuss these first and then consider the methods of reducing information processing requirements.

VERTICAL INFORMATION SYSTEMS

One approach to improve coordination is to improve the capacity of the existing hierarchical structure to process information by creating information systems. Information systems are mechanisms that collect data about organizational functioning and distribute those data to a predetermined network of organizational members (Cammann, 1974; Lawler and Rhode, 1976). Budgets, for example, are information systems that enable the monitoring of expenditures (compared to previously determined standards) and that alert managers to take corrective action when the actual expenditures differ greatly from the expected ones.

Many complex types of information systems exist, but those aimed at increasing the capacity to coordinate and control activity in the organization (frequently called *control systems*) have certain elements in common (see Figure 11.3). In this model of a control system, an organizational work unit is seen as a system that takes some form of input, subjects it to a transformation process, and produces an output. For example, the systems development department takes some inputs (technologies from the applied research department, effort and knowledge by the staff, and resources in the form of equipment and supplies) and transforms those into plans for finished products that can then be produced and sold by the company. The control system itself has certain key elements. First, it has a *sensor* that serves to collect information about various aspects of the unit's functioning. Also present are *standards*, benchmarks against which data can be compared. These standards may originate from a variety of sources, for example, the planning or goal-setting process. In systems development, there may be goals concerning how much progress will be made on a product and at what cost during a certain period. These serve as standards against which actual performance can be compared. This activates a *comparison* process and a *decision process* where decisions are made concern-

Figure 11.3 *Basic Components of Formal Control Systems*

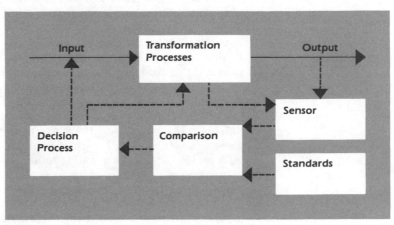

Nadler, 1977a; adapted from Lawler and Rhode, 1976.

ing corrective action if discrepancies occur between planned and actual performance. Such corrective action may include changing work assignments, changing the amount of resources available, changing personnel, and reexamining or perhaps changing the goals.

The creation and operation of information and control systems enables the processing of much more information than might otherwise be possible. If such systems were used in the Technical Division, for example, it would be possible to make changes quickly and to adjust for problems in one department when problems were indicated in the other department. In CNB, such systems are used extensively. The lending activities of the bank's branches are monitored so that when problems arise (for instance, when loan delinquency rates go up) corrective action can be taken by upper management. A range of such systems enables the control of a large number of branches.

As will be expanded upon later, the costs of information systems can be high, especially where large amounts of information need to be handled. Individual decision makers can be overloaded with information and unable to act. In addition, information and control systems run the risk of unintended and sometimes adverse motivational effects (see Lawler, 1976; Lawler and Rhode, 1976).

LATERAL RELATIONS

An alternative to the creation of more extensive vertical information systems is to create ways in which units can exchange information directly and coordinate their activities by mutual adjustment (Thompson, 1967) rather than by moving information up and down the hierarchy. This, of course, moves discretion and control downward in the organization and may result in some loss of direct managerial control. On the other hand, it may enhance the movement of information that is critical in highly uncertain and highly interdependent tasks. Galbraith (1977) has provided an extensive list of approaches for developing lateral relations. Instead of dealing with all of these in detail, we will discuss a few of the general lateral relations types to illustrate how this kind of mechanism works.

The simplest form of lateral relations is *direct contact* between individuals in different work units. This can occur informally or through formally designated liaison roles. For example, in each of the two departments in the Technical Division, individuals might be designated as contact persons or as having liaison roles with the other group. When interunit problems arise, these individuals would contact each other to exchange information and work out the problems (see Figure 11.4).

A somewhat more extensive approach is the creation of *cross-unit groups*. These are groups, either temporary or permanent, that are composed of people from different units. Such a group provides a forum for the exchange of information, for coordination, and for conflict resolution that crosses work unit

Figure 11.4 *Coordination and Control by Contact*

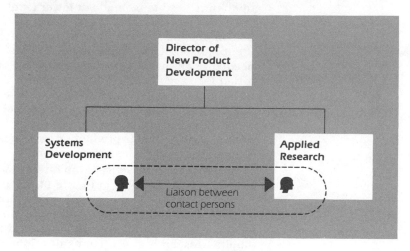

boundaries. For example, in the Technical Division, several individuals from each unit who are working on the same product might be designated as members of a product team or task force. This group would have the role of coordinating the work and information flow related to that product, thereby involving the two departments (see Figure 11.5).

Figure 11.5 *Coordination and Control by Cross-Unit Groups*

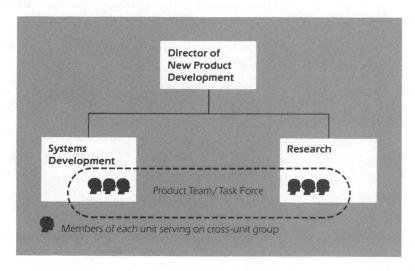

As uncertainty increases and more decisions that affect multiple units need to be made at lower levels, problems sometimes arise around leadership. Cross-unit teams may result in no one person feeling accountable for the total performance of the group. In addition, sometimes conflicts arise and someone is needed to aid in the effective resolution of the conflict. One solution is to specifically appoint someone as an *integrator* (Lawrence and Lorsch, 1967b), with the direct responsibility for integrating or coordinating the activities of multiple work units around the performance of a task (such as a specific product or project). Jobs such as product or project manager in large organizations are examples of integrators.

In the Technical Division, an integrator could be used in several ways. As illustrated in Figure 11.6, a product manager could be designated to coordinate or lead the product team, which includes members of the two units. The product team members, however, are primarily members of their functional departments (applied research and systems development), and the product manager does not have direct managerial control over them. Thus, the integrator cannot rely on the rewards system as a source of power and must use expertise or some other form of power in order to coordinate their efforts. Individual integrators can be created, as can integrating departments or groups. In this case, the integrator is used in conjunction with cross-unit teams, but that may or may not be the best solution in other organizations.

MATRIX ORGANIZATIONS

In highly uncertain environments with highly interdependent tasks, great pressures for coordination and control may come both from the functional side (that is, systems development and applied research) of the organization and from the product side. In these cases, it may aid coordination to balance the power between the two perspectives. For example, in the Technical

Figure 11.6 *Coordination and Control by Integrator Roles/Units*

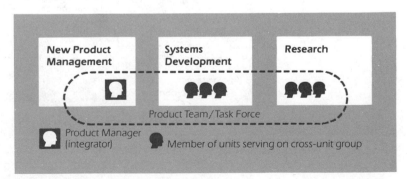

Division, it may be useful to give the product manager additional power in the form of some type of managerial authority over the people on the product team. This is not complete authority, since those people would still report to managers in the functional departments. Team members would essentially have two bosses. This form of organization is called a *matrix organization design* (see Davis and Lawrence, 1977, for an in depth discussion of the matrix and its use). Figure 11.7 presents a matrix organization structure for the Technical Division case. It has two chains of command. On the right side, the functional departments continue to exist. The organization still benefits from the information exchange and control provided by having people grouped by function. On the left is another chain of command, with a product manager for each major new product coordinating the activ-

Figure 11.7 *Coordination and Control by Matrix*

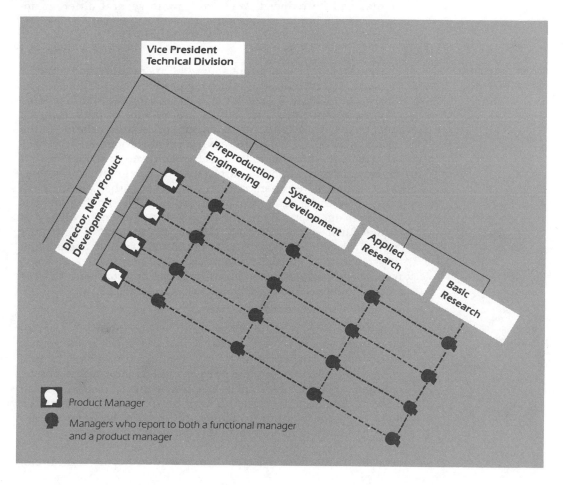

Product Manager

Managers who report to both a functional manager and a product manager

ities of individuals across the functional groups. Thus, those managers within each function who head up the product activities report to two bosses at once, a functional boss and a product boss. In this way, information is processed both within and across functional groups, and coordination of different product-oriented activities is achieved.

Designing to Reduce Information Processing Needs

The design mechanisms considered so far all aim to improve the capacity of the organization to process information, either up and down the hierarchy or laterally across organizational boundaries. An alternative design strategy is to make changes in the organizational structure so that the need to process information among work units (that is, the information processing requirements) will be reduced. We turn now to several different approaches including environmental management, slack resources, and self-contained units (Galbraith, 1977).

ENVIRONMENTAL MANAGEMENT

The environment is a prime source of uncertainty and a major factor in determining the information processing requirements that an organization or a set of organizational units face. One way an organization can reduce the amount of uncertainty it must cope with is to attempt to control or reduce variation in the critical portions of the larger environment through environmental management. This may be achieved through strategies that enable an organization to gain a hold on a segment of the market, through government regulation or some other similar measures. The management of relations with the environment is similar to questions of organizational strategy which will be discussed further in Chapter 13. The important point to remember from our brief discussion here is that an alternative to changing the structure to process more information is to reduce, in some way, the uncertainty that stems from the environment, thereby reducing the need for additional structural devices.

SLACK RESOURCES

Another way organizations frequently reduce their information processing needs is by the use of slack resources. By adding slack into the organization — by extending timetables, by providing more resources — the need to process information can be reduced. If, for example, it is not important to meet a certain delivery date for a new product from the Technical Division, the need to coordinate and exchange information between the applied research and systems development departments is reduced. Without the pressure of time, one department does not need to know where a project is in the other department. It can afford to wait until the project is finally handed over and then worry about dealing with it.

Creating slack resources uses resources, leads to longer time spans for the same amount of performance, and costs more. On the other hand, it reduces the need for the structure to process information, and many organizations do make use of slack as an approach to coordination. Where there is little competition in the marketplace, adding slack becomes a more feasible approach than in a case where competitors are able to take away business by delivering earlier or at a lower cost. Essentially, slack is the process of using up more resources in place of coordinating and processing information.

SELF-CONTAINED
UNITS

A third information processing reduction strategy is to create new self-contained units. This can also be seen as another description of reforming units around new information processing requirements. For example, the Technical Division is organized functionally, where several departments contain individuals who do the same kind of work or perform the same kinds of functions (that is, applied research, systems development, preproduction engineering). Implicit in this structure is the assumption that the most critical information processing needs are among people doing the same functions, even though working on different projects or products. The various coordination and control mechanisms are thus designed to deal with the remaining information processing needs that exist once groups have been formed around functions.

An alternative to functional groups with various coordination and control mechanisms (up to and including a matrix linking those who work on similar products) is to organize around what is the other axis of the matrix, in this case, the product rather than the function. In the Technical Division, we could create several small departments, each department responsible for a product going from research to systems development to preproduction engineering. In this case, only basic research and support functions such as the library might be left separate. In fact, what this does is to create several small technical divisions, one for each major product that is being developed. The information processing needs across the functional departments are now reduced because everyone working on the same product is in the same department (see Figure 11.8).

There are costs associated with creating product-oriented departments. Part of the rationale for creating functional departments in the first place is that such an approach frequently permits the best and most cost-effective use of resources. To create small product departments may require the duplication of resources at extra costs. For example, each department may need a chemical engineer, requiring four chemical engineers for four products, when the technologies are similar enough so that two

Figure 11.8 *Improving Coordination and Control by Reducing Information Processing Requirements — Self-contained Units*

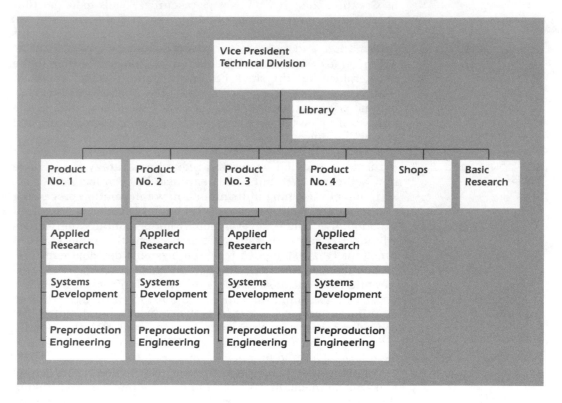

chemical engineers could have done the work in the original research department. Thus, coordination is achieved by reducing the need to process information but at the cost of duplication or poor utilization of available resources.

Additional Design Mechanisms

The design mechanisms that have been discussed are major tools which can be used to structure organizations so that the desired coordination and control can be achieved. These mechanisms, however, are not the only available approaches. As has been mentioned throughout this chapter and Chapter 10, two types of design tools, the design of reward systems and the design of tasks, are both powerful and directly related to the design mechanisms already discussed.

In the early chapters of this book, the point was made that the use of various kinds of rewards (as extrinsic motivators) and various types of work design and goal-setting arrangements (as intrinsic motivators) could lead to major changes in the patterns of behavior of individuals and groups. This was based on the view that much of the behavior of individuals is based on their expectancies of what kinds of outcomes (rewards) will be obtained as a result of different levels of work performance. Clearly, then, the design of reward systems (pay systems, career paths, and the like) and the design of tasks (including the types of goals people strive for) are important aspects of design that affect behavior.

Indeed, the use of work design and reward systems is inherent in a number of coordination and control mechanisms that have already been described. The use of rules and procedures, the creation of goals, and the development of product teams all have an impact on the skill variety, autonomy, task identity, meaningfulness, and feedback of both individual and group tasks. Similarly, the issue of measurement and evaluation in control systems and the use of rules and goals all assume that some rewards or sanctions are designed into those systems to motivate people to follow rules, to attempt to achieve goals, and to behave in ways that will improve performance as measured by the control system.

The implication is that the task design and rewards systems should be reexamined during the design process. Many times, a new organization design is developed with new roles, relationships, and work units but no change is made in the existing reward system. Similarly, new designs often have consequences for the nature of individual tasks, but these are not considered. Consequently, following changes in the basic composition of groups, internal unit structure, and coordination and control mechanisms, it is important to examine both the reward systems and the resultant task design to ensure that the behavior motivated by these structural factors is consistent with that facilitated or constrained by the other primary organization design variables. The crucial issue is consistency; all the elements of the structure should be consistent in the behavior that is motivated, facilitated, and constrained.

Choosing Appropriate Coordination and Control Mechanisms

**CHOICE FROM
A RANGE**

Going back to the basic information processing model, the designer of organizations needs to choose among combinations of mechanisms. The ultimate aim is to match the information processing capacity of the resulting structure with the information processing requirements of the critical organizational tasks.

Given this approach, the coordination and control mechanisms can be thought of as a continuum (see Figure 11.9). The mechanisms vary in their extensiveness — how many resources need to be devoted to coordination — with hierarchy and rules at the low end of the range and vertical information systems and the more complex lateral relations at the high end. Similarly, the different mechanisms vary in the cost to the organization and in their capacity to process information.

The criteria for choice involves a tradeoff between cost and the effect of the mechanism on information processing capacity or requirements. Mechanisms should be extensive enough to effect information processing as needed, but not too extensive, or the organization will pay more for coordination and control (both directly and indirectly) than it needs to.

As suggested in Chapter 10, the designer of organizations should first determine how the lowest level units should be composed and internally structured. Following that step, sets of units should be examined. In each case, the question is asked, What are the information processing requirements that exist among the work units in this set? Given those requirements, a set of coordination and control devices should be chosen which will meet those requirements at minimum cost to the organization. This process should then continue with successively larger sets of units being considered.

Figure 11.9 *A Continuum of Coordination and Control Mechanisms*

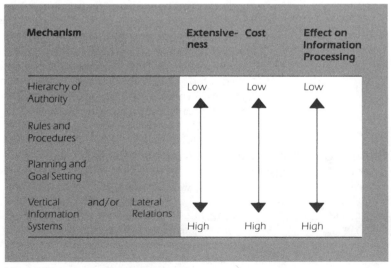

Adapted from Tushman and Nadler, 1978.

In the final analysis, the choice of coordination and control mechanisms is a question of fit. As indicated in Figure 10.9, the objective is to achieve a fit between the information processing requirements posed by the task and the information processing capacity of the organizational structure.

THE DESIGN MODEL REVISITED

Now that we have completed our discussion of coordination and control mechanisms, we need to go back and review our overall design process. It should now be clear that the combination of work-unit composition, work-unit structuring, and coordination and control mechanisms allows the designer of organizations to create many combinations which can equally process information.

Since a number of designs will probably provide equal amounts of information processing capacity, how are decisions to be made? Previously, several factors such as the informal organization, political issues, and the costs of changing structure to various new designs were mentioned. In reviewing the design model and thinking about how it might be used, two other guidelines should be kept in mind.

First, it is important to identify what are the dominant competitive issues or questions facing the organization. This relates to questions of organizational strategy, which will be introduced here and considered in more detail in Chapter 13. Organizations perform many different tasks. Some tasks, given the nature of the product/service, the environment, and so on, are more crucial than others. Some tasks can be done poorly and the organization will still survive. Other tasks are central to the organization and must be done well. The implication is that designs should be built around those *critical tasks* that the organization must do well if it is to continue to survive and function effectively. The information processing needs associated with doing those critical tasks should be the ones to which the structure responds first.

A second guideline concerns the work flow. Much can be determined by tracing how work moves through the organization. In the case of the Technical Division, this is relatively easy, since one can see a product develop as it moves from research through systems development to preproduction engineering over to the manufacturing department. In other cases, the work flow may be more difficult, as in the case of a large hospital where there are multiple work flows that are interconnected.

This concept of examining the work flow and related interactions is not a new one (see, for example, Chapple and Sayles, 1958); however, it is worth keeping in mind as one looks at an existing organizational structure. While examining the work flow, it is important to identify the critical interactions occurring between people and work units as the work moves through the organization. How much uncertainty is associated with the work at different points? Where do problems such as breakdowns in communications, missed targets, or delays occur? All of these may be indicators of unmet information processing needs.

In summary, identifying crucial competitive issues and tracing the work flow are starting points for applying the design model. The goal is to determine what the information processing requirements are that are posed by the critical tasks, and then to assess whether the current organizational structure has adequate information processing capacity. Where there are needs to increase information processing capacity, three factors — the composition of work units, the internal structuring of work units, and the various mechanisms for coordination and control — are tools available for improvement of organizational structure, and, in turn, the enhancement of organizational functioning.

Summary

An important aspect of organization design is the methods used to bring about coordination of the efforts of work units. If an organization is to be effective, the structure must somehow assure that each unit is performing as planned, and that different units will effectively mesh their performances together.

Organization designers have a variety of different coordination and control mechanisms with which to work. They range from fairly simple devices such as rules, programs, and hierarchies, to more complex approaches such as matrix organizations, self-contained units, and so on. An information processing model can guide the choice of mechanisms. As uncertainty increases, more complex and elaborate mechanisms need to be employed so that the information processing capacity of the structure will match the information processing requirements of the tasks to be done.

Suggested Readings

Davis, S. M., and Lawrence, P. R. *Matrix*. Reading, Mass.: Addison-Wesley, 1977.

Galbraith, J. R. *Organizational Design*, Reading, Mass.: Addison-Wesley, 1977.

Lawler, E. E., and Rhode, J. G. *Information and Control in Organizations*. Pacific Palisades, Cal.: Goodyear, 1976.

Newman, W. H. *Constructive Control*. Englewood Cliffs, N.J.: Prentice-Hall, 1976.

Newman, W. H., and Warren, E. K. *The Process of Management*. 3rd ed. Englewood Cliffs, N.J.: Prentice-Hall, 1977.

Chapter **12**

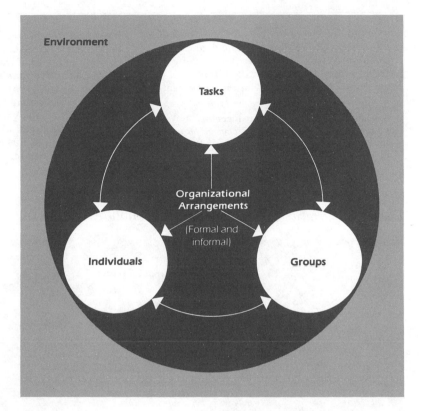

Managing Conflict
in Organizations

Household Products Inc.[1] is a large producer of food products and related household goods. The company grew to its present size over a period of fifteen years, under the direction of the company President, M. Norman. In the lat-

[1] Adapted from Household Products Inc., in W. H. Newman and E. K. Warren, *The Process of Management*. 3rd edition. Englewood Cliffs, N.J.: Prentice-Hall, 1977.

ter part of that period, however, the company leveled off in growth, and many of the members of the Board of Directors became concerned about Norman's capacity to continue to run the company. After much discussion and maneuvering among the board members, Norman was "kicked upstairs" to become Chairman of the Board, and John Saxon, previously Vice President in charge of the consumer products group was promoted to President.

Figure 12.1 *Organization Chart of Household Products Inc.*

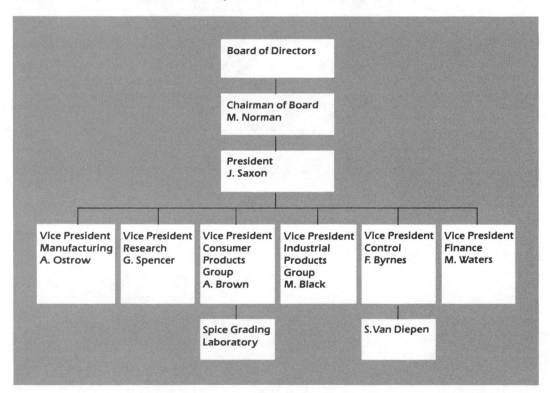

Saxon spent a few months orienting himself to the new job and then began a massive round of cuts in the organization. Several thousand people were laid off or fired, including fifty people in middle and upper management positions. For several weeks, each Monday would be marked by a new set of memos from Saxon's office, indicating where the next group of cuts would come from and who would be involved.

After three months of "cutting out the fat," the organization became stabilized (see the organization chart shown in Figure 12.1). Saxon, however, was still convinced that there was much fat in the organization and that a number of "frills" could be cut out with no harm to organizational performance. He gave Fred Byrnes, a former member of Saxon's staff and current Vice President for Control, the mission of finding other areas where cost reductions could be made.

Byrnes, in turn, gave the assignment to look for "frills" to a new member of his staff, Sam Van Diepen, who had just joined Household straight out of school. After several weeks Van Diepen gave Byrnes a report which included a number of areas for additional cost reductions.

One which stood out was the Spice Grading Lab, buried in the Consumer Products Group. This lab, set up by M. Norman about ten years ago, did tests on different spice products and published reports used industry-wide. Since then, however, Household had drastically reduced its spice line so the lab had limited use. By eliminating it, immediate savings of $150,000 a year could be realized.

Byrnes agreed with Van Diepen's analysis and sent a memo to Art Brown, Vice President for Consumer Products, outlining the analysis and directing him to eliminate the lab from his budget.

A few days later, Byrnes received a visit from the President, Saxon, who was agitated. In his hand, he had memos from the Vice Presidents of Manufacturing and R & D, as well as from Brown, protesting the elimination of the Spice Grading Lab. In addition, Saxon had received a call at home the previous evening from Norman, who said that he was "very interested in the analysis of the Spice Grading Lab operation." Saxon wanted to know how all of this mess had gotten started.

INCIDENTS SUCH AS THIS are familiar in organizations. Conflict between individuals, groups, or units is frequent, and at Household Products, it is consuming top management time, effort, and attention. If it continues unresolved, it may further damage the working relationships of the top management group, a group that needs to work together effectively if the company is to succeed. The individual managers may become so involved in the Spice Grading Lab question that "winning" on this issue may become more important than doing what is in the best interests of the organization.

One of the realities of organizational life is that as organizations grow and groups develop their own perspectives, conflict tends to develop among groups (March and Simon, 1958; Katz and Kahn, 1966). This is natural as groups develop over time (see Chapters 6 and 7). Contrary to popular belief, conflict is not necessarily undesirable. As we will see, conflict has both constructive and destructive effects. For example, in Household Products, the conflict over the spice lab could stimulate the search for new and creative solutions, result in improvements in production methods, or lead to insights that might not have been made otherwise. On the other hand, a continuation of the conflict may cause damage to the effectiveness of the top management group. Given that conflict is inevitable in organizations, the question each manager must answer is how to react to, respond to, and manage conflict between groups in organizations so that positive effects will be realized and negative effects minimized.

In this chapter, we will answer this question by examining the nature of conflict between individuals and groups in organizations. First, we will define what conflict is. Second, we will look at the organizational and political context of conflict. Following that, we will outline a model that describes how conflict develops in organizations, one that will help us to understand both how conflict comes about and how it can be managed. Also, we will examine the various positive and negative effects of conflict. Finally, we will use the model to identify different approaches for dealing with and managing intergroup conflict.

What Is Conflict?

The word conflict brings to mind images such as antagonism, struggles between parties, opposition processes, threats to cooperation, and so on. As we consider conflict between groups in organizations, however, we need to define the concept more specifically. One approach to the concept which seems to include most of the important characteristics defines conflict as:

> "overt behavior arising out of a process in which one unit seeks the advance of its own interests in its relationships with others. . . . Units are not in conflict when deliberate interference is absent . . . the interference must be deliberate and goal directed by at least one party" (Schmidt and Kochan, 1972, p. 363).

Conflict, therefore, exists when one party (group or individual) attempts to attain its own goals relative to some other party, *and* where the party interferes with the other party's attempts to reach goals. The interference, while a necessary condition for conflict, may be active or passive. For example, Art Brown, the Vice President for Consumer Goods, could have blocked Byrnes's attempts to cut costs by not providing data about the spice lab (passive) or by writing memos to Saxon (active). Therefore, it is more than disagreement; it is the deliberate interference of another party's attempts to meet its goals.

When conflict occurs, it can be seen and experienced in many ways. Three levels of conflict have been identified (Filley, 1975). First, conflict is *perceived*. The parties realize that conflict exists, because they see that their goals are different from the goals of other groups and that the opportunity for interference exists. Second, conflict is *felt*. The conflict brings about feelings of hostility, anger, fear, or mistrust between one party and the other. Third, conflict is expressed through *behavior* which is the active or passive interference by at least one party. All three of these levels, perceived conflict, felt conflict, and conflict behavior exist in conflict situations.

Finally, conflict occurs in the context of a relationship between two or more parties, in this case, groups. Conflict can occur between individuals, or it can occur between sets of individuals. Conflict can also occur among more than two parties at one point in time. As will be seen, the context of conflict can be important in understanding why conflict occurs and in determining what to do about it.

The Political Context of Conflict

A DIFFERENT PERSPECTIVE

It is important to remember that conflict in an organization occurs within the context of an ongoing system, and thus within the context of continuing relationships among people, groups, and work units. In Household Products, the conflict goes beyond Byrnes and Brown and even beyond Control and Consumer Products. It involves other people, since each of the key actors has relationships with other individuals who, in turn, have relationships with yet others. Each individual may have developed working alliances with other managers out of opportunity, necessity, or fear.

To understand these dynamics, a somewhat different perspective on organizational behavior is needed. Up to now, we have concentrated on the relatively rational and purposeful nature of organizations, especially in our discussions of organization design and structure. Such an approach assumes that individuals, when given full information, will do what is in the best interests of the total larger organization, since that will ultimately be of benefit to them. In Household Products, for example, if it were possible to objectively determine whether the spice lab is worth $150,000 a year, then a clear and rational decision could be made about whether it should be eliminated.

While a rational perspective makes sense, it unfortunately does not describe much of the behavior that occurs in organizations. Other factors, particularly questions of relative power, come into play. The existence of power as an issue to be considered suggests a political perspective for interpreting patterns of behavior (see Allison, 1971; Tushman, 1977). Politics refers to the use of authority and power to affect definitions of goals, directions, and other major aspects of the organization (Wamsley and Zald, 1973). The political perspective emphasizes the view that many decisions in organizations are not made in a rational or formal way but rather through continued conflict, compromise, accommodation, and bargaining. This occurs because groups have very different desired outcomes, and they behave in ways that will enable them to realize their own goals.

Traditionally, when talking about groups within organizations, we think of the formal organizational groupings, the subunits that appear on an organization chart. Experience and research indicate, however, that these formally constructed groups frequently are not the elements that operate on a day-to-day basis. Rather, another organization structure emerges over time and cuts across the formally prescribed boundaries and territories. One way of thinking about this emergent organization structure is to think of networks that exist within organizations (Tichy, 1973, 1979).

Organizations are made up of individuals who are linked to other individuals in many ways. First, individuals can be linked together by information. The simple flow of data between two individuals constitutes a form of linkage. Second, individuals can be connected by influence. The ability of one individual to induce behavior in another is another form of linkage. Third, individuals can be linked together by affect, or positive and negative feelings that they hold toward each other. The patterns of linkages among individuals are called a *network*. Some individuals have many connections or linkages to other individuals, while others have very few. One way to think about networks is to portray them graphically. For example, if we determined who Byrnes, the Vice President for Control at Household, exchanges information with frequently, and subsequently with whom those other individuals also exchange information, we could identify ten different individuals who are linked together in a network of information. That network then could be laid out graphically (see Figure 12.2), with points representing people and the lines connecting them indicating the linkages.

When network maps of organizations are constructed, a number of patterns frequently appear. First, when the network is plotted, sets of points (individuals) tend to emerge that are highly interconnected. These dense areas in the network represent the key subunits, which we described in the previous two chapters. These dense areas are referred to as *cliques* (Tichy, 1973). Cliques are the basic building blocks of political structures, much as the formal work group or subunit is seen as the major building block of the formal organization. They operate as one form of group (see Chapters 6 and 7), developing norms and influencing the behavior of members.

Cliques tend to develop cooperative action strategies with other cliques. They act in concert on certain issues. When a number of cliques group together to take cooperative action, they are called a *coalition*. Coalitions, being sets of cliques, tend to be less stable than cliques, although some may endure over relatively long periods of time. Coalitions tend to develop around specific issues, values, events, or decisions. Thus, the nature

Figure 12.2 *An Example of a Simple Network*

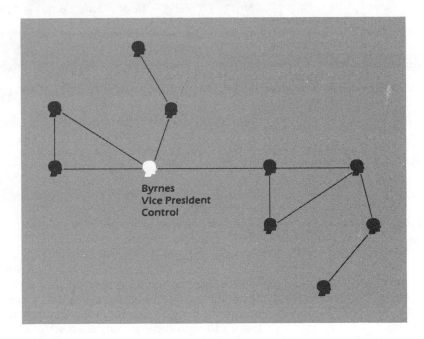

Byrnes
Vice President
Control

and composition of coalitions may change over time as different issues become salient. For example, a set of cliques that cooperate with regard to one particular conflict (that is, the Spice Grading Lab at Household Products) may dissolve and reform with a different composition when another question (Who will succeed Norman as president?) comes up. Thus, the membership of cliques in coalitions may be multiple and overlapping. Similarly, individuals may have relationships with several cliques and coalitions, and may, therefore, be spanning boundaries among a number of groups.

The network approach can be helpful in understanding behavior. If, for example, we were to plot the networks in Household Products, we would come up with a picture of an organizational structure that is very different from the official chart (see Figure 12.3). The conflict between Byrnes and Brown can be seen within the context of two cliques that exist, which may have different goals, views, or needs.

DYNAMICS OF NETWORKS

Perhaps the most interesting aspect of networks is not their existence but their dynamics — how they operate over time. While research in this area is still in early stages, a number of patterns of interaction that tend to characterize the relations among cliques and coalitions have been identified.

1. *Cliques and coalitions tend to compete for power.* One of

Figure 12.3 *A Network Map of Household Products Inc.*
(Note: Circled sets of names are cliques.)

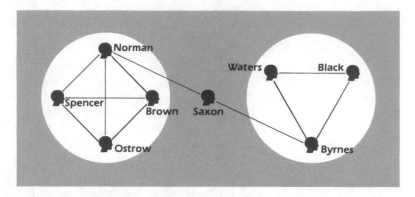

the most pervasive patterns is that cliques and coalitions expend energy competing for power relative to other groups (Tushman, 1977). This competition for power is the essence of political behavior. Political behavior manifests itself in a variety of ways, including more frequent conflict, energy directed toward acquiring and controlling resources, tests of other groups' power, and the like. This again is not a pattern that is either inherently good or bad but a natural tendency of groups within organizational settings. The spice lab controversy might be seen, for example, as a test of power among two cliques.

2. *Political behavior increases under conditions of uncertainty.* Where there is certainty, political behavior tends to be less evident. When, for example, there are clear and enforced rules and procedures, where performance criteria are clear and measurable, or where there is a very evident and stable distribution of power among different groups, there is less political behavior. As uncertainty increases, political behavior also increases (Thompson and Tuden, 1959). Uncertainty provides an opportunity for individual cliques or groups to improve their power positions. It is not surprising that the Spice Lab incident emerged following major organizational cost reductions, restructuring, and other instability.

3. *Groups vary in their power.* Groups within the organization vary greatly in their power and in their ability to operate effectively in the political arena. A number of factors may contribute to the relative power of a group, clique, or coalition. Specifically, three factors have been identified as important. First, to the extent that a group has control, or is the source, of a critical organizational resource, it will tend to be perceived as powerful (Pfeffer and Salancik, 1974). If, for example, a university is very dependent on research grants for support of its activ-

ities, then departments that bring in more research money will tend to have more power and exercise more influence over key decisions.

A second and similar source of power is the ability of a group to cope with uncertainty (Thompson, 1967; Hickson et al., 1971). To the extent that one group has the capacity to deal with uncertainty that is critical for the entire organization, that group will be powerful. For example, in a consumer products organization, when consumer tastes are rapidly changing, those who control information about the nature of those changing tastes and buying patterns may tend to be powerful. Finally, groups gain power by building alliances with other groups, so that together they may exert more power than any one could individually. Hence, allies are another source of power for a group (Pfeffer, 1977; Thompson, 1967).

POLITICS AND CONFLICT

Given a political perspective on organizations, it is not surprising that conflict is pervasive. Organizations as political systems have a general disposition to move toward states of conflict. Within this general perspective, however, specific factors may exacerbate or mediate the kind of conflict that emerges. The next questions, then, are, What are the origins of conflict, and how does conflict develop over time?

How Conflict Comes About — A Model

Conditions exist in organizations which tend to create conflict. These *antecedent conditions* are inherent in the nature of organizations, and they tend to create perceptions between groups that in turn lead to *conflict*. As is shown in Figure 12.4, conflict leads to *outcomes* that can be both positive and negative and that can influence the perceptions which brought about the conflict in the first place.

Three antecedent conditions tend to be present in most organizations. A first condition is the *differentiation of groups*. As organizations grow, they not only get bigger, but they also develop more individual parts or components; these components tend to become more and more specialized (Katz and Kahn, 1966). Groups specialize because it is more efficient to have one group worry about market products (consumer products group), for example, and one group worry about containing costs (control) than to have everyone trying to do everything. Marketing people can develop as specialists in selling (salespeople) and create relationships with customers and clients while the control people can become specialists in information and cost analysis (accountants).

The idea of creating specialized groups makes sense within some of the limits discussed earlier in the chapters on job design

Figure 12.4 *A Model of Intergroup Conflict*

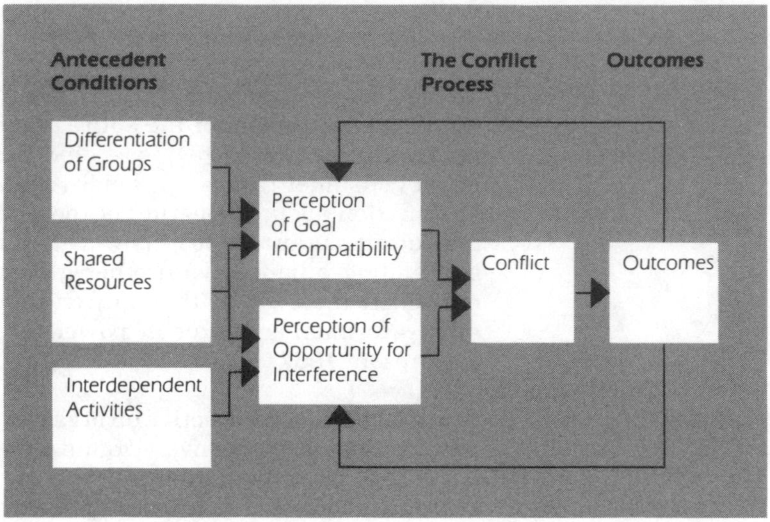

Adapted from Schmidt and Kochan, 1972.

and work group functioning. A result of this specialization, however, is that over time, groups doing different tasks and relating to different parts of the environment begin to develop unique ways of thinking about the world. They have their own special language, goals, and ways of working together. This process of developing a specific perspective as the result of specializing is called *differentiation* (March and Simon, 1958; Lawrence and Lorsch, 1967a). Differentiation is not necessarily bad; it helps the group to get its work done. If a group of salespeople, for example, knows that the term *cold call* means to call unannounced on a new perspective customer, it helps them to communicate more effectively and efficiently with each other.

Differentiation, however, presents potential problems. One group (say, marketers) may begin to see themselves as having very divergent goals and interests from another group (say, cost accountants). The two groups may encounter problems communicating with each other because they have their own goals in mind, they think in separate time frames, or they use their special language or coding schemes.

A second condition is that the resources available to groups are usually limited (March and Simon, 1958). During any period, a relatively fixed amount of organizational resources (dollars, budget lines, people, machines, space) can be allocated among groups within the organization. The result is that if one group is to increase the amount of resources it has, another group will have to lose or forgo resources. This contributes to the perception that some groups have different and perhaps incompatible goals.

A third condition is that individuals and groups in the same organization typically are dependent on each other to perform their activities (Thompson, 1967). Interdependence exists where one individual group cannot do its work unless another group also does its work. For example, the manufacturing department at Household Products cannot begin to make products until it gets orders from the product group, indicating what products to manufacture. Similarly, the product group cannot deliver the products to the customers until production finishes manufacturing them. All groups within an organization are interdependent in at least some ways, even if slightly. When groups become highly interdependent, an opportunity is provided for one group to either aid or hinder the work of the other groups.

Most organizations are made up of differentiated groups that must make use of limited resources and whose activities are interdependent. The problem, however, is that the presence of these conditions can create perceptions that lead to the emergence of conflict. As already noted, differentiation of groups leads to the perception that the goals of the groups are dissimilar and, in some cases, incompatible. Likewise, the existence of scarce and limited resources also creates the perception that if another group meets its goal of acquiring more resources, our group will have to lose some of the resources that we want. Thus, these two factors contribute to the *perception of goal incompatibility* between groups.

Shared resources also provide an opportunity for one group to interfere with the goal attainment of another group. By using resources, one group can keep those same resources away from another. Similarly, the existence of interdependence creates the opportunity to interfere with another group's performance by not providing the materials, information, and so on, needed to do the job. Together, then, shared resources and interdependent activities create the *perception that there is the opportunity for interference.*

In Household Products, many of the antecedent conditions were present. The product group and the control department represent differentiated cliques or units. The recent cuts in expenses and staff have created a situation where resources are especially scarce. Finally, the two departments are to some degree dependent on each other, although they are not highly interdependent.

These two perceptions — the perception of incompatible goals and the perception of opportunity for interference — tend to lead to conflict (Schmidt and Kochan, 1972), a process where one group attempts to advance its own interests in relation to another group through deliberate interference.

Figure 12.5 *The Process of Conflict*

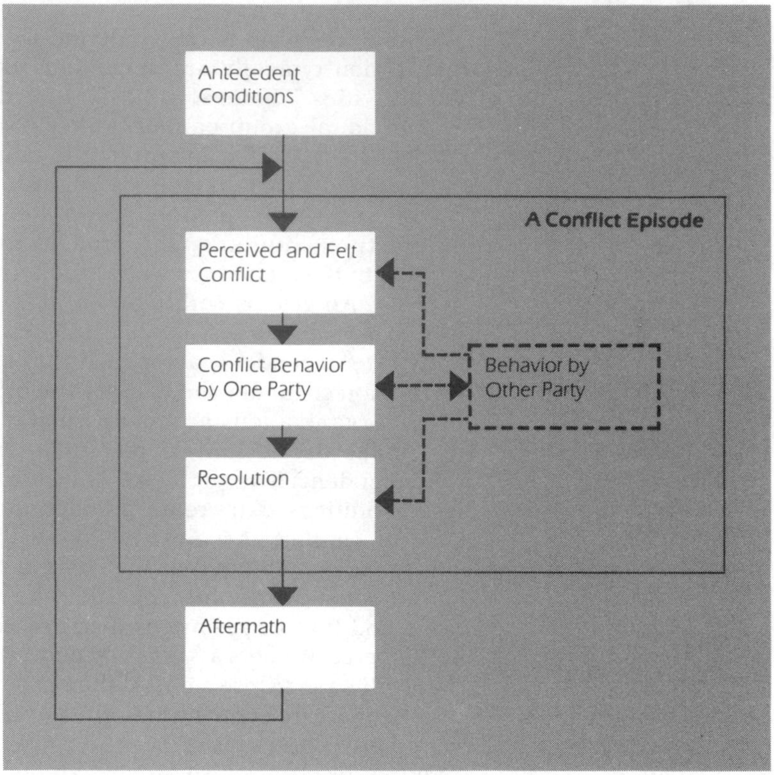

The Conflict Episode

So far, we have talked about conflict in general terms. Now we would like to consider what actually happens in the conflict situation. As is shown in Figure 12.5 (Filley, 1975; Thomas, 1976) antecedent conditions (group differentiation, shared resources, and interdependence) lead to the creation of conditions where conflict episodes are likely to occur. One of the potential parties in the conflict perceives a conflict situation to exist (perceives goal incompatibility and the opportunity for interference) and has feelings of conflict with the other party. This leads to the one party engaging in conflict behavior. Groups employ a number of different conflict tactics to achieve their goals, ranging from active blocking of the other party's work to passive resistance.

Action by one party usually leads to some form of behavior in reaction by the other party. The response of the other party is important. Depending on how the other party reacts, a number of events may occur (indicated by the dotted lines in Figure 12.5). The behavior of the other party may affect the feelings and perceptions of conflict held by the first party (in either a positive or negative direction), may result in additional conflict behavior by the first party, or may lead to some form of resolution of the conflict.

Resolution marks the end of the conflict episode. Resolution does not indicate that the conflict is solved or effectively managed; it only means that the conflict episode has ended in some way. Resolution may come about by one group winning and the other losing, by compromise, or through other means. As a result of the conflict behavior by the parties and the way in which the conflict is resolved, there are residual feelings and perceptions, called the *aftermath* of the conflict (Pondy, 1967). The aftermath of conflict is important, because it leads to the perceptions and feelings that the parties hold as the next episode of conflict begins. Indeed, the actual conflict episode is a repeated cycle of events (Thomas, 1976), where the resolution and aftermath of one episode determines the nature and scope of the next.

Conflict Outcomes

The way the parties react in the conflict and the way the conflict is resolved have a major influence on the perceptions, feelings, and behaviors to follow (Deutsch, 1973). In general, the manner in which the conflict proceeds and is resolved affects the task performance of the groups, the feelings the group members have, the perceptions they hold, and the quality of the communication between the groups.

CONSTRUCTIVE OUTCOMES OF CONFLICT

Conflict can have a number of potentially positive effects in the organization. First, conflict causes the arousal of feelings and energy in the individual group members. Watching a group move into a conflict situation, one can see evidence of increased energy — people become more attentive, voices are raised, more effort is exerted. This arousal of energy can have beneficial effects. It can stimulate interest and curiosity in finding more effective ways of doing tasks and new and creative approaches to solving problems. Second, conflict can stimulate greater feelings of identity within the group. Defining a group of people "out there" whom we are in conflict with as "them" also helps to define "us" as the group here. As groups move into conflict situations, they, therefore, tend to become tighter or more cohesive. Individual members feel more like a part of the group. Finally, cohesiveness and the energy that is created can contribute to increased motivation to perform the group task. As part of "winning," individuals may be motivated to do their jobs more effectively.

Conflict also serves some constructive purposes in the functioning of the larger organizational system. Conflict is a way of calling attention to problems that exist. The occurrence of conflict between groups may bring about the application of resources (such as managerial time) to the areas where conflict is taking place and, as a result, cause a serious problem to be solved. Conflict also can serve as a way of diffusing larger or more serious problems. By engaging in conflict over symbolic or minor issues, two groups may be able to avoid conflict over more serious matters with larger consequences. Finally, conflict is a means for groups to test and adjust the existing balance of power.

Thus, conflict has its constructive functions, both for the performance of the conflicting groups and for the functioning of the larger system in which they are embedded. It generates energy and can serve as a correction mechanism.

DESTRUCTIVE EFFECTS OF CONFLICT

While conflict does create some desirable conditions, it clearly has undesirable consequences for the functioning of an organization. In conflict, individuals and groups see their efforts blocked by other groups in the face of pressure to win. Feelings of frustration, hostility, and stress develop. This atmosphere is stressful and can impair judgment and the ability to perform as well as have negative consequences for individual well-being. Similarly, while cohesiveness increases in the group, so does pressure to conform. As conformity pressures increase, individual freedom decreases, and the group may not solve problems or perform effectively. Finally, much of the energy that is created in conflict is energy that is directed toward working on the conflict, as opposed to doing other productive work. Winning the conflict becomes more important than working effectively.

The destructive effects of conflict are also seen in the patterns of behavior that are characteristic of conflict between groups. As in the spice lab affair, groups begin to block the activities of other groups or refuse to cooperate with each other. In many cases, this results in decreased performance of the total system or organization.

Finally, conflict affects the nature of the relationship that exists between the conflicting groups. Conflict feeds on itself. As conflict increases, communication between the groups tends to become distorted. One group tends to stereotype, to see the other group as "the enemy," and to attribute negative motives and intentions to that other group. All of this increases the perceptions that the other group's goals are incompatible with "our" group's goals and that we, therefore, cannot cooperate with them. The decreased communication and perceptual distortion tends to lead to the magnification of the conflict and, in turn, to the magnification of the detrimental effects of the conflict.

In summary, conflict can have both constructive and destructive outcomes for particular groups, for individuals, and for the total organization (see Table 12.1). The question then is how to manage conflict to obtain constructive effects while minimizing destructive ones.

Approaches to Conflict Management

METHODS OF CONFLICT RESOLUTION

The way a conflict is resolved affects the nature of the outcomes it produces and thus future conflict episodes (Blake, Shephard, and Mouton, 1964; Deutsch, 1973). A conflict episode can be resolved in a number of ways. By examining methods of resolution, an initial understanding of approaches to conflict management can be obtained.

There are basically three ways in which a conflict can be resolved. Filley (1975) has identified these:

1. *The win/lose resolution:* Using various methods, one group manages to win the conflict by obtaining its goals and frustrating the other group in its attempt to meet its goals. The other group therefore loses.
2. *The lose/lose resolution:* Each group gives up some of its desired goals through some form of compromise. Neither group gets all of what it wants; therefore both groups lose.
3. *The win/win resolution:* The groups succeed in identifying solutions to the problem that will allow both groups to achieve their desired goals. Thus, both sides to the conflict are able to win.

Table 12.1 *Some Outcomes of Intergroup Conflict in Organizations*

Potentially constructive outcomes	*Potentially destructive outcomes*
Stimulates interest and curiosity	Frustration, stress, hostility
Increases group cohesion	Conformity pressures in the group
Increases group task motivation	
Calls attention to problems	Diversion of energy
Diffuses more serious conflict	Blocking activities
Tests and adjusts power differences	Refusal to cooperate
	Decreased communication
	Perceptual distortion
	Magnification of conflict

The first two patterns of resolution tend to lead toward a continuation or maintenance of the conflict. Since at least one group (and sometimes both groups) has not achieved its desired goals, it perceives the conflict as unfinished and is motivated to initiate another conflict episode where it can win. In win/win situations, however, the conflict magnification cycle is broken, and the probability of conflict in the future is lessened.

Three general approaches to conflict management fall into the win/win category. The first is to prevent conflict from occurring or to keep it within bounds by modifying or changing the antecedent conditions which bring it about. This is the *structural* approach to conflict management, since many of the techniques make use of structural devices such as those used for coordination and control. The second approach, the *process* approach, involves interventions into the actual process of the conflict episode itself rather than changing antecedent conditions (Thomas, 1976). The third approach involves the use of both structural and process interventions and is a *mixed* approach to conflict management. Under each of these three categories — structure, process and mixed — a number of specific conflict management tools and techniques exist (see Table 12.2).

STRUCTURAL APPROACHES

The structural approach is based on the fact that conflict arises from perceptions that are created by the antecedent conditions of differentiation, scarce limited resources, and interdependence. If these elements can be changed, the resulting perceptions and conflict can be affected. One of the simplest and most frequently used approaches is to attempt to minimize differences among groups by identifying goals that are held by the two groups. If the two groups can be made aware of interests that they have in common they may not perceive their own goals as incompatible with those of the other groups. A classic example can be seen in the "common enemy" effect, where conflict groups suddenly begin to cooperate in the face of a serious threat from a common enemy. The problem with the common enemy

Table 12.2 *Approaches to Conflict Management*

Structural approaches	Process approaches	Mixed approaches
Common goals	Deescalation	Rules
Reward systems	Confrontation	Liaison roles
Regrouping	Collaboration	Task forces/teams
Rotation		Integrator roles
Separation		

approach is that once the external threat is gone, the parties may move back toward conflict. A common goal, however, may be a lasting one and thus may have a permanent impact.

Another structural device which can impact on both group goals and shared resources is the use of formal organizational reward systems (Lawler, 1971). As was stressed in Chapter 4, by using pay systems to reward the combined performance of two or more groups, the organization creates a common goal, and it creates the perception that the pie of resources to be distributed is not fixed. Quite the contrary, it is possible for one group to gain resources without causing the other group to lose, and indeed it becomes advantageous to all for groups to perform well and to cooperate.

The group differences problem can also be dealt with through the regrouping of individuals, so that the conflicting groups are now encompassed within a larger unit. For example, as was discussed earlier, production and marketing people might be put together on a product team with responsibility for producing and selling the product and be rewarded on the basis of total product performance, rather than individual group performance (such as the autonomous work group design presented in Chapter 5). Furthermore, group members might be rotated between groups so that individuals gain an understanding of other perspectives and an appreciation for the common goals that exist.

Finally, if other approaches are not successful or feasible, the groups can be physically and structurally separated in order to reduce their interdependence and their opportunities for interference. Although groups might still feel in conflict and that their goals are incompatible, the low level of interdependence of activity makes interference difficult and the probability of conflict actually occurring is lessened.

PROCESS APPROACHES

Another approach to reducing conflict involves intervention in the episode to modify the process of the conflict. This approach can be used by one of the parties in conflict, by an outsider, or by a third party (a consultant, a neutral manager, someone higher in the organization). Many tools, techniques, and processes have been developed for dealing with conflict (Walton, 1969; Beckhard, 1969). They fall into one of three general approaches.

First, the conflict can be deescalated. One party, by reacting to the conflict behavior of the other party in a cooperative rather than conflicting manner, can begin to stop the escalation of conflict and even encourage less conflict behavior. As Deutsch (1973) points out, conflict or cooperative behavior by one party tends to elicit the same kind of behavior on the part of the other party. This is easily seen in the escalation stage, where one party's conflict behavior motivates conflict behavior by the other party, but the same is true for cooperative or nonconflict behavior.

When the conflict has gone so far, deescalation cannot be effected and a second approach is needed. It starts with making the conflict visible in a direct confrontation between the hostile parties. This step is at the heart of a number of process intervention approaches; for example, the confrontation meeting (Beckhard, 1969). The premise is that the parties need to vent their emotions and identify the conflict areas before they can begin resolution. Only by identifying the areas of conflict can the parties then begin to work on identifying win/win solutions.

A third approach, often used following deescalation or confrontation, is collaboration (Filley, 1975; Likert and Likert, 1976). The two parties work together to solve problems and to identify win/win solutions or integrative approaches (Walton and McKersie, 1965) that will integrate the goals of both parties.

In all of these approaches, a third party or consultant is used for a very good reason. Since conflict frequently results in decreased communication, perceptual distortion, and mistrust, it is difficult for groups to communicate adequately for purposes of deescalation, confrontation, or collaboration. Thus, a skilled outsider or "process consultant" is needed to ensure that communication remains clear and to help the parties learn to trust each other (Schein, 1969).

MIXED APPROACHES

A number of approaches to conflict management incorporate both process and structural elements. One method is to influence the process of the conflict by structural means through the development of rules for working out conflicts (Deutsch, 1973). By specifying the procedures and bounds for working on conflict, it can be contained and the parties can be moved toward problem solving.

Another approach is to build third parties into organizations so that they are available at all times to aid in the win/win resolution of conflicts that arise. For example, conflict groups may identify specific individuals as having the task of communicating with the other group, in the form of a liaison role or assignment. Despite differences between the groups, the liaison personnel can continue to communicate clearly and without distortion and have a greater appreciation for the perspective of the other group than the rest of the group members. Similarly, cross-group teams or task forces may be created that span the boundaries of normal groups (such as a project task force) that might normally move toward conflict if they had to work together unaided. In many cases, organizations identify individuals whose jobs are to resolve conflict between groups. These integrator roles (Lawrence and Lorsch, 1967b) include jobs such as a product or project manager, account executives, and so forth. Their job is to coordinate the effort of potentially conflicting groups toward effective performance of a total task. They do many of the same things that a process consultant or third party would do, but they are built in as a permanent part of the organization. (See also the discussion of integrators in Chapter 11.)

The Manager and Conflict

An individual manager can either be in the role of conflict resolver or in the role of actor in a continuing conflict. Returning to the spice lab controversy, one managerial perspective would be that of John Saxon, the President, who is a member of neither of the two cliques and would like to see the conflict constructively resolved. Another perspective would be that of Byrnes, the Vice President for Control, who would like to win in the conflict with the opposing clique. To some extent there is overlap in that Saxon is not completely disinterested or objective, and Byrnes would also like to see the conflict resolved. However, in our discussion of how managers should deal with conflict, we will consider the two perspectives separately.

CHOICE OF RESOLUTION STRATEGIES

Assuming that a manager is approaching the conflict with the goal of successful resolution, there is a choice among three types of methods — structural, process, and mixed. In general, it is best to use the mixed method when attempting to resolve conflict. Conflict is so inherent in organizational life and thus so persistent that constructive resolution may require the use of several approaches concurrently. Structural approaches may help by changing antecedent conditions, but perceptions and feelings of conflict may continue to exist as the result of earlier conflict episodes. Moreover, process work alone may "cool out" a current conflict, but if the antecedent conditions remain, the conflict may only rise up again in another form or at another time.

In some cases, only one approach can be used. It may be difficult to find a third party that all trust, or physical or organizational changes may not be feasible. Another constraint on action is skill. Managers may want to function as third parties; this role, though, requires a good deal of skill in dealing with feelings and problems in interpersonal relations. Managers, therefore, are at times constrained from using all of the approaches that they might want to, and they then need to make choices.

As a general guideline, it may be most profitable to focus on the structural approaches to resolution. Structural approaches deal with the antecedents of conflict, and structural changes may prevent destructive conflict from occurring in the first place. Structural changes are usually easier to bring about and require less specialized skill than process approaches.

THE MANAGER AS ACTOR IN THE CONFLICT

Frequently, managers are involved as principals in a conflict. In some cases, they may want to seek constructive resolution, but the other party does not. In other cases, the individual manager may not want to resolve the conflict for political reasons. In Household Products, Byrnes is in this position. In these cases, the manager is concerned with how to successfully resolve the conflict from his or her perspective, or how to win. Building on the network approach, power can be amassed by controlling critical organizational resources, by being able to cope with uncertainty better than other groups, and by building alliances with other groups, cliques, or coalitions. By accurately understanding the political topography of the organization and by using various tactics to increase power relative to other groups, the manager can increase the chances of resolving a conflict to his or her own benefit.

Summary

Conflict between groups is an inevitable fact of life in organizations. Conflict arises from the inherent nature of organizations, being composed of different groups, linked together in their activities but sharing limited resources. These conditions lead to perceptions of incompatibility of goals and opportunities for interference that cause the emergence of conflict which is perceived, felt, and acted out. Conflict can have both constructive and destructive outcomes, the method of resolution determining much of the outcome. Conflict between groups and individuals is also a manifestation of the political nature of organizations. Informal groups evolve over time and function within a larger network of organizational relationships. Uncertainty causes increases in political behavior and the groups may vary widely in their ability to exercise power. Thus, the manager relates to conflict in two ways. In many cases, the manager is involved in managing conflict to limit destructive effects and promote problem solving between groups, while in other circumstances, managers may function within the political system to maximize the power of their own group relative to others. In either event, an understanding of the dynamics of conflict specifically and political behavior in general is crucial.

Suggested Readings

Allison, G. T. *Essence of Decision: Explaining the Cuban Missile Crisis.* Boston: Little, Brown, 1971.

Filley, A. *Interpersonal Conflict Resolution.* Glenview, Ill.: Scott Foresman, 1975.

Pettigrew, A. *The Politics of Organizational Decision-making.* London: Tavistock, 1973.

Walton, R. *Interpersonal Peacemaking: Confrontations and Third Party Consultation.* Reading, Mass.: Addison-Wesley, 1969.

Chapter 13

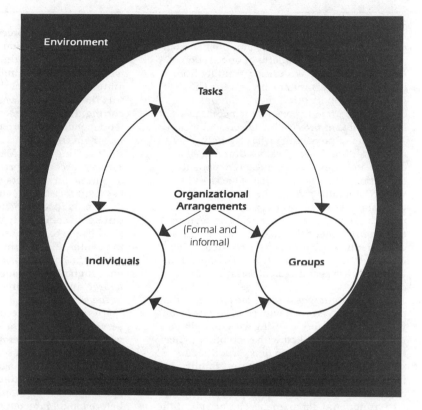

Organizational Strategy and Behavior

The Neighborhood Health Center was formed in the late 1960s to provide comprehensive outpatient care to the residents of one section of a large eastern city. With heavy funding from the federal government (through the Office of Economic Opportunity) the center was designed to provide care for the poor that went far beyond that provided in hospital clinics. The group of physicians who originally formed the center had a set of values that placed an emphasis on preventive medicine, patient education, and the provision of services by a variety of health practitioners, not just the physician. As the center began to grow and prosper, an organization design was developed to help implement the goal of comprehensive care. Health care teams were created which included physicians, nurse practitioners, family health workers, medical assistants and dentists.

Each patient was assigned to a team so that patients received care with continuity; the different practitioners working with an individual or a family worked with each other to help treat cases. At the same time, practitioners were grouped by function (nurses, family health workers, physicians, and so on) into departments. The result was a matrix design with functional departments on one side of the structure and interdisciplinary health care teams on the other. By the mid-1970s the center had grown to about 300 employees and had an annual operating budget of about $8 million.

By the late 1970s, however, a number of changes had occurred in the environment of the center, which forced management to reevaluate the mission and structure of the organization. First, the direct federal funding for support of the center began to decline annually. The goal of the federal government was that the center would become self-supporting. Reduced direct funding made the center dependent on third party payments (payment from sources other than the patient, such as Blue Cross, Medicaid, Medicare). These sources only provided reimbursement for physician contacts with patients, with no payment for other health practitioners. The remaining federal money was channeled through a community advisory board that was established to serve as a board of directors for the center. Finally, the area of the city in which the center was located began to experience high rates of housing abandonment, with a large and continuing drop in the population in the service area.

In response to these changes, cutbacks in service were made, layoffs were instituted, while the center attempted to continue providing the same type of service as best it could. Finally, the top management group began to realize that if it continued on its current course, the center would be out of business before long. Management began to explore actively some alternative actions that would enable the center to continue to provide comprehensive service within a changed environment. Alternatives such as setting up satellite centers in more populated areas and finding special funding for nonphysician based activities were considered.

THE NEIGHBORHOOD HEALTH CENTER is a graphic example of how an organization may have to make significant changes if it is to continue to exist as environmental conditions change. The case underscores the need to consider the nature of the environment and how the organization relates to that environment as critical factors in understanding organizational behavior. Until this point, our focus has been on the organization and its components. Relatively little attention has been given to what lies beyond the boundaries of the organization — namely, the larger environment. In fact, the environment is extremely important.

In the first chapter, we argued for thinking about organizations as open social systems (Katz and Kahn, 1966). This open-systems view takes account of the fact that organizations continually conduct transactions with different parts of the environment. The health center, for example, conducts transactions with its clients or patients; it also has to deal with financial institutions, regulatory bodies, community organizations, professional societies, and so on. If the organization is to survive, it must develop approaches to deal with these many elements of its environment. If the health center were to continue to provide the same kind of service, with the same kind of team structure, to the same service area, in the face of declining population and changing funding formulas, it could not last for long.

It, therefore, becomes clear that environmental relations are important for understanding and managing patterns of organizational behavior. Environmental relations and organizational behavior are related in several ways. First, the nature of environmental relations and how they are managed determines many of the patterns of organizational behavior. Depending on the way in which the health center decides to cope with its changing environment, very different types of organizational behavior will be required. Moving to satellites will require different types of individual performance, team functioning, and organizational design. On the other hand, patterns of organizational behavior may influence the nature of environmental relations. The effectiveness of the top management work team, for example, critically affects what kinds of decisions are made about environmental relations. Similarly, the types of coalitions and cliques that exist and the patterns of conflict management and resolution determine the way in which key decisions are made and implemented. Thus, environmental relations and organizational behavior influence one another.

One way of thinking about the interactions between the organization and the environment is to consider the various *strategies* that organizations develop for relating with the rest of the world. In this chapter, we will employ a strategic perspective, and the emphasis will be on understanding how strategy influences organizational behavior and vice versa. First, we will define the general concepts of strategy. Second, we will examine the ways in which strategy develops in organizations. Third, we will discuss some of the specific components of strategy, and finally, we will consider the relationship between strategy and organizational behavior.

Throughout this discussion, the emphasis will be on recognizing strategy and understanding its implications for managing organizational behavior. We will not consider in detail how to formulate and evaluate strategy, as these issues are considered in depth elsewhere (see, for example, Hofer and Schendel, 1978; Newman and Logan, 1976; Andrews, 1971).

What Is Organizational Strategy?

RELATING TO THE ENVIRONMENT

In its simplest and most basic form, strategy is the approach organizations take to managing the relationship between them and their environments (Ansoff, 1969). While we speak of organizations operating within an environment, in actuality the environment is made up of many groups, individuals, organizations, and other institutions. Figure 13.1 illustrates some of the key elements in the environment of most organizations. Clearly, an organization must relate to its employees both as individuals and through the groups that may represent their interests, such

Figure 13.1 *Critical Elements of the Organization's Environment*

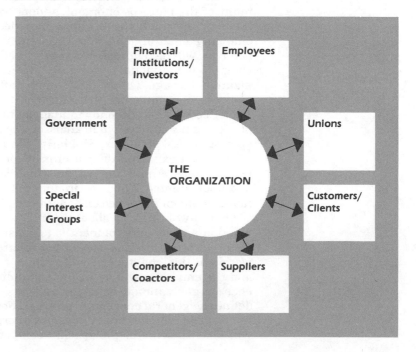

as unions. Organizations have customers or clients with which they must interact. Further, organizations depend on other organizations to supply the needed materials, information, energy, and so on, necessary to produce a product or service. Within the environment, other organizations are also acting. Some act as competitors, while others act as either allies or coactors. Special interest groups have their own constituencies, such as professional groups, lobbies, environmental groups, and others. Various levels of government have great impact through taxation, regulation, and government spending. Lastly, in some way organizations relate to financial institutions and, in some cases, to individual financial investors.

We can illustrate some of these relationships by recalling the health center. The center must find individuals who can be hired as physicians, dentists, nurses, family health workers, and others. It has contractual relations with a labor union, which represents the employees other than dentists, doctors, and nurses. It has a client/patient population to which it provides services, and it relies on a variety of different suppliers for materials ranging from stethoscopes to electric power. Within this section of the city, there are what is known as "medicaid mills" (small physicians' offices aimed at providing minimum service to medicaid patients), which compete with the center as well as other health care organizations which provide complementary types of care. Within the community, political groups make demands on the center; some of these factions are represented on the center board. In addition, groups such as the local medical board and third-party payment agencies have both a direct and indirect effect on the center. The government plays a major role through regulation of service, funding procedures, and other methods. Finally, the management of the organization's financial assets requires interaction with banks in the area.

In summary, organizations face a domain or a set of relationships with institutions that exist in their environment, many of which are critical for the organization's survival (Evan, 1966; Thompson, 1967; Starbuck, 1976). Together, the components of the environment put *constraints* on organizational action and make *demands* on the organization (Katz, 1970); but, at the same time, the environment provides *opportunities* (Andrews, 1971) for the organization to make use of its own unique or distinctive resources and competencies.

USING A SET OF RESOURCES

Organizations face environments with sets of resources at their disposal. Every organization has a special combination of competencies, assets, and experiences, that it can put to use in meeting environmental demands, working within constraints, and taking advantage of opportunities. These resources can vary in nature and value. Referring again to the health center, it has its own set of resources. Clearly, it has individuals with skills, experience, and a commitment to a concept of providing health care. It also has physical assets such as buildings, medical equipment, and the like. It has a number of less tangible resources, such as the image it has in the community with health planners and with funding agencies.

Organizations can make very different use of their resources. Resources can be concentrated in one specific area (such as one product, one market, or one technology) or spread over a variety of areas of activity. Through patterns of use, resources can be depleted or can be strengthened and increased. Thus, a crucial question is what is called *resource allocation* (Bower, 1970) or *strategic choice* (Child, 1972, 1973): the way in which the organization decides to allocate its existing resources among alternative projects, programs, products, or courses of action. Again, the health care center's possible decision to open satellite centers and to invest dollars and energy in the project is a decision to allocate resources in a different manner than they were in the past.

STRATEGY AS THE ENVIRONMENT– RESOURCES MATCH

Now that we have established a view of organizations as functioning within environments and working with a set of available resources, we can define strategy in more detail. To begin with, strategy is the process by which the organization attempts to match its use of resources effectively to the demands, constraints, and opportunities in the environment (Hofer, 1976). This matching of the organization's resources to the environment is essentially a determination by the organization about what its role will be within that environment. As Andrews (1971) states, strategy is the "pattern of purposes and policies defining the company and its business."[1]

More specifically, beyond deciding "what business we're in," the formulation of strategy involves identifying the things that an organization needs to do in order to compete successfully. Consequently, strategy is also "the determination of the basic long-term goals and objectives of the enterprise, and the adoption of courses of action and allocation of resources necessary for carrying out these goals" (Chandler, 1962). Making decisions about strategy involves the identification of goals for the organization, the allocation of resources to achieve those goals, and thus, the determination of the specific *tasks* that the organization needs to accomplish or perform.

Putting together the views and definitions of strategy, we can devise a framework or model for thinking about how strategy is formed and how it relates to organizational behavior (see Figure 13.2). Organizations scan their environments to identify con-

[1] Much of the strategy literature has been developed from observations of private sector organizations. Thus, the terms *business policy* or *corporate strategy* are used. The concepts are, of course, applicable to public and not-for-profit organizations.

Figure 13.2 *A Basic Strategy Model*

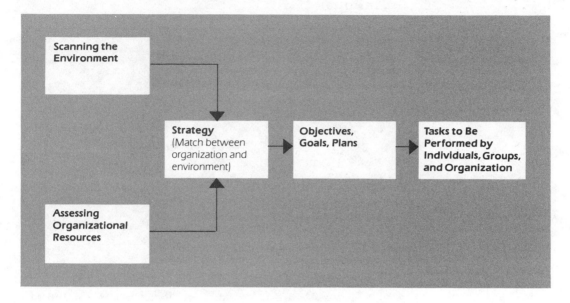

straints, demands, and opportunities. This scanning is sometimes very detailed and systematic (Aguillar, 1967). At the same
time, the organization assesses its own resources and the way in
which those resources are utilized. Out of this dual examination,
a match between the organization's resources and an environment (present or future) is identified, and decisions are made
about the allocation of resources needed to obtain that match.
That set of decisions is the course of a strategy. From these decisions flows a set of objectives, goals, and plans that represent
how the organization will attempt to implement the strategy. By
implication, these objectives, goals, and plans define a set of
tasks that must be performed.

In a broad sense, then, strategy is the determination of *what*
the organization needs to do. As a result of developing a strategy,
it becomes clear which of the tasks that individuals, groups, and
the total organization could perform are the most critical. Having identified such tasks, the organizational issues concern *how*
those tasks will be done. Thus, strategy and organization interact and combine to determine how effective the organization
will be (see Figure 13.3). For an organization to be effective, it
needs to have both an appropriate strategy and the means to
implement that strategy (that is, performing critical tasks)
through the use of individuals, groups, and organization design.
As we will see, strategy has implications for how an organization
is designed, and organizational behavior has implications for

Figure 13.3 *The Relationship between Strategy and Organization*

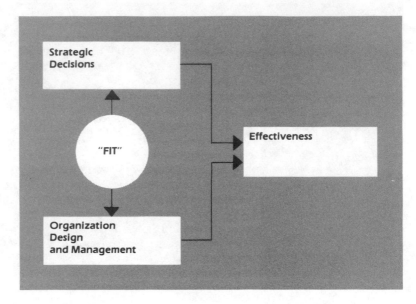

what kind of strategies develop. Strategy, organizational design, and management need to be consistent (Galbraith and Nathanson, 1978).

While the model of strategy development shown in Figure 13.2 does reflect a general view of strategy, it has two major drawbacks. First, the model implies that strategy emerges from a preplanned and rational process of environmental scanning, organizational assessment, and strategy formulation by the organization. In truth, the process by which strategies emerge is frequently much more complex and haphazard than this. Second, strategy has been talked about in relatively vague and abstract terms. To understand what strategy is and how it influences organizational behavior, a clearer and more detailed understanding is needed of how strategy is formulated and of the components of strategy.

Methods of Strategy Formulation

How does strategy actually develop in organizations? Specifically, how do organizations go about scanning the environment, assessing resources, and forecasting a pattern of resource allocation that will create a match between environment and resources? The model of strategy development presented in Figure

13.2 implies that strategic decisions are made in a sequential and rational basis and that the systematic determination of strategy precedes the implementation of those strategies by the organization.

In truth, there are a number of ways in which strategy is formulated in organizations. Three general approaches that have been observed are the rational planning approach, the political processes approach, and the adaptive approach.

RATIONAL PLANNING APPROACH

This most traditional approach conceives of strategy formulation as a process of rational and sequential thought that leads to the development of plans which are then executed. The environment is systematically scanned, the organization's resources are assessed, and decisions are made among alternative courses of action and their long-range implications. This rational process may be carried out in at least two ways. One way is by having top management serve as the strategic planners, either as individuals or in working groups. A second method is to use some form of planning staff, either through a planning department or group. This group, sometimes with the aid of outside consultants, develops environmental forecasts, explores several strategic options, and makes recommendations for top management decisions.

The health center, at first glance, provides an example of the beginning of the rational planning approach to strategy. Faced with problems in the environment, the top management group has begun to meet regularly to analyze the environment and to explore strategic options such as the creation of satellite centers, the search for new funding sources for nonphysician care, and the like. Were this approach to be carried through, the group might create a set of long-range plans with specific objectives (for example, four satellites handling 30 percent of the patient load to be in place by the end of three years). Each year, the plan might be reexamined by this group and changes made in light of new developments in the environment and the relative success to date in implementing the existing plan.

POLITICAL PROCESSES APPROACH

Recently, the observation has been made that the rational planning approach does not adequately describe how decisions actually are made or how strategic planning is conducted within many organizations. A more accurate view might be one that takes account of the various political processes that occur within organizations and how these processes affect the development of strategies (Allison, 1971; MacMillan, 1978).

If we think of organizations as being made up of cliques, coalitions, and networks, as proposed in Chapter 12, then it is only natural that these aspects of the emergent or informal organization will come to play when strategic decisions are being made. Strategic decisions often involve issues of personal or group values, since such decisions may alter the sense of what constitutes the organization's mission, function, or goals. Groups may attempt to influence such decisions so that the organization will move in a direction consistent with their values. Thus, strategy is not necessarily the result of rational planning (although it may frequently have those trappings); rather, often it is the outcome of competition, conflict, coalition formation, and bargaining (such as those discussed in Chapter 12) among numerous interest groups within the organization (see, for example, studies by Bower, 1970; Aharoni, 1966).

The health center case provides an illustration of political processes and strategy formulation. While on the surface the center's top management appears to be starting a process of rational planning of strategy, various political factors have influenced strategy in the past and no doubt will continue to influence how strategy evolves in the future. In the top management group, a number of people represent the supporting practitioners, such as family health workers or nurse practitioners. These groups form a coalition highly committed to the team-care approach and would rather see the organization go out of business than give up the team-care approach. On the other hand, a number of physicians in the management group are much less committed to the team concept and would prefer to see the center survive, even if some of the work of nonphysicians had to be greatly deemphasized. In the middle is a group composed of several top managers who are not physicians and whose views fall somewhere in between the two other factions. All three are important for continued functioning of the center and all three have different bases of power.

The strategy that eventually emerges from top management, probably, will be the result of negotiation, bargaining, and compromise among the three key power groups. The strategy may thus be very different than what would emerge if we assumed that this group was to be completely rational and objective in its analysis and decision making, or if we assumed that all of the group members shared a set of common goals for the organization.

ADAPTIVE PROCESSES APPROACH

In many instances, strategy simply seems to emerge over time. In the extreme, nobody is explicitly formulating strategy, so it is formed as a result of a stream of decisions, none of which are oriented toward or based on a larger strategic perspective. This approach is what some have called "muddling through" (Lindblom, 1959). Strategy is never consciously or explicitly formulated, but as a result of sets of implicitly strategic decisions, strategies are indeed created. They may be effective or ineffective strategies, but they are still strategies.

During the early 1970s, the health center used an adaptive or muddling-through approach. No one in top management ever gave much thought to long-range trends in the environment and their implications for the center. No long-run plans to cope with environmental changes were formed; rather, sets of decisions were made in response to crises that occurred. As funding decreased and no other sources of revenue appeared, staff were cut and services curtailed. These were indeed strategic decisions, but they were made in response to a short-run crisis with little attention to long-range questions such as, If we continue to cut services in response to decreasing funding and demand, at what point will we be out of business? In some cases, such an approach may be effective. In this instance it was not because the changes in the environment were too severe and harmful to enable the center to maintain adequate environmental relations.

An Expanded View of Strategy Formulation

To some extent, organizations tend to make use of all three approaches to strategy formulation. If one examined strategic decisions for any organization, one would find that a combination of rational planning, political processes, and muddling-through was used. The difference among organizations lies in which of the approaches is used most extensively and for which types of decisions. In reality, some strategies are explicitly and rationally developed but do not ever become implemented because of political processes. Some strategies never are explicitly formulated, but somehow do become implemented. In some cases, no planning is done, but a set of decisions are labeled as a strategy after the fact.

One approach to untangling the types of strategies is to use a recently proposed typology of strategies (Mintzberg, 1976). It expands on our discussion so far because it considers both strategy formulation and implementation. In it the explicit and formally preplanned strategies are called *intended strategies*. In the health care case, the founders had an explicit strategy for providing a certain kind of unique medical care to the specific market. This is an example of an intended strategy.

A strategy that emerges from the stream of decisions made and implemented in actuality is called a *realized strategy*. In the early years of the health center, the originally intended strategy was achieved and thus was a realized strategy. In other cases, strategies that are planned are not achieved for various reasons; such strategies can be called *unrealized strategies*. Finally, where an adaptive or muddling-through approach is used, there is no explicit strategy and no formal planning, but after the fact, it is possible to look at the set of decisions that were made and label them as a strategy. For example, in the health center case, during the mid-1970s, the center did not have a definite plan or strategy, but looking back at the organization, the individual short-term decisions added up to a strategy of contraction of resources and services in response to the environment. A strategy that is not explicitly developed but that can be labeled after the fact is called a *retroactive strategy*.

Building on this broader view of strategy development and formulation, it is possible to expand the model presented earlier in Figure 13.2. A number of factors are potential components of the strategy-formulation process. As mentioned earlier, scanning the environment and assessing organizational resources are important elements. In addition, the individual values of key decision makers and the political processes that exist in the organization are also important in influencing the type of strategy that evolves.

In any organization, some combination of these factors will influence how strategy is developed, whether or not the process is rational, political, or adaptive. What results is a set of decisions. These may be an intended strategy that is explicit or a set of decisions with no explicit strategic component, but which will later be seen as a retroactive strategy. As an outcome of these decisions, critical tasks are identified for the organization to perform. Depending on how the organization is designed, how groups function, and how individuals behave, different patterns of organizational functioning will result. These, in turn, influence the components of strategy formulation and may lead to changes in strategy, particularly depending on whether original strategies (intended or not) are either realized or unrealized. Figure 13.4 presents this view of strategy formation.

The Components of Strategy

So far, strategy has been described as a set of decisions about the organization vis-à-vis its environment. This is consistent with the views of a number of strategy theorists (Mintzberg, 1976), that a strategy is, in reality, a stream of decisions. The question that still remains, however, is, Decisions about what?

A number of theorists have attempted to identify the critical components of a strategy (see Hofer, 1976). One approach is that used by Katz (1970) which views strategy as a set of decisions by which an organization moves from a current posture or set of environmental relations to a desired future posture, by deploying resources according to a plan. Specifically, he distinguishes three types of decisions which fall under the heading of strategy (see Table 13.1).

The first type of decision are those concerning the *scope* of the organization. Decisions about scope concern the type of environment in which the organization will operate and what will be the distinctive characteristics of that organization in that environment. It involves the identification of the specific competitive

Figure 13.4 *An Expanded Strategy Determination Model*

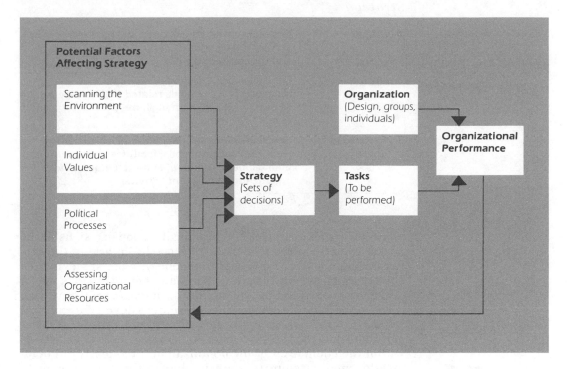

advantage or distinctive competence of the organization. The health center, for example, began by identifying a geographical area that needed service and by defining team care as the competitive advantage that it offered over other providers of health care. The decision was also made within the larger context of federal funding policies; team care that involved community residents in the health care team as family health workers made the center an attractive project for the government to fund during the 1960s. The strategic issue facing the center in the late 1970s was how to change the scope of its strategy in order to remain effective in a changed environment.

The second type of decision concerns the development of *objectives* that reflect performance characteristics needed if scope of strategy is to be realized. This might translate into specific goals such as rate of growth, market share, capital structure, and so on. For example, the objectives of the health center might be the number of patients served, satellites in service, additional inflow of funds, and the like.

The third type of decision concerns *resource allocation* within the organization so that objectives can be reached. Decisions about expense budgets, facilities, human resources planning,

Table 13.1 *Basic Components of an Organizational Strategy*

1. Scope	Decisions about the *markets* and *customers* to be served, the types and characteristics of *products*, and the *competitive basis*.
2. Objectives	Decisions about desired *performance characteristics* or goals related to the scope, such as rate of growth, market share, profitability, and so on.
3. Resource allocation	Decisions about the *allocation* of *organization resources* such as funds, facilities, personnel, management attention, and such among the organization's different activities.

Adapted from Katz, 1970.

and such are all examples of resource allocation decisions. If the health center decides to expand its scope by enlarging the geographical area served and sees that done through achieving the objectives of establishing new satellite centers, then a set of decisions about funding the satellites, management time allocated to the satellite development, resources devoted to political relations in the new communities all need to be made. It is important to note that resource allocation means more than actions within the boundaries of the organization. Frequently, an organization may attempt to actively change the environment in some way; for example, through lobbying or joining together with other organizations in coalitions (MacMillan, 1978). In these cases, organizational resources (management time, money, and reputation) are also being allocated in support of a strategy.

In summary, a strategy is a set of decisions concerning the scope of the organization's activities, objectives to be reached if the scope is to be realized, and resource allocations to be made in order to achieve objectives. These decisions involve action both inside and outside the boundaries of the organization.

Implications for Organizational Behavior

The aim of our examination of strategy has been to gain an understanding of what strategy is so that the relationship between strategy and the management of organizational behavior can be better understood. For some time, many models of organizational behavior have ignored the role of the environment and the role of strategy as an influence on patterns of behavior. The existence of strategy and the fact that managers make strategic decisions, impacts on organizational behavior in a number of ways.

1. *Strategic decisions determine organizational tasks.* As a result of strategic decisions about scope, objectives, and resource allocation, the critical tasks that an organization needs to perform are defined. Strategic decisions also spell out the critical dimensions of organizational tasks (for example, providing comprehensive health care as opposed to minimal health care). Going back to the organizational framework presented in Chapter 1 and used throughout each chapter of this book, tasks are a central concern in understanding patterns of organizational behavior. Ultimately, it is the job of the manager to get individuals and groups to perform tasks effectively. The attention given to reward systems, staffing, job design, group design, and organization design occurs in order to accomplish tasks. The organizational designer must consider the question of "designing to do what?" The recognition of the existence of strategy helps, in that strategy defines the "what" that is critical.

The implication is that managers at all levels need to become aware of what organizational strategy is. Efforts to solve problems and improve organizational effectiveness through job redesign, group design, or organization design, for example, need to be done within the context of total organizational strategy as well as the specific portions of that strategy implemented by individual organizational units.

2. *Strategic decisions influence organizational design.* The choices of scope, objectives, and resource allocations are especially influential in organizational design (as discussed in Chapters 10, 11, and 12). Research indicates that the effectiveness of organizational designs depends on which strategies are chosen (Aldrich and Pfeffer, 1976). Ideally, there should be consistency or "fit" between the demands and requirements of a strategy and the characteristics of an organizational design (Galbraith and Nathanson, 1978).

An example of the potential effect of strategy on organizational design can be seen in the health center. Clearly, the organizational structure that has been devised to manage the health center at one location during a period of contraction will need to be altered if the center undertakes a strategy of expansion through the implementation of satellites. As the organization changes its scope, different kinds of individual performance will be needed, new groups will need to be designed and managed, and new organizational groupings will need to be created, along with new and more appropriate mechanisms for coordination and control. A change in strategy can create the need for profound changes in organizational design. Conversely, to consider organizational design without also heeding potential changes in strategy can lead to problems, as changes may be made to create an organization that is consistent with a strategy no longer operational.

3. *Strategic decisions influence and are influenced by or-*

ganizational power questions. Organizational strategy is directly related to questions of power, politics, and conflict (MacMillan, 1978). First, strategic choices and the relations that exist within the environment have implications for the distribution of power internally among different cliques, coalitions, and groups (Hickson et al., 1971; Aldrich and Pfeffer, 1976). Depending on the nature of the environment and the demands of strategy, disparate groups can vary in their relative power in the organization. For example, in the health center, the dependence on federal funding based on physician-contact hours with patients may increase the power of physicians relative to other groups in the facility. The physicians as a group control a critical resource (that is, reimbursable contact hours with patients) and, therefore, are more critical to the survival of the center. Similarly, those administrators who are adept at finding and obtaining federal funding that is not tied to physician contact may be more powerful than administrators who are less able to bring funds into the center. As a result of strategic issues and choices, therefore, groups will become more or less powerful in the organization.

The relationship between strategy and power is somewhat circular. As groups become more powerful, they may also be able to influence the determination of strategy to a greater extent. We mentioned earlier that strategy develops not only through rational and preplanned processes, but also as the result of political processes between individuals, groups, or cliques. Strategic choices influence power relationships internally, and these relationships frequently influence subsequent strategic choices.

4. *Organizational effectiveness is jointly determined by strategic and organizational design decisions.* It should be apparent by now that decisions about strategy and decisions about organizational design (at the individual, group, and system level) are very much interdependent and combine *jointly* to determine how effective an organization will be. A potentially successful strategy may fail if the organizational structure is poorly designed, if groups function ineffectively, or if individuals are not motivated. Likewise, an organization may not be effective even though it has motivated workers and productive groups, if that organization is attempting to implement an inappropriate strategy. In the most general terms, organizational effectiveness is a reflection of both strategic and organizational design decisions.

Summary

Organizations are open systems; thus, organizational behavior cannot be considered in a vacuum. To survive, any organization must adapt to changes in its environment, and this process of adapting what the organization does and how it does it, to compensate for (or anticipate) changes in the environment, is the process of strategy development. Strategy defines what the organization does and, therefore, provides an important factor in understanding organizational behavior by defining what the purpose of the organization will be.

Suggested Readings

Andrews, K. R. *The Concept of Corporate Strategy*. Homewood, Ill.: Dow-Jones Irwin, 1971.

Galbraith, J. R., and Nathanson, D. A. *Strategy Implementation: The Role of Structure and Process*. St. Paul, Minn.: West Publishing, 1978.

Hofer, C. W., and Schendel, D. *Strategy Formulation: Analytical Concepts*. St. Paul, Minn.: West Publishing, 1978.

MacMillan, I. C. *Strategy Formulation: Political Concepts*. St. Paul, Minn.: West Publishing, 1978.

Miles, R. E., and Snow, E. E. *Organizational Strategy, Structure, and Process*. New York: McGraw-Hill, 1978.

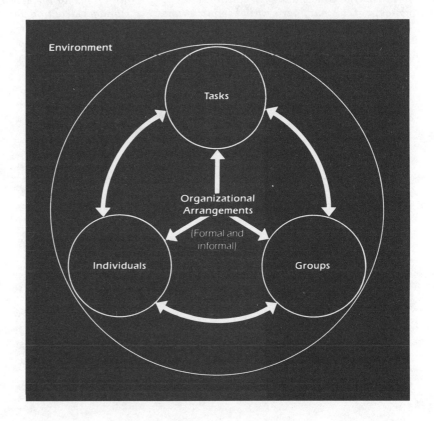

Effective Management of Organizational Behavior

OVERVIEW / The manager is ultimately responsible for the effectiveness of the organization. If we conceive of an organization as individuals and groups performing tasks, aided by organizational arrangements, all within the context of a larger environment, then the manager is the one who is charged with making this whole system work. The concept of the manager's job has implications for the kinds of skills, perspectives, and capacities that managers need to be effective. In this final section, the emphasis will be on how the manager makes use of tools and concepts such as those presented in this book to diagnose patterns of organizational behavior and to take managerial action. A broad view of the manager's role will be discussed and directions for the development of effective managerial action will be considered.

Chapter 14

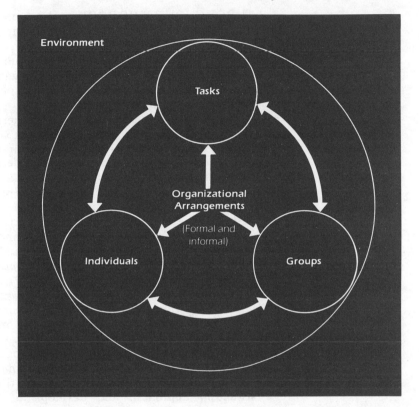

Managing Human Systems: Diagnosis and Action

THROUGHOUT THIS BOOK, we have presented ideas and tools that can help a manager, or a manager-to-be, to understand and influence what happens in organizations. We have considered, in turn, concepts that relate to individual behavior, group processes and performance, and the organization as a whole. Throughout, we have tried to draw out of this material specific implications for managerial action.

How can all these ideas be put together and applied on a day-to-day basis? Actually, managers do not spend one day contemplating organizational strategy, the next deciding about a recruitment program, and the third redesigning jobs. Managerial work is not that compartmentalized and not that easy. Managers must somehow use bits and pieces of knowledge about this and that organizational issue as they are confronted with a kaleidoscope of changing organizational crises and opportunities. There are always many balls in the air and, like the juggler, the manager must use considerable skill (and knowledge of which balls are where) to keep the system functioning more or less as intended.

In this chapter, we will focus on ways managers can *integrate* what they know about organizational behavior to understand and constructively influence the organizational units or functions for which they are responsible. We will begin by examining what managers actually do at work — and what various theorists feel they *should* be doing. Then, we will take one perspective on that question, a perspective that we call the diagnosis-action approach, and develop the implications of that approach for day-to-day managerial behavior. Finally, we will address some of the limitations of effective managerial action, and suggest what managers can do when (as is often the case) their goals and aspirations outstrip the resources available to them.

Perspectives on the Manager's Job

People who study management and organizational behavior have expended considerable effort trying to describe just what the manager's job entails, and how management jobs ideally should be set up. Some very different approaches have been used, drawing on different assumptions about managerial work and using different methods of investigation. Each approach adds to our understanding of what is involved in managing organizational behavior. We will briefly review two of these approaches, and then describe a third that we find especially helpful in thinking about the process of management.

CLASSICAL PERSPECTIVES

Management theorists in the classical tradition are primarily concerned with what managers *should* do (see, for example, Miner, 1978; Newman and Warren, 1977). While classical theorists use different terminology to describe the key tasks of managers, there is general agreement that a manager should be performing two basic tasks. One is *strategy formulation* (see Chapter 13). Managers should assess the organization and the environment in which it exists, and make decisions about the scope of the organization's activities and the allocation of resources to these various activities. A second basic task is *strategy implementation*. Managers should see that plans, goals, and objectives that derive from strategy choices are implemented effectively. Much of what we have discussed in this book (for example, designing jobs and organizational units, establishing compensation and control practices, and so on) would be seen by classical theorists as having mainly to do with strategy implementation.

Several functions have been specified by these theorists as being central to the implementation process. One is *planning*, determining the steps that must be taken to bring about future states of affairs that have been deemed as desirable. Another function is *organizing*; that is, developing structures and practices that will help actualize the plans. A third is *controlling*, setting in place systems and control mechanisms to assure that what happens within the organization is consistent with organizational plans and helpful in achieving them. A fourth is *directing*, leading and motivating people to behave in ways that are consistent with the imperatives of the organization's strategy.

Analyses of managerial functions, such as those suggested above, are pervasive in the management literature. Indeed, it would be possible to discuss almost all of the topics covered in this book in terms of one or another of these four functions, and it would be informative to do so. Yet by placing such a heavy emphasis on what managers *should* do, one risks overlooking another equally important perspective on managerial work; namely, what managers *actually* do at work.

EMPIRICAL PERSPECTIVES

What do managers do when they come to work? How do they spend their time? How much of their work involves dealing directly with people, and how much has to do with such impersonal matters as data and reports? Do managers spend their time taking initiatives and following them up, or in reacting to the initiatives of others?

These are the kinds of questions that are addressed in descriptive, empirical approaches to understanding managerial work. One of the most comprehensive empirical studies of what managers do has been carried out by Mintzberg (1973, 1975). Mintzberg actually observed a number of high-level managers over a substantial period of time and then combined his observations with those of other researchers to construct a detailed profile of how managers spend their time at work. The picture that emerges is strikingly different from the rational, normative view of the classical theorists. Planning, organizing, controlling, and directing turn out to be less central to actual managerial work than are putting out fires — dealing with problems brought by colleagues and subordinates — and juggling a multitude of short and diverse interactions with numerous other people. The pace is hectic, and the time spent on any one item is short. Managers rely far more heavily on telephone calls and meetings for information than they do on reports and other documents, and they are more intuitive than systematic in dealing with problems and in making decisions.

These findings have led a number of commentators to conclude that thinking of management in terms of normative functions, such as planning, controlling, and so on, is misleading, because so few managers actually behave as the classical theorists say they should (presumably because the immediate demands of the job don't allow them to). Instead, empiricists prefer to think about management as the *roles* that managers perform in doing their work. For example, Mintzberg (1975) has used three specific roles in summarizing managerial activities.

The first is the *interpersonal role*, having mainly to do with interactions with other people. The manager is viewed as a figurehead or symbol of the organization, as the hands-on leader of specific individuals and groups, and as the liaison with individuals and organizational units other than his or her own subordinates. Second, the manager plays an *informational role*, serving as a major source and channel of information within the organization. The manager collects information that is needed for decision making or action, disseminates information to others, and serves as a spokesperson to individuals outside his or her organizational unit or outside the organization itself. Finally, the manager has a *decisional role*, making or contributing to decisions that affect the organization and what happens within it. Many of these decisions concern the allocation of scarce resources to individuals and groups within the organization; others involve attempts to improve a given work unit, to adapt a unit to changing environmental circumstances, or to deal with conflicts and other disturbances within the organization.

Empirical studies of managers show that a given manager typically is involved in these three different roles more or less constantly and often simultaneously. As organizational and environmental circumstances change, the manager must jump back and forth from one role to another, dealing with a diversity of demands on his or her attention with very little time for reflective contemplation.

A DIAGNOSIS-ACTION PERSPECTIVE

The third perspective on managerial work is, like the classical approach, prescriptive. Yet like the empirical approach, it is based on research data and highlights the roles that managers play. This approach assumes that most managers spend little of their time formulating strategy for the organization as a whole. In most cases, determining the strategic directions of an organization (or of a unit within the organization) is done by members of top management.

The activities of most managers, then, mainly have to do with creating conditions within the organization so that individuals and groups can carry out their work as effectively as possible. These activities can be characterized by two managerial roles. The first role is that of a *diagnostician.* As a diagnostician, a manager collects and analyzes information about how the organization and the people within it are functioning, and determines what changes need to be made to improve organizational effectiveness. The second role is that of *change agent.* In this role, the manager attempts to bring about changes in the organization that will improve its effectiveness. The focus of these changes can be an individual, group, or system; their content (for example, changing jobs vs. redesigning control systems vs. hiring or firing someone), of course, depends on what the diagnostic data indicate is needed.

The diagnosis-action perspective is not a replacement for either the classical or the empirical approaches to understanding managerial work. Instead, the three approaches complement and inform one another. While managers ultimately must determine strategy (and then plan, organize, control, and direct to implement that strategy), they frequently have to do this in a disjointed and fragmented way. Such implementing activities can be described using the notion of informational, interpersonal, and decisional roles. And, while all of this is going on, the manager is collecting data, drawing diagnostic conclusions, and taking action to affect behavior in the organization.

The concepts and ideas presented in this book can be linked both to the classical and the empirical approaches to management. Our focus for the remainder of this chapter, however, will be on the diagnostic-action approach. We will turn first to the diagnostic activities that managers can perform and then to managerial action.

The Diagnosis of Organizational Behavior

It is hard to overemphasize the importance of basing managerial actions on solid diagnostic information. Too often changes are made or actions are taken in response to a vague intuition that a certain change will help. Changes undertaken without the benefit of some kind of systematic diagnosis are more like gambling than they are like management.

As will be seen below, there are at least two approaches to organizational diagnosis, one that focuses on symptoms of existing organizational problems, and one that is more general and comprehensive in nature. Both can be helpful because both involve the systematic use of *data* about the organization. On the other hand, intuitive diagnoses, in which the manager decides on his or her own what is wrong and why, are about as risky as no diagnosis at all. Consider, for example, a manager who observes signs of poor quality work by rank-and-file employees. Because of the pervasive human tendency to attribute the reasons for observed problems to the people who are associated with them, the manager decides that there is a "people problem." The action that derives from this intuitive diagnosis is to change the people — either by hiring "better" people or by training the people presently on the job to behave more competently. If, however, the *real* root of the observed problem is that the people are overqualified for their work (and therefore chaffing at the monotony of their job), or that the compensation system provides disincentives for effective work, then the solutions that flow from the manager's diagnosis may worsen the situation rather than improve it. If the manager were to collect some systematic data about the relationship between the people and their work, then the chances of a missed diagnosis and an incorrect action would be lessened.

TYPES OF ORGANIZATIONAL DIAGNOSIS

Central to the diagnosis of organizational behavior is the identification and analysis of problems. It is the process by which a manager finds out what is wrong or what needs action within the organization. This is analogous to diagnosis in medicine, where the body is examined, the functioning of different systems is assessed, and based upon symptoms, hypotheses are generated about possible ailments.

An organizational diagnosis can be undertaken for a variety of reasons. It might be initiated because of obvious symptoms of problems. For example, poor quality production, increased costs, interdepartmental conflict, or any number of other observed difficulties might prompt a manager to undertake a diagnosis to discover the reasons for these problems. Alternatively, a diagnosis might be initiated when managers believe that organizational changes are needed to respond to changes in the environment (such as changes in available resources, in the labor market, in the economic climate, or in customer/client preferences). Finally, a diagnosis might be done as part of a regular program to monitor organizational functioning and performance. Much as an individual might visit a physician for an annual checkup, or a vehicle might be taken in for routine maintenance, a manager might choose to assess the state of the organization periodically. Such checkups can identify problems before undesirable symptoms are present, and can point out exploitable opportunities for organizational growth and development.

In general, there are two ways to approach the diagnostic task. First, the diagnosis can be symptom-based, beginning with (and limited to) the problems or issues that initially prompted the diagnostic activity. Alternatively, the diagnosis can be comprehensive, dealing with the full range of organizational variables, from organizational strategy to the needs of individual members. Both approaches have value and are considered separately below.[1]

SYMPTOM-BASED DIAGNOSIS

When specific symptoms of organizational problems are present, a manager can elect to organize diagnostic activities around those symptoms, rather than to conduct a large-scale and comprehensive diagnosis of an entire organizational unit. The symptom-based approach is actually a form of action research (cf. French and Bell, 1973). The manager develops and carries out an informal research design that involves (1) noting and documenting a problem of interest, (2) developing some hypotheses about the causal roots of the problem based on its symptoms and the manager's knowledge of organizational behavior, (3) developing a data collection plan, and (4) gathering and analyzing data to test the hypotheses. When done well, the symptom-based approach can provide a basis for managerial action that is both efficient and trustworthy. Doing it well involves:

1. *Identifying the symptoms.* Determine just what the signs are that problems exist, and make sure that the information being used is valid and reliable. Sometimes a manager will report a crisis that, on further exploration, turns out to reflect the manager's momentary anxieties more than any real organizational problem. It is always advisable to use at least two different sources of data to get a "fix" on the symptoms (for example, supervisory reports of quality problems *plus* high reject rates from quality control records).

2. *Identifying the focus and range of diagnostic activity.* What are possible reasons why the symptoms appeared? What kinds of data are, therefore, needed to find and understand

[1] For guidelines that are useful in designing and executing a comprehensive diagnostic process, see Levinson (1972), Nadler (1977b), or Lawler, Nadler, and Cammann (1980).

underlying problems? This is one of the most critical stages of the diagnostic process, and one where many diagnoses go wrong. It is very tempting to define problems *only* by their symptoms: If a person performs poorly, something is wrong with the person (but perhaps the real difficulty has to do with the organizational circumstances in which he or she works); if people complain about their supervisor, then something is wrong with how the supervisor is acting (but perhaps the real difficulty has to do with excessive production pressures on the supervisor from other managers). It is at this stage in the diagnostic process that managers need to draw heavily on their understanding of organizational behavior to ensure that all reasonable explanations for the observed symptoms are addressed in the diagnosis.

It is always somewhat risky to carry out a symptom-based diagnosis. Organizations are complex and things that happen in one part of the system affect other parts of the system, sometimes in nonobvious ways. Just as a physician might examine the feet when a patient reports a backache (because the physician knows that foot problems cause alterations in posture which, in turn, can cause backaches), a knowledgeable manager may collect diagnostic data about a seemingly unrelated organizational system in response to a specific organizational complaint.

3. *Collecting the diagnostic data.* After the manager has decided what factors *might* be responsible for the observed symptoms, data to check out these possibilities should be collected. Sometimes this involves merely checking available records and reports; other times, it will be necessary to observe or interview people in the organization to obtain their views of what is going on. Whatever the focus of the diagnosis, it is always a good idea to collect data from several sources (Nadler, 1977b). This allows the manager to make sure that different kinds of data lead to the same conclusion and makes the manager less dependent on any one source of information. Explorations of the reason for a quality problem, for example, might involve discussions with employees, supervisors, and inspectors as well as on-site observations of the work being done. If the data do converge, then the manager can be confident that he or she has a good "fix" on the problem; if they do not, then the manager should delay forming any conclusions about the root of the difficulty until the reasons for the discrepancies are understood.

4. *Analyzing the data.* When the manager is convinced that the diagnostic data are trustworthy, it is time to use those data, along with appropriate conceptual models, to identify the probable causes of core problems. Action plans for improving the situation can be proposed on the basis of this analysis.

COMPREHENSIVE DIAGNOSIS

While the presence of specific symptoms may indicate the need for a focused symptom-based diagnosis, other occasions require a broader, more comprehensive approach. It may be, for example, that the initial stages of symptom-based diagnosis indicate the existence of multiple problems that relate to a number of aspects of the organization. A few symptoms may only be the tip of a much larger iceberg of organizational problems. Or it may be that shifts in organizational strategy, changes in the environment, or needs for periodic monitoring of the organization will prompt a diagnosis that focuses on an entire organization or on the functioning of a major organizational unit.

While comprehensive organizational diagnosis involves basically the same steps as symptom-based diagnosis, the collection of data should be driven primarily by an organizational model or framework which defines what data to collect and how to interpret the data once collected. Many different frameworks for diagnosis exist (see Levinson, 1972; Weisbord, 1978). The approach presented below is based on the organizational framework that we have used throughout the book.

As shown in Figure 14.1, there is a logical flow of what aspects of the organization should be examined in what order. The starting point is strategy. Before digging into what goes on within the organization, it is important to understand what the strategy of the organization is; that is, what the organization is attempting to accomplish (see Chapter 13). The next question has to do with the critical tasks of the organization: Given the strategy, what are various parts of the organization required to do and which of these tasks are most critical?

After identifying the critical tasks for organizational units, the next step is to examine the organizational structure and determine whether the organization is designed appropriately to meet the demands of the task (see Chapters 10, 11, and 12). Analysis of the organizational structure should include how individuals and work units are grouped as well as various mechanisms for coordination and control that link individuals and work units. Similarly, the informal organization and methods of conflict resolution should be reviewed.

Having determined the nature and appropriateness of the organization structure, diagnostic activities should next turn to the patterns of individual and group behavior that exist within the organization (see Sections II and III of this book). Special attention should be given to three issues: (1) the characteristics of the individuals who work in the organization, including their perceptions of the work and the organization and their on-the-job behaviors, (2) organizational practices that influence individual behavior — ranging from the design of jobs to reward systems to control mechanisms, and (3) the design and management of work groups, including informal controls used by groups to influence their members. It is important to address these three factors simultaneously, since the people, the groups in which they work, and the organizational structures and practices that affect their behavior should, in most cases, fit together and complement one another.

Figure 14.1 *A Sequence for Comprehensive Diagnosis*

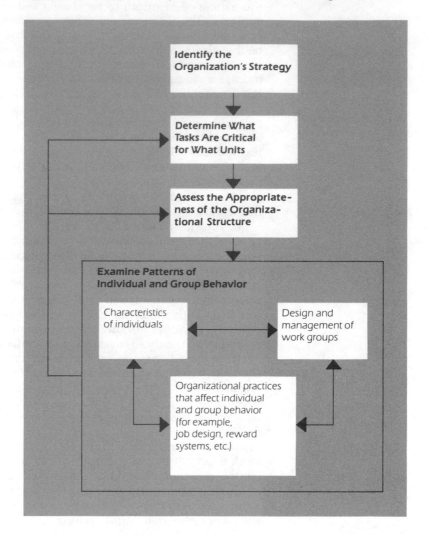

As individual and group level phenomena are examined, some recycling of diagnostic activities may be called for. It may be discovered, for example, that while the structure of the organization is appropriate for the task to be done, it is inconsistent with the needs or the skills of the individuals who perform the work. This could suggest a reexamination of the structure itself, the way tasks are defined and broken up, or the staffing policies and practices.

At each point in the diagnostic process, different conceptual tools are used. For example, when examining the fit between organizational tasks and structure, the information processing model discussed in Chapters 10 and 11 is relevant. When examining how informal social norms support or contradict formal organizational practices, models from Chapters 7 and 8 on small group behavior may be helpful. The sequence suggested in Figure 14.1, then, is a way of organizing and applying the various models and tools that have been presented throughout this book.

Finally, it should be noted that the process by which a diagnosis is carried out is equally as important for comprehensive diagnosis as it is for symptom-based diagnosis. If the data are unreliable, collected only from favored informants, or otherwise distorted when gathered or analyzed, then the conclusions reached will form a poor basis on which to take action.

Managerial Action: Bringing About Organizational Change

When organizational problems (and opportunities) have been clearly identified and their probable causes determined, the manager makes a transition from diagnostic activities to actual plans for change. In the change-agent role, the manager takes conceptual tools and frameworks and uses them to design and install changes in how the organization operates.

There is much more to bringing about change in organizations than merely thinking up solutions and installing them. Research and experience suggest that two issues require considerable thought and ingenuity if changes have a chance for long-term success.

1. The *content* of the change. What will be changed: people, relationships, tasks, structures, or many aspects of the organization simultaneously? How can one tell if the planned changes are adequate in focus, scope, and magnitude to bring about hoped-for results?
2. The *process* of the change. How will the changes be planned, announced, installed, and followed up? Is the method of implementation appropriate for the content of the change? Will implementation processes deal adequately with resistance to change?

It is important to understand that content issues (what is done) and process issues (how it is done) are closely related. When content and process are not synchronized, problems are sure to follow. An attempt to increase the degree to which lower-level managers are to participate in dealing with their subordinates, for example, is *not* appropriately installed by a directive from higher management. Nor is it appropriate to try to resolve interdepartmental conflict by asking representatives of the antagonistic departments to sit on opposite sides of a table and decide which group was more to blame for the difficulties between them. In short, how you go about dealing with a problem is often as important, if not more so, than the objective changes you make. A small but well-executed change, in many cases, will have a more positive and lasting effect on an organizational unit than will a poorly executed blockbuster.

THE CONTENT OF MANAGERIAL ACTION

We have discussed the content of possible organizational changes throughout this book. In virtually every chapter, models or prescriptions have been presented that can be used to generate specific ideas for improving the functioning of organizations. At this point, the reader should have in mind numerous kinds of tools and techniques that could be used to influence what happens in organizations. Indeed, the problem may be having so many tools available for change that selecting among them is a confusing and intimidating prospect. As a means of integrating some of these points of leverage for managerial action, it is useful to think of a scheme for classifying possible changes into two groups: (1) those involving alterations of *structures*, and (2) those that attempt to change directly *people and their behavior*. (See Table 14.1)

Structural changes are changes in the design of the organization, in organizational tasks, in the composition of groups that make up the organization, or in the specific structures that influence, regulate, and control behavior. Such structural features comprise one major point of leverage for altering organizational behavior. Specific structural changes that might be made include redesigning the overall structure of the organization; altering various coordination and control mechanisms; forming, abolishing or redesigning work groups; enriching or simplifying jobs; revising measurement and control systems; modifying personnel systems (including recruitment, placement, and career paths); and so on. The focus for structural changes is on tangible aspects of the structure of the organization or its components.

A second approach is to attempt to change behavior by influencing individual attitudes, perceptions, and capabilities. For

Table 14.1 *Leverage Points for Managers to Bring About Organizational Change*

1. Leverage points based in the content of the change	Structural changes in the organization
	Changes in people and their behavior
2. Leverage points based in the process of how the change is implemented	Motivation to change
	Participation in the change design and implementation
	Power

example, a manager might decide to recruit new people to the organization or to transfer out existing personnel; training programs might be instituted to upgrade the skills of people or to alter individuals' organization-related attitudes and perceptions; or a manager might intervene directly to change patterns of interpersonal behavior and interaction (such as group norms, leadership behavior, and so on).

Obviously, when attempting to bring about *major* shifts in patterns of organizational behavior, both of these leverage points need to be considered and used. Because behavior is affected *both* by the characteristics of the person and the environment in which he or she is functioning, making changes in organizational behavior ultimately must deal both with people as well as the organizational context.

To change either the person or the environment without attention to the other is risky. Modifications in the structural features of an individual's environment, for example, can have a very powerful effect on behavior (such as who deals with whom, what the tasks are that people work on, and so on). But when such changes are implemented without attention to the needs, perceptions, and attitudes of the individuals who will be affected by them, they may have unintended and undesired consequences. More than one major reorganization of a department or function has failed because the changes did not take into account the needs and special interests of key individuals who were affected by the reorganization.

It also works the other way. Changes dealing directly with the behavior of individual organization members can have great impact on what people do in the short run. But unless organizational structures and systems support them, person-focused changes often fade out in a relatively short period of time. As mentioned in Chapter 3, leadership training programs are a good case in point. They often are conducted off premises, in an environment designed to provide support for individual experimentation, risk taking, and learning. End-of-course assessments invariably show (for well-conceived and well-run courses) that people have learned new behaviors and that they firmly intend to use these behaviors in their management activities when they return to the organization.

The problem arises when the manager-student attempts to carry out those intentions: In many cases, he or she discovers that they simply do not work for the people and the tasks that must be dealt with on a day-to-day basis. The back-home environment is *not* supportive of the new behaviors, and despite high aspirations and good intentions, the manager soon slips back into the old ways of behaving because those behaviors are supported by the organization's unchanged structures and systems.

In sum, if a manager hopes to bring about major changes in an organization, changes that will persist and take root over time, then those changes must deal with both the persons involved and with the organizational environment.

THE PROCESS OF MAKING CHANGES

The manager can make changes in various ways. The simplest method is simply to command or mandate change. In some cases, this may be effective, notably when the change is tangible and involves mainly structural aspects of the organization. In many situations, however, mandated changes simply do not work. One reason is that most organizational changes are met with resistance from powerful individuals or groups within the organization (see Lawrence, 1969). There are many good reasons why such resistance occurs, reasons which do *not* imply that the people involved are backward, opposed to progress, or basically uncooperative human beings.

Change almost always creates instability in the organization, at least temporarily, and thus is fraught with risks for people who see important policies, practices and structures going up in the air without any assurance of where they will come down. Organizational changes often generate alterations in power relations among individuals and groups, or changes in the networks, cliques, and coalitions that provide stability and security for organization members. Disturbing those arrangements risks disturbing individuals' own niches in the social system — and perhaps diminishing their power to influence the things they care about. At the same time, the general uncertainty that accompanies organizational change reduces the clarity of individual expectancies about "what leads to what" in the organization and, therefore, can simultaneously increase ambiguity about what people should do at work and reduce the motivation to perform well.

It should be understood that these difficulties come about because of the *process* of change, pretty much regardless of what the change actually is. Resistance may also develop if people find that they disagree with the specific content of the changes. If a manager believes that integrating the engineering and the production planning groups is a bad idea, that person may be invested in maintaining the status quo regardless of how competently the change is carried out.

There are, then, many good reasons why individuals feel it is in their own best interest to resist change. Those who attempt to bring about changes in organizations should structure the process of change to acknowledge the likelihood that some individuals will behave in ways that impede rather than foster meaningful change. At least three approaches can be used. First, managers can create conditions to increase the *motivation* of people to change. Second, the use of *participation* in the planning and execution of change can help overcome resistance. And third, it sometimes is appropriate to use existing centers of *power* in the organization to facilitate the implementation of change.

Motivation. Resistance to change sometimes can be dealt with by providing the people affected with a strong motivation to cooperate. One way to do this is to build on people's dissatisfactions with the existing situation, and to provide them with an ideal or vision of how the contemplated changes can lead to improved working conditions and valued rewards. The key is to provide information that causes individuals to develop expectancies connecting the current situation with undesirable outcomes and future (postchange) states with desirable outcomes. A wide range of methods can be used to collect information about the present situation, and to help people understand how things will be improved (Nadler, 1977b). Especially useful in pointing out the problem with the present situation are data from managerial audits, attitude surveys, and interviews. Extensive communications programs which use approaches such as group discussions and written statements of policy can be very helpful in pointing out the advantages of this change.

While the devices suggested above can be powerful in affecting the motivation of people to cooperate in change activities, they all presume that the postchange circumstances will, in fact, be experienced as an improvement over the status quo. If there is reason for doubt or uncertainty about the desirability of postchange outcomes for organization members (for example, when the changes may involve a substantial cutback of personnel), then these motivational devices are wholly inappropriate. If negative outcomes for participants are highlighted prior to the change, resistance can be expected to increase; if they are not discussed (or, worse, if a false, glowing picture of the postchange state of affairs is painted), then a backfire is a near certainty when people find out that things did not turn out favorably for them. The backfire will be especially destructive to organizational effectiveness if people feel that they were hoodwinked when the change and its likely effects were first described to them.

Participation. A related method for dealing with resistance to change involves the use of participative change techniques. By inviting people in the organization to become involved in the design and implementation of changes, resistance may be reduced in several ways. First, participation in the process of change may create feelings of ownership over proposed changes. The change becomes "our" change, and thus people are motivated to make it a success, rather than "their" change which people may be motivated to make fail. Participation also makes it possible for people to share with one another (and with the change agent or manager) special information they have that bears on how the changes should be designed. In many cases this leads to the content of the change being improved. Moreover, because information is shared, people involved in the change are likely to understand it better. This can eliminate resistance based on misunderstanding, and help people comprehend just how things will work after the changes are made.

Many specific devices or mechanisms can be used to help people participate in a change process. One way is large-scale data collection through interviews, voting, surveys, and so on. Alternatively, ideas can be generated using representatives (either formal or informal) of existing groups, which provides a way for large numbers of people to have at least an indirect say in the decision-making process. Finally, pilot projects, in which the findings are shared with involved individuals, can be useful in testing out ideas for change prior to large-scale implementation. Such projects provide people with a genuine opportunity both to learn about and shape the planned changes, and for that reason can be an especially powerful device for dealing with resistance to change that stems primarily from ignorance about what the changes may entail.

Use of Power. A third way to proceed with the implementation of changes is to link them closely to sources of power in the organization. Because powerful figures in the organization can often influence the attitudes and behaviors of large numbers of people, they can play a key role in reducing resistance to change. Moreover, by developing linkages with power figures, those responsible for implementing the changes may be better able to weather the turbulence that typically accompanies major changes.

Indeed, there are so many possible sources of resistance to change, and so many vested interests in the status quo, that major changes are unlikely to be installed and persist unless powerful individuals or groups are engaged to help see the project through the inevitable troubles and uncertainties that accompany them. Sometimes, top management can serve this function; other times, it is the involvement of a union that provides the push to keep changes going; still other times, the personal commitment of individual opinion leaders within the organization does the trick. But the manager who is contemplating major changes in his or her work unit is well advised to line up *some* powerful source of support. The risk of not doing so is changes that are smaller in scope and magnitude than hoped for, and changes that fail to persist in the organization after they have been installed.

Limitations on Managerial Action

Up to this point, we have assumed that the manager has a great number of options for change, and that if managers make the proper choices, they can substantially alter how their organizations function. This is often not the case. Any manager is but one actor in a large and interdependent social system, and he or she is limited by a number of factors, some of which have to do with the manager as an individual, some with inherent limits on how rational any manager can actually be in his or her role, and some with the way the manager's job is defined. It is important for managers to be aware of these limitations and to consider them when contemplating plans for organizational change.

INDIVIDUAL SKILLS

The ability of managers to diagnose, analyze, and solve problems through action is limited by their specific skills and talents. Depending on differences in background, training, experience, and sensitivity, some people find it much easier than others to apply the kinds of analytic and diagnostic tools discussed throughout this book. For starters, the amount of knowledge and experience a person has are important. If one understands the concepts and managerial tools that can be used in managing organizations, and if that person has a rich set of experiences to use in assessing the usefulness of these concepts and tools in specific settings, then he or she has a real advantage in both the diagnostic and action parts of the managerial job.

Beyond knowledge and experience, however, specific behavioral skills can make great differences in how well a manager actually executes what he or she cognitively knows. The capability of a manager to sensitively handle difficult interpersonal relations, for example, can powerfully influence how effective that person is at managing conflict within a work unit, in dealing with the political aspects of an organization, in helping a group deal competently with matters of interpersonal process, or in dealing with subordinates' resistance to planned organizational change. Thus, two managers who have equal amounts of knowledge and experience, but who differ in interpersonal skill will and probably should deal differently with situations such as those described above.

Interpersonal skills are but one of a number of behavioral skills affecting managerial performance. Others include the knack for assimilating and making sense of large amounts of data, the ability to help others understand organizational problems in terms more general than their manifest symptoms, and so on. Fortunately, many of these skills can be learned, but they cannot be mastered by reading any book. We have tried to provide here a knowledge base for effective managerial behavior. With that knowledge in hand, and with an adequate array of organizational experiences, the manager or manager-to-be should be in a good position to work with colleagues or teachers to develop the *behavioral* skills needed to use effectively the knowledge we have tried to provide. Only when such skills have been developed, we believe, can conceptual knowledge be applied effectively to concrete and specific managerial problems.

The models presented in this book are quite rational. They involve identifying desired goals or end states, designing tasks and structures consistent with those aspirations, and then managing individuals and groups in ways that foster rather than impede effective work toward those aspirations. They require attention to a multiplicity of factors that can influence what happens in organizations, and place on the manager a substantial and at times impossible data collection and data processing load. The human manager is not a computer and has limited capacity to process information. Moreover, managers must deal with the reality of Mintzberg's findings: the hectic pace, the uninvited crises, and the barrage of messages, memos, and meetings. Even if they cognitively could handle the task of making rational decisions about management strategy and technique in an information-abundant environment, most would have nowhere near the time required to do so.

What, then, are the alternatives? One, not very satisfactory from our perspective, is to back off from tools and models of the type presented in this book. Many managers decide that they can make do with the set of managerial concepts and techniques they happen to have developed in their professional lives, simply because they do not have the time to learn new ideas and approaches. They pretend that behavioral science knowledge about individuals, groups, and social systems is not really very relevant to day-to-day work, and they make avoidable and serious mistakes because of that view.

A second alternative is to learn to blend day-to-day "business as usual" with a selective use of the concepts and tools discussed here. Managers who follow this strategy take time from the hectic pace of work to reflect on what they are doing and how they might behave differently in the future. They do not try to "follow the book" all the time, because they realize that is impossible; but frequently they do use the materials they have learned to test and to inform their actions.

The third alternative, "developing informed intuition," is really an extension of the second. In Chapter 1, we raised questions about the value of intuitive managerial decision making, because intuitive theories often are incorrect and because the data on which intuitive decisions are based often are incomplete and biased. Yet many managers who do their reflective homework are able to develop an *informed* intuition that can shortcut the need to systematically and rationally consider all the factors that may be relevant.

When a manager has, over months or years, worked through the implications of various models or management tools, he or she develops the capability to provide a seemingly quick, intuitive response to organizational issues. Such managers may say, after only a few minutes of conversation, "We ought to check out how those people are paid, because I'm guessing that they don't see the link between what they do and what they get," or "It sounds to me like he ought to be let go — I'm doubtful that he's up to the job. What do you think?" Such quick responses *sound* as if they are arbitrary judgments of the worst kind. In fact, they may be the result of years of very thoughtful experience and experimentation, and they may reflect overlearning (rather than naiveté) about organizational behavior. It is just that the accumulated wisdom of such individuals operates, at times, subconsciously rather than through deliberate and conscious processing of all relevant managerial options and alternatives.

In summary, we are not suggesting that this book, or any book, can serve as a day-to-day guide for managerial behavior. Instead, we are suggesting that books such as this will help managers get started toward developing the kind of informed intuition that can make the process of management efficient, effective, and rewarding.

THE MANAGERIAL ROLE

A third limitation on managerial action stems from the way the management role itself is defined. As we have seen, behavior in organizations is powerfully constrained by forces in the internal and the external environments. Managers, like rank-and-file workers, are limited by these forces. Even members of top management often report that their freedom to carry out the kinds of changes that they believe to be in the best interest of the organization is far too restricted. The situation for lower managers is, in most cases, far more constraining.

Middle- and lower-level managers who are knowledgeable about the forces shaping organizational behavior sometimes find that knowledge more frustrating than empowering, simply because their role does not allow them to *use* what they know to make a constructive difference. If a manager diagnoses his or her work unit and discovers that productivity is being impeded by a faulty control system, inappropriate compensation arrangements, poorly designed jobs, and seemingly capricious placement procedures, *what is that manager to do if he or she has no power to alter those organizational systems?* Or, even more distressing, what if a lower-level manager senses a discrepancy between the strategy and the structure of the organization? Even the manager's boss's boss may not have the authority to deal with that key issue.

In fact, organizations are often structured in ways that assign responsibility for organizational performance to middle- and lower-level managers without providing them influence over those organizational structures and systems that most powerfully affect how well their units actually perform. Under such circumstances, some managers attempt to threaten, inspire, or otherwise cajole their subordinates into the best level of performance that possibly can be achieved under the circumstances. Others, who may be either braver or wiser, choose not to direct their attention and energy downward, but instead look upward. They try to create, by persuasion or by political behavior, change in those organizational systems that most strongly influence what happens within their own domain. Often, there are ways that managerial roles can be enriched and improved. An important task for higher managers is to review the jobs of their subordinate managers and, when possible, to restructure them so that lower-level managers are provided greater influence over the organizational policies and practices that affect the effectiveness of their work units.

VALUES AND THE MULTIPLE CONSTITUENTS OF ORGANIZATIONS

Organizations are large and complex systems that are constructed to implement strategies and serve the needs of a number of individuals and groups. The very nature of an organization's business affects the lives of the people who receive the organization's products or services, not to mention the lives of people who have invested in it. The way an organization is structured and managed also touches on the lives of those who are employed by the organization and the lives of their families. Any enterprise that so centrally involves people necessarily deals with questions of human values, whether those questions are addressed implicitly or explicitly.

Questions of values in management cannot be avoided. They can be ignored only if one chooses not to address the implications for people and for society of what organizations do. Value questions can be viewed as another set of limits that constrain managerial actions. In many situations these constraints are quite real since they have been translated into law and organization policy.

It is also possible and we feel desirable to conceive of *all* management actions as having value consequences, as creating conditions that are "good" or "bad" for some persons, groups, or social systems. If management involves making changes in organizations, then this view suggests that who benefits (and who does not) from those changes is always a relevant question. What kind of product or service do we want to provide for the people in our society? What kind of worklife do we want to provide for the people we manage? How do we want to balance our aspiration for organizational efficiency and our aspirations for a high quality of worklife?

Obviously such questions have no easy answers, and we would not presume to suggest what we see as right and wrong ways of responding to them. But we do believe that struggling with questions such as these is one of the most important, and most easily overlooked, aspects of the manager's job.

Summary

Organizations are complex and intricate mechanisms created to get work done, composed of individuals and groups performing tasks, and aided by various types of organizational structures. The effectiveness of any organization is ultimately affected by the patterns of behavior that develop and emerge over time. How individuals and groups behave has a major impact on how well an organization meets its many goals. The manager in an organization sits at the center of all of this. Management actions and decisions are crucial determinants of the patterns of organizational behavior. Managers select individuals to work in organizations, motivate and reward them, guide them, and build organization structures to coordinate and control their work.

We have attempted to provide students and managers with a set of concepts to help understand how organizational behavior comes about. In this chapter, we have attempted to provide guides for using those concepts within the context of real organizations and actual everyday pressures. The manager's role has been examined, and an approach to managing has been advocated based on the roles of diagnostician and change agent. Leverage points for change have been discussed related to both the content of changes and the process of implementing changes. Finally, we have identified some of the limitations on managerial action within organizations.

The task of managing organizations is important. Concepts of organizational behavior will continue to be critical in the development of effective management. Our hope is that managers who are equipped with tools rooted in the scientific study of organizational behavior will be able to create more effective organizations. These will be organizations that use resources well, perform needed tasks efficiently, enable individuals to fulfill their needs, and make positive contributions to the larger society.

Suggested Readings

Beckhard, R., and Harris, R. T. *Organizational Transitions: Managing Complex Change.* Reading, Mass.: Addison-Wesley, 1977.

French, W., and Bell, C. *Organization Development: Behavioral Science Interventions for Organizational Change.* 2nd ed. Englewood Cliffs, N.J.: Prentice-Hall, 1978.

Levinson, H. *Organizational Diagnosis.* Cambridge, Mass.: Harvard University Press, 1972.

Mintzberg, H. *The Nature of Managerial Work.* New York: Harper and Row, 1973.

Weisbord, M. *Organizational Diagnosis.* Reading, Mass.: Addison-Wesley, 1978.

References

A

Aguillar, F. J. *Scanning the Business Environment*. New York: Macmillan, 1967.

Aharoni, J. *The Foreign Investment Decision Process*. Boston: Division of Research, Harvard Business School, 1966.

Aldrich, H. E., and Pfeffer, J. "Environments of Organizations," *Annual Review of Sociology*, 1976, 2, 79–105.

Allison, G. T. *Essence of Decision: Explaining the Cuban Missile Crisis*. Boston: Little, Brown, 1971.

Andrews, K. R. *The Concept of Corporate Strategy*. Homewood, Ill.: Dow Jones-Irwin, 1971.

Ansoff, H. I. "Toward a Strategic Theory of the Firm." In *Business Strategy*, edited by H. I. Ansoff. Baltimore: Penguin, 1969.

Argyris, C. *Interpersonal Competence and Organizational Effectiveness*. Homewood, Ill.: Irwin-Dorsey, 1962.

B

Beckhard, R. *Organization Development: Strategies and Models*. Reading, Mass.: Addison-Wesley, 1969.

Bem, D. J. "An Experimental Analysis of Self-persuasion," *Journal of Experimental Social Psychology*, 1965, 1, 199–218.

Blake, R. R., and Mouton, J. S. "Group and Organizational Team Building: A Theoretical Model for Intervening." In *Theories of Group Processes*, edited by C. L. Cooper. London: Wiley, 1975.

Blake, R. R., Shepard, H. A., and Mouton, J. S. *Managing Intergroup Conflict in Industry*. Houston: Gulf Publishing, 1964.

Bower, J. L. *Managing the Resource Allocation Process: A Study of Corporate Planning and Investment*. Boston: Division of Research, Harvard Business School, 1970.

Burns, T., and Stalker, G. M. *The Management of Innovation*. London: Tavistock Publications, 1961.

C

Cammann, C. "The Impact of a Feedback System on Managerial Attitudes and Performance." Unpublished doctoral dissertation, Yale University, 1974.

Campbell, J. P., Dunnette, M. D., Lawler, E. E., and Weick, K. *Managerial Behavior, Performances and Effectiveness*. New York: McGraw-Hill, 1970.

Chandler, A. D. *Strategy and Structure*. Cambridge, Mass.: M.I.T. Press, 1962.

Chapple, E. D., and Sayles, L. R. *The Measure of Management*. New York: Macmillan, 1961.

Child, J. "Organization Structure and Strategies of Control: A Replication of the Aston Study," *Administrative Science Quarterly*, 1972, 17, 163–177.

———. "Strategies of Control and Organizational Behavior," *Administrative Science Quarterly*, 1973, 18, 1–17.

Collins, B. E., and Guetzkow, H. *A Social Psychology of Group Processes for Decision-making*. New York: Wiley, 1964.

D

Davis, K. *Human Society*. New York: Macmillan, 1950.

Davis, L. E., and Trist, E. L. "Improving the Quality of Work Life: Sociotechnical Case Studies." In *Work and the Quality of Life*, edited by J. O'Toole. Cambridge, Mass.: M.I.T. Press, 1974.

Davis, S. M., and Lawrence, P. R. *Matrix*. Reading, Mass.: Addison-Wesley, 1977.

Delbecq, A. L., Van de Ven, A. H., and Gustafson, D. H. *Group Techniques for Program Planning*. Glenview, Ill.: Scott, Foresman, 1975.

Deutsch, M. *The Resolution of Conflict: Constructive and Destructive Processes*. New Haven: Yale University Press, 1973.

Duncan, R. "Characteristics of Organizational

Environments," *Administrative Science Quarterly*, 1972, *17*, 313–327.

———. "Multiple Decision Making Structure in Adapting to Environmental Uncertainty," *Human Relations*, 1973, *26*, 273–291.

Dunnette, M. D. *Personnel Selection and Placement*. Belmont, Cal.: Wadsworth, 1966.

Dunnette, M. D., and Bass, B. M. "Behavioral Scientists and Personnel Management," *Industrial Relations*, 1963, *2*(3), 115–130.

Dunnette, M. D., Campbell, J., and Jaastad, K. "The Effect of Group Participation on Brainstorming Effectiveness for Two Industrial Samples," *Journal of Applied Psychology*, 1963, *47*, 30–37.

E

Emerson, R. M. "Power-dependence Relations," *American Sociological Review*, 1962, *27*, 31–40.

Evan, W. "The Organization Set: Toward a Theory of Interorganizational Relations." In *Approaches to Organization Design*, edited by J. Thompson. Pittsburgh: University of Pittsburgh Press, 1966.

F

Farris, G. F., and Lim, F. G., Jr. "Effects of Performance on Leadership, Cohesiveness, Influence, Satisfaction, and Subsequent Performance," *Journal of Applied Psychology*, 1969, *53*, 490–497.

Feldman, D. C. "A Contingency of Socialization," *Administrative Science Quarterly*, 1976, *21*, 433–452.

Festinger, L. A. "A Theory of Social Comparison Processes," *Human Relations*, 1954, *7*, 117–140.

———. *A Theory of Cognitive Dissonance*. Stanford: Stanford University Press, 1957.

Fiedler, F. E. *Leadership*. New York: General Learning Press, 1971.

Filley, A. C. *Interpersonal Conflict Resolution*. Glenview, Ill.: Scott, Foresman, 1975.

Fishbein, M. "A Behavior Theory Approach to the Relations Between Beliefs about an Object and the Attitude toward the Object." In *Readings in Attitude Theory and Measurement*, edited by M. Fishbein. New York: Wiley, 1967.

French, J. R. P., Jr., and Raven, B. "The Bases of Social Power." In *Group Dynamics* (3rd ed.), edited by D. Cartwright and A. Zander. New York: Harper and Row, 1958.

French, W. L., and Bell, C. H. *Organization Development*. Englewood Cliffs, N.J.: Prentice-Hall, 1973.

G

Galbraith, J. R. *Designing Complex Organizations*. Reading, Mass.: Addison-Wesley, 1973.

———. *Organization Design*. Reading, Mass.: Addison-Wesley, 1977.

Galbraith, J. R., and Nathanson, D. A. *Strategy Implementation: The Role of Structure and Process*. St. Paul, Minn.: West, 1978.

Ghiselli, E. E. *The Validity of Occupational Aptitude Tests*. New York: Wiley, 1966.

Gomersall, E. R., and Myers, M. S. "Breakthrough in On-the-job Training," *Harvard Business Review*, 1966, *44*(4), 62–72.

Graen, G. "Role-making Processes within Complex Organizations." In *Handbook of Industrial and Organizational Psychology*, edited by M. D. Dunnette. Chicago: Rand McNally, 1976.

Guion, R. M. *Personnel Testing*. New York: McGraw-Hill, 1965.

H

Hackman, J. R. "Group Influences on Individuals in Organizations." In *Handbook of Industrial and Organizational Psychology*, edited by M. D. Dunnette. Chicago: Rand McNally, 1976.

———. "The Design of Self-managing Work Groups." In *Managerial Control and Organizational Democracy*, edited by B. T. King, S. S. Streufert, and F. E. Fiedler. Washington, D.C.: Winston and Sons, 1978.

Hackman, J. R., and Morris, C. G. "Group Tasks, Group Interaction Process, and Group Performance Effectiveness: A Review and Proposed Integration." In *Advances in Experimental Social Psychology* (Vol. 8), edited by L. Berkowitz. New York: Academic Press, 1975.

Hackman, J. R., and Oldham, G. R. "Development of the Job Diagnostic Survey," *Journal of Applied Psychology*, 1975, *60*, 159–170.

———. "Motivation through the Design of Work: Test of a Theory," *Organizational Behavior and Human Performance*, 1976, *16*, 250–279.

―――. *Work Redesign*. Reading, Mass.: Addison-Wesley, 1979.

Hackman, J. R., Oldham, G., Janson, R., and Purdy, K. "A New Strategy for Job Enrichment," *California Management Review*, 1975, *17*(4), 57–71.

Hall, D. T. *Careers in Organizations*. Pacific Palisades, Cal.: Goodyear, 1976.

Hall, R. H. *Organizations: Structure and Process*. Englewood Cliffs, N.J.: Prentice-Hall, 1972.

Herzberg, F. *Work and the Nature of Man*. Cleveland: World Publishing Company, 1966.

Hickson, D. J., Hinings, C. R., Lee, C. A., Schneck, R. E., and Pennings, J. M. "Strategic Contingencies Theory of Intraorganizational Power," *Administrative Science Quarterly*, 1971, *16*, 216–229.

Hofer, C. W. "Research on Strategic Planning: A Survey of Past Studies and Suggestions for Future Efforts," *Journal of Economics and Business*, 1976, *28*(3), 261–285.

Hofer, C. W., and Schendel, D. *Strategy Formulation: Analytical Concepts*. St. Paul, Minn.: West, 1978.

Hollander, E. P. "Conformity, Status, and Idiosyncracy Credit," *Psychological Review*, 1958, *65*, 117–127.

House, R. J., and Mitchell, T. R. "Path-goal Theory of Leadership." In *Organizational Behavior and Industrial Psychology*, edited by K. N. Wexley and G. A. Yukl. New York: Oxford University Press, 1975.

J

Jackson, J. "Structural Characteristics of Norms." In *Current Studies in Social Psychology*, edited by I. D. Steiner and M. Fishbein. New York: Holt, Rinehart and Winston, 1965.

―――. "Normative Power and Conflict Potential," *Sociological Methods and Research*, 1975, *4*, 237–263.

Janis, I. L. *Victims of Groupthink: A Psychological Study of Foreign-Policy Decisions and Fiascos*. Boston: Houghton Mifflin, 1972.

K

Kane, J. S., and Lawler, E. E. "Performance Appraisal Effectiveness: Its Assessment and Determinants." In *Research in Organizational Behavior: An Annual Series of Analytical Essays and Critical Reviews*, edited by B. Staw. Greenwich, Conn.: Jai Press, 1979.

Katz, D., and Kahn, R. L. *The Social Psychology of Organizations*. New York: Wiley, 1966.

―――. *The Social Psychology of Organizations* (2nd ed.). New York: Wiley, 1978.

Katz, R. L. *Cases and Concepts in Corporate Strategy*. Englewood Cliffs, N.J.: Prentice-Hall, 1970.

Kelman, H. C. "Processes of Opinion Change," *Public Opinion Quarterly*, 1961, *25*, 57–78.

L

Lawler, E. E. "Job Design and Employee Motivation," *Personnel Psychology*, 1969, 426–435.

―――. *Pay and Organizational Effectiveness: A Psychological View*. New York: McGraw-Hill, 1971.

―――. *Motivation in Work Organizations*. Monterey, Cal.: Brooks/Cole, 1973.

―――. "The Individualized Organization: Problems and Promise," *California Management Review*, 1974, *17*(2), 31–39.

―――. "Control Systems in Organizations." In *Handbook of Industrial and Organizational Psychology*, edited by M. D. Dunnette. Chicago: Rand McNally, 1976.

―――. "Reward Systems." In *Improving Life at Work: Behavioral Science Approaches to Organizational Change*, edited by J. R. Hackman and J. L. Suttle. Pacific Palisades, Cal.: Goodyear, 1977.

―――. "The New Plant Revolution," *Organizational Dynamics*, 1978, *6*(3), 2–12.

Lawler, E. E., Nadler, D. A., and Cammann, C. *Organizational Assessment: Perspectives on the Measurement of Organizational Behavior and the Quality of Working Life*. New York: Wiley-Interscience, 1980.

Lawler, E. E., and Rhode, J. G. *Information and Control in Organizations*. Pacific Palisades, Cal.: Goodyear, 1976.

Lawrence, P. R. "How to Deal with Resistance to Change," *Harvard Business Review*, 1969, *47*(1), 1–16.

Lawrence, P. R., and Lorsch, J. W. *Organization and Environment: Managing Differentiation and Integration*. Homewood, Ill.: Richard D. Irwin, 1967a.

————. "New Management Job: The Integrator," *Harvard Business Review*, 1967b, *45*(6), 142–151.

Levinson, H. *Organizational Diagnosis*. Cambridge: Harvard University Press, 1972.

Levinson, H., Price, C. R., Munden, H. J., and Solley, C. M. *Men, Management and Mental Health*. Cambridge: Harvard University Press, 1962.

Lieberman, S. "The Effects of Changes in Roles on the Attitudes of Role Occupants," *Human Relations*, 1956, *9*, 385–402.

Likert, R., and Likert, J. G. *New Ways of Managing Conflict*. New York: McGraw-Hill, 1976.

Lindblom, C. E. "The Science of 'Muddling Through,' " *Public Administration Review*, 1959, *19*, 79–88.

Lowin, B., and Craig, J. R. "The Influence of Level of Performance on Managerial Style: An Experimental Object-Lesson in the Ambiguity of Correlational Data," *Organizational Behavior and Human Performance*, 1968, *3*, 440–458.

M

MacMillan, I. C. *Strategy Formulation: Political Concepts*. St. Paul, Minn.: West, 1978.

McGregor, D. "An Uneasy Look at Performance Appraisal," *Harvard Business Review*, 1957, *35*(3), 89–94.

Maier, N. R. F., and Solem, A. R. "The Contribution of a Discussion Leader to the Quality of Group Thinking," *Human Relations*, 1952, *5*, 277–288.

March, J. G., and Simon, H. A. *Organizations*. New York: Wiley, 1958.

Maslow, A. H. *Motivation and Personality*. New York: Harper and Row, 1954.

Meyer, H. H., Kay, E., and French, J. R. P., Jr. "Split Roles in Performance Appraisal," *Harvard Business Review*, 1965, *43*(1), 123–129.

Miner, J. *The Management Process*. New York: Macmillan, 1978.

Mintzberg, H. *The Nature of Managerial Work*. New York: Harper and Row, 1973.

————. "The Manager's Job: Folklore and Fact," *Harvard Business Review*, 1975, *53*(4), 49–61.

————. *Patterns in Strategy Formation*. Montreal: McGill University, 1976.

N

Nadler, D. A. "Organizational Control Systems and Behavior: The Interaction of Behavioral and Informational Components." Paper delivered at the 37th Annual Meeting of the Academy of Management, Orlando, Fla., August 1977a.

————. *Feedback and Organization Development: Using Data Based Methods*. Reading, Mass.: Addison-Wesley, 1977b.

Newman, W. H., and Logan, J. P. *Strategy, Policy, and Central Management* (7th ed.). Cincinnati: South-Western, 1976.

Newman, W. H., and Warren, E. K. *The Process of Management*. Englewood Cliffs, N.J.: Prentice-Hall, 1977.

P

Patchen, M. *The Choice of Wage Comparisons*. Englewood Cliffs, N.J.: Prentice-Hall, 1961.

Perrow, C. B. *Organizational Analysis: A Sociological View*. Belmont, Cal.: Brooks/Cole, 1970.

Pettigrew, T. F. "Social Evaluation Theory: Convergences and Applications." In *Nebraska Symposium on Motivation* (Vol. 15), edited by D. Levine. Lincoln: University of Nebraska Press, 1967, 241–311.

Pfeffer, J. "Power and Resource Allocation in Organization." In *New Directions in Organizational Behavior*, edited by B. M. Staw and G. R. Salancik. Chicago: St. Clair Press, 1977, 235–266.

Pfeffer, J., and Salancik, G. R. "Organizational Decision Making as a Political Process: The Case of a University Budget," *Administrative Science Quarterly*, 1974, *19*, 135–151.

Pondy, L. R. "Organizational Conflict: Concepts and Models," *Administrative Science Quarterly*, 1967, *12*, 296–320.

Porter, L. W., Lawler, E. E., and Hackman, J. R. *Behavior in Organizations*. New York: McGraw-Hill, 1975.

Porter, L. W., and Steers, R. M. "Organizational, Work and Personal Factors in Employee Turnover and Absenteeism," *Psychological Bulletin*, 1973, *80*, 151–176.

R

Rice, A. K. *Productivity and Social Organization: The Ahmedabad Experiment*. London: Tavistock Publications, 1958.

Roethlisberger, F. J., and Dickson, W. J. *Management and the Worker*. Cambridge: Harvard University Press, 1939.

Roy, D. F. "Banana Time," *Human Organization*, 1959, *18*, 158–168.

S

Schein, E. H. *Process Consultation*. Reading, Mass.: Addison-Wesley, 1969.

———. *Career Dynamics*. Reading, Mass.: Addison-Wesley, 1978.

Schmidt, S., and Kochan, T. "Conflict: Toward Conceptual Clarity," *Administrative Science Quarterly*, 1972, *17*, 359.

Scott, W. E. "Activation Theory and Task Design," *Organizational Behavior and Human Performance*, 1966, *1*, 3–30.

Schneider, B. S. *Staffing Organizations*. Pacific Palisades, Cal.: Goodyear, 1976.

Seashore, S. *Group Cohesiveness in the Industrial Work Group*. Ann Arbor: Institute for Social Research, University of Michigan, 1954.

Simon, H. A. *Administrative Behavior* (2nd ed.). New York: Macmillan, 1957.

Starbuck, W. H. "Organizations and Their Environments." In *Handbook of Industrial and Organizational Psychology*, edited by M. D. Dunnette. Chicago: Rand McNally, 1976, 1069–1124.

Stein, M. I. *Stimulating Creativity* (Vol. 2). New York: Academic Press, 1975.

Steiner, I. D. *Group Process and Productivity*. New York: Academic Press, 1972.

T

Taylor, F. W. *The Principles of Scientific Management*. New York: Harper, 1911.

Thomas, K. "Conflict and Conflict Management." In *Handbook of Industrial and Organizational Psychology*, edited by M. D. Dunnette. Chicago: Rand McNally, 1976, 889–935.

Thompson, J. D. *Organizations in Action*. New York: McGraw-Hill, 1967.

Thompson, J. D., and Tuden, A. "Strategies, Structures and Processes of Organizational Decision." In *Comparative Studies in Administration*, edited by J. D. Thompson et al. Pittsburgh: University of Pittsburgh Press, 1959.

Tichy, N. M. "An Analysis of Clique Formation and Structure in Organizations," *Administrative Science Quarterly*, 1973, *18*, 194–208.

———. "Networks in Organizations." In *Handbook of Organizational Design*, edited by W. Starbuck and P. Nystrom. New York: Oxford University Press, 1979.

Tichy, N. M., Hornstein, H., and Nisberg, J. N. "Participative Organization Diagnosis and Intervention Strategies: Developing Emergent Pragmatic Theories of Change," *Academy of Management Review*, 1976, *1*, 109–119.

Trist, E. L., Higgin, G. W., Murray, H., and Pollack, A. B. *Organizational Choice*. London: Tavistock Publications, 1963.

Tushman, M. L. "Communication in Research and Development Organizations: An Information Processing Approach." Unpublished doctoral dissertation, Massachusetts Institute of Technology, 1976.

———. "A Political Approach to Organizations: A Review and Rationale," *Academy of Management Review*, 1977, *2*, 206–216.

Tushman, M. L., and Nadler, D. A. "Information Processing as an Integrating Concept in Organizational Design," *Academy of Management Review*, 1978, *3*, 613–624.

V

Van de Ven, A., Delbecq, A., and Koenig, R. "Determinants of Coordination Modes within Organizations," *American Sociological Review*, 1976, *41*, 322–338.

Vroom, V. H., and Yetton, P. W. *Leadership and Decision-Making*. Pittsburgh: University of Pittsburgh Press, 1973.

W

Walton, R. E. *Interpersonal Peacemaking: Confrontations and Third Party Consultation*. Reading, Mass.: Addison-Wesley, 1969.

———. "How to Counter Alienation in the Plant," *Harvard Business Review*, 1972, *50*(6), 70–81.

Walton, R. E., and McKersie, R. B. *A Behavioral Theory of Labor Negotiations: An Analysis of a Social Interaction System*. New York: McGraw-Hill, 1965.

Wamsley, G., and Zald, M. *The Political Economy of Public Organizations*. Lexington, Mass.: D. C. Heath, 1973.

Wanous, J. P. "Job Preview Makes Recruiting More Effective," *Harvard Business Review*, 1975, 53(5), 16, 166–168.

———. "Organizational Entry: Newcomers Moving from Outside to Inside," *Psychological Bulletin*, 1977a, 84, 601–618.

———. "Who Wants Job Enrichment?" In *Perspectives on Behavior in Organizations*, edited by J. R. Hackman, E. E. Lawler, and L. W. Porter. New York: McGraw-Hill, 1977b.

Weisbord, M. R. *Organizational Diagnosis: A Workbook of Theory and Practice*. Reading, Mass.: Addison-Welsey, 1978.

Whyte, W. F., ed. *Money and Motivation: An Analysis of Incentives in Industry*. New York: Harper, 1955.

Z

Zander, A. *Motives and Goals in Groups*. New York: Academic Press, 1971.

Author Index

A

Aguillar, F. J., 245
Aharoni, J., 248
Aldrich, H. E., 253, 254
Allison, G. T., 223, 247
Andrews, K. R., 242, 243, 244
Ansoff, H. I., 242
Argyris, C., 147

B

Bass, B. M., 47
Beckhard, R., 235, 236
Bell, C. H., 265
Bem, D. J., 118
Blake, R. R., 147, 233
Bower, J. L., 244, 248
Burns, T., 186, 192

C

Cammann, C., 207, 265n
Campbell, J. P., 47, 52, 53, 59, 61, 152
Chandler, A. D., 244
Chapple, E. D., 217
Child, J., 244
Collins, B. E., 108
Craig, J. R., 159

D

Davis, K., 120
Davis, L. E., 86
Davis, S. M., 211
Delbecq, A. L., 151, 190, 193
Deutsch, M., 231, 233, 235, 236
Dickson, W. J., 59
Duncan, R., 190, 193
Dunnette, M. D., 47, 52, 53, 59, 61, 152

E

Emerson, R. M., 163, 164
Evan, W., 243

F

Farris, G. F., 159
Feldman, D. C., 49
Festinger, L., 59, 118
Fiedler, F. E., 166
Filley, A. C., 222, 230, 233, 236
French, J. R. P., Jr., 60, 160
French, W. L., 265

G

Galbraith, J. R., 186, 190, 195, 203, 208, 246, 253
Ghiselli, E. E., 47
Gomersall, E. R., 46, 47, 50
Graen, G., 159
Guetzkow, H., 108
Guion, R. M., 47
Gustafson, D. H., 151

H

Hackman, J. R., 81, 84, 87, 90, 108, 115, 137n, 148, 182
Hall, D. T., 48, 49, 66
Hall, R. H., 182
Herzberg, F., 81
Hickson, D. J., 227, 254
Higgin, G. W., 86
Hinings, C. R., 227, 254
Hofer, C. W., 242, 244, 250
Hollander, E. P., 128
Hornstein, H. A., 13
House, R. J., 166

J

Jaastad, K., 152
Jackson, J., 122, 126
Janis, I. L., 109
Janson, R., 84

K

Kahn, R. L., 15, 221, 227, 241

Kane, J. S., 61
Katz, D., 15, 221, 227, 241
Katz, R. L., 243, 250
Kay, E., 60
Kelman, H. C., 128
Kochan, T., 222, 228n, 229
Koenig, R., 190, 193

L

Lawler, E. E., 35, 37, 52, 53, 59, 61, 66, 81, 89,
    90, 145, 152, 182, 207, 208, 235, 265
Lawrence, P. R., 190, 192, 210, 211, 228, 236,
    272
Lee, C. A., 227, 254
Levinson, A., 48, 265n, 267
Lieberman, S., 117
Likert, J. G., 236
Likert, R., 236
Lim, F. G., Jr., 159
Lindblom, C. E., 248
Logan, J. P., 242
Lorsch, J. W., 190, 192, 210, 228, 236
Lowin, B., 159

M

McGregor, D., 62
McKersie, R. B., 236
MacMillan, I. C., 247, 254
Maier, N. R. F., 149
March, J. G., 221, 228
Maslow, A. H., 30
Meyer, H. H., 60
Miner, J., 261
Mintzberg, H., 249, 250, 262, 276
Mitchell, T. R., 166
Morris, C. G., 148
Mouton, J. S., 147, 233
Munden, H. J., 48
Murray, H., 86
Myers, M. S., 46, 47, 50

N

Nadler, D. A., 186, 190, 191n, 194n, 195n, 265,
    266, 273
Nathanson, D. A., 246, 253
Newman, W. H., 205, 242, 261
Nisberg, J. N., 13

O

Oldham, G. R., 81, 84, 137n

P

Patchen, M., 67
Pennings, J. M., 227, 254
Perrow, C. B., 190
Pettigrew, T. F., 59
Pfeffer, J., 226, 227, 253, 254
Pollack, A. B., 86
Pondy, L. R., 231
Porter, L. W., 35, 66, 90, 182
Price, C. R., 48
Purdy, K., 84

R

Raven, B., 160
Rhode, J. G., 207, 208
Rice, A. K., 86
Roethlisberger, F. J., 59
Roy, D. F., 80

S

Salancik, G. R., 226
Sayles, L. R., 217
Schein, E. H., 48, 49, 236
Schendel, D., 242
Schmidt, S., 222, 228n, 229
Schneck, R. E., 227, 254
Schneider, B. S., 43
Scott, W. E., 80
Seashore, S., 108
Shephard, H. A., 233
Simon, H. A., 33, 221, 228
Solem, A. R., 149
Solley, C. M., 48
Stalker, G. M., 186, 192
Starbuck, W. H., 243
Steers, R. M., 35, 66
Stein, M. I., 151
Steiner, I. D., 142

T

Taylor, F. W., 78
Thomas, K., 230, 231, 234
Thompson, J. D., 182, 190, 203, 208, 226, 227,
    229, 243
Tichy, N. M., 13, 224
Trist, E. L., 86
Tuden, A., 226
Tushman, M. L., 186, 190, 191n, 194n, 195n,
    223, 226

V

Van de Ven, A., 151, 190, 193
Vroom, V. H., 169, 170, 171

W

Walton, R. E., 104, 235, 236
Wamsley, G., 223
Wanous, J. P., 45, 46
Warren, E. K., 205, 261
Weick, K. E., 47, 52, 53, 59, 61, 152

Weisbord, M. R., 267
Whyte, W. F., 73

Y

Yetton, P. W., 169, 170, 171

Z

Zald, M., 223
Zander, A., 146

Subject Index

A

Ability, 8, 16
Absenteeism, 67–68
Accurate information exchange, 43–46, 60
Achievement motivation, 62–63
Adaptive planning, 248–249
Affective reactions, 34–35, 37, 67. *See also* Job satisfaction
Aggregation, of jobs, 185
Appraisal. *See* Performance appraisal
Aptitude tests, 29
Assembly effects, 108–109
Attitudes, 16, 117
Attitude change, 117–118
Attraction-selection process, 42, 44–45
Autonomous work groups, 86–88, 235
Autonomy, 81–82, 86–87

B

Behavior
  as motivated by needs, 29–31
  determination of, 27–37
  influences on, 36–38
Behavioral changes, 270–272
Beliefs, 117
Brainstorming, 151–152

C

Career development, 53–54
Change-agent role, 269–274
Change process, 272–274
Classical management theory, 261
Cliques, 224, 247
Coacting groups, 107, 167–171, 173–174
Coalitions, 224–225, 247
Communication, 18, 186–187
Comprehensive diagnosis, 266–267
Conceptual tools, 9–10, 21, 268–269
Conflict
  antecedent conditions of, 227
  and control systems, 203, 210
  definition of, 222
  levels of, 222–223

outcomes of, 231–233
  in performance appraisals, 59
  resolution of, 233–238
Conformity, 108, 129
Confrontation, 236
Consultation
  and group performance, 146–147
  and leadership, 165
Contingency approach
  to conflict resolution, 237–238
  to job design, 88–92
  to leadership, 171–174
  to organization behavior, 12–13
  to organization structure, 187–198
Control, definition of, 202
Control mechanisms, 193, 203–212
Control systems, 207–208
Coordination, definition of, 202
Coordination mechanism, 17, 193, 203–212
Critical tasks, 217
Cross-unit groups, 208–209

D

Decision making
  involving subordinates in, 168–171
  process of, 7–8
  and work design, 91
Delphi method, 151
Design of work, 78–88
Design process, 217–218
Deviance, 128–129, 130–131
Diagnosis, 70, 91–92
Diagnosis-action perspective, 263
Discretionary stimuli, 114–118

E

Elements of organizational behavior, 15–17
Empirical management theory, 261–262
Environment
  characteristics of, 18
  importance of, 18
  and organizational behavior, 27–28
  organizational relations with, 242–243

Environment [*cont.*]
  perceptions of, 33–34
  and systems theory, 15
  of the work group, 131–133
Environmental management, 212
E→P expectancy, 31
Equity, 168
Evaluation. *See* Performance appraisal
Expectancies
  effort to performance, 31
  performance to outcome, 32
Expectancy theory
  and absenteeism, 68
  and control systems, 205
  definition of, 31–33
  and discretionary stimuli, 115
  and individual expectancies, 31–38
  and job design, 77–78, 88–89
  and leadership, 161–163
  and organization structure, 182–184
  as related to reward systems, 66
  as related to staffing, 43
Experiential models, 10–12
Extrinsic motivators, 215
Extrinsic rewards, 30, 66–74

F

Feedback
  and job design, 81–82, 86
  and leadership, 165
  about performance, 63
  and performance appraisal, 59
Formal authority relations, 10
Frameworks, 8, 14–20. *See also* Models and
  frameworks

G

Global ratings, 64
Goal incompatibility, 229
Goals, 62–63, 165, 244
Goal-setting, 205–206, 215
Group building activities, 109
Group cohesiveness. *See* Social intensity
Group design, 153
Group effectiveness, 147–152
Group environment, 145–147, 153–154
Group identity, 231
Group-individual relationships, 129–133
Group influences, 118–119
Group internal processes, 154
Group norms, 143–144
Groups
  balancing goals of, 105–106

  designing work for, 86–88
  as an element of organizational behavior,
    16–17
  functions of, 101–105
  homogeneity of, 129
  social intensity of, 106–109
  types of, 99–100
Groupthink phenomenon, 109

H

Halo effect, 61
Hierarchy of authority, 204
Hierarchy of needs. *See* Needs, hierarchy of
Human resources development, 59
Human response capacity, 28–29, 37

I

Idiosyncracy credits, 128
Individual differences
  role in job design, 83–84
  and work design choices, 88–89
Individual-organization adaptation, 48–49
Individuals
  as an element of organizational behavior, 16
  nature of, 10
  as rational decision makers, 33
Individual work effectiveness, 17
Influence, as a network linkage, 224
Informal organization, 17
Informal relationships, 10
Information, as a network linkage, 224
Information processing
  reducing needs for, 212–214
  theory of, 186–187
  types of mechanism, 203–210
Information systems. *See* Control systems
Informed intuition, 276–277
Inputs, definition of, 15
Intact work teams. *See* Work teams
Integrator role, 210, 236
Intended strategy, 249
Interference, 222, 229
Interpersonal conflict, 130
Interpersonal process, 147–152
Interunit relationships, 186
Interventions
  into conflict situations, 235–237
  for team effectiveness, 144
Interviews, 47
Intraunit relationships, 185–186, 192–193
Intrinsic motivators, 215
Intrinsic rewards, 30

J

Job design
  choice process for, 92–93
  principles of, 84–86
Job design characteristics, 81–82
Job enrichment, 81–84
Job satisfaction, 34–35, 67, 79–88

L

Lateral relations, 208–210
Leadership
  of coacting groups, 167–171
  contingent nature of, 171, 172–174
  and control systems, 210
  historical review of research on, 157–160
  of individuals, 164–167
  and organizational systems, 166–167
  as a social influence process, 160–164
  of work teams, 171–172
Leadership failure, 166–167
Leader-subordinate relationship, 160–164
Leverage points, 185–186
Level of capability, 38
Level of effort, 38, 137, 148
Liaison roles, 208, 236

M

Management by objectives, 64–65
Manager
  as change agent, 263
  as diagnostician, 263
  limitations on, 274–278
Manager-group relations, 132–133
Managerial role, 277–278
Managerial tools. *See also* Models and
    frameworks
  attraction-selection, 42–48
  career development, 53–54
  conflict resolution, 233–238
  coordination and control, 202–218
  design mechanisms, 214–215
  design of work, 88–93
  extrinsic rewards, 66–74
  organizational change, 269–274
  organizational design, 181–197
  organizational diagnosis, 264–269
  performance appraisal, 58–66
  socialization, 48–51
  training, 52–53
Manager's job, perspectives on, 260–263
Matrix organizations, 210–212

M (continued)

Mechanistic organization, 186
Models, 8–14
Models and frameworks
  of behavior in organizations, 27–28, 38
  of a control system, 207
  of decision making, 169–171
  of groups in organizations, 109–110
  of information processing, 180–195
  of job characteristics, 81–84
  of leadership, 160–164
  of motivation-ability-performance, 13
  of norms, 120–124
  of the organization, 14–20
  for organizational design, 186–195
  of strategy formulation, 244–245
  of work group effectiveness, 152–154
Motivation
  to comply with leader, 161–163
  and conflict, 231
  and job design, 77–93
  and needs, 29–31
  and organizational behavior, 31–38
  and organization structure, 182–184
  and performance, 8–9
  and reduction of resistance, 272

N

Needs
  definition of, 29–31
  hierarchy of, 30
  higher-order type of, 30–31, 37
  list of, 30
  lower-order type of, 30–31, 37
  two-step hierarchy of, 31, 37
Network linkages, 224
Networks, 17, 224–227, 238, 247
Nominal group technique, 151
Norms
  and cliques, 224
  crystallization of, 122–124
  definition of, 120
  development of, 124–126
  group member compliance with, 126–129
  intensity of, 122
  properties of, 120–124

O

Objectives, 251
Open systems, 15, 241
Organismic organization, 186

Organizational arrangements, 17–19
Organizational behavior
    elements of, 15–17
Organizational diagnosis, 264–269
Organizational effectiveness, 4–8, 194, 254
Organizational structure
    and individual behavior, 182–184
    and information processing capacity,
        191–193
    and work design choice, 89–90
Organization chart, 17, 224
Organization design
    definition of, 17, 182
    and information processing, 186–195
    as a managerial function, 198–199
    as a managerial tool, 181
    the process of, 196–198
    and strategy, 253
Organizations
    definition of, 17
    as social systems, 14–15
Outcomes, 38, 227
Outputs, definition of, 15

P

Path-goal theory, 166
Pay, 70–73
Pay plans, 70–72
Perceptions, 33–35, 37–38, 168
Performance appraisal, 58–66
Performance motivation, 73
Performance-reward process, 34–35, 38
Performance strategies, 143–144, 151–152
Personalization process, 49
P→O expectancy, 32
Point of maximum return, 122
Political perspective on organizations, 223
Political planning, 247–248
Power
    bases of, 160–161
    and conflict management, 235
    and dependence on others, 163–164
    distribution of, 10
    and political behavior, 226–227
    and reduction of resistance, 274
    and strategy, 254
    types of, 160–161
Pragmatic models, 13–14
Pressures to conform, 232
Problem-solving techniques, 151
Psychological contract, 48–49

R

Range of tolerable behavior, 122
Rational perspective on organizations, 223
Rational planning, 247
Realized strategy, 249
Recruiting, 46
Reference groups, 107–108
Resistance, to organizational change, 272–274
Resource allocation, 243–244, 251–252
Retroactive strategy, 250
Return potential curves, 122
Rewards
    as design mechanisms for control, 215
    and group performance, 87–88, 145
Reward systems
    and conflict resolution, 235
    and effective control, 205
    as a managerial tool, 58
    and performance motivation, 68–74
    and work group productivity, 132
Roles
    change agent, 269–274
    integrator, 210, 236
    leadership, 172–174
    liaison, 208, 236
    managerial, 262, 277–278
    supervisory, 50

S

Satisfaction. See Job satisfaction
Scientific management, 78–80
Scientific models, 12
Selection instruments, 47–48
Self-contained units, 213–214
Self-esteem, 116
Self-realization, 30
Sensitivity training, 147–148
Scope, 250–251
Skill tests, 29
Skill variety, 81–82
Slack resources, 212
Social influence, 17
Social intensity, 106–109, 128–129
Socialization process, 48–51
Staffing, 40–55
Strategy
    components of, 250–252
    definition of, 242–246
    formulation of, 246–250
    impact of on organizations, 252–254
    and systems theory, 15
    typology of, 249–250

Strategic choice. *See* Resource allocation
Structural changes, 270–272
Symptom-based diagnosis, 265–266
System perspective, 15

T
Targets, 205–206
Task design, 140–142
Task-effective group processes, 145–154
Task identity, 81–82
Task performance strategies, 137
Task-relevant skills, 143, 149–150
Tasks
    degree of uncertainty of, 187–190
    as an element of organizational behavior,
        15–16
    information processing requirements of,
        189–190
    interdependence of, 190
    motivating potential of, 140–141, 206
    predictability of, 190
    and strategy, 253
    and work group productivity, 131–132
Task significance, 81–82
Team building, 147–148
Technology, 89, 139, 152
Traditional groups, 106–107
Training, 146–147
Training programs, 52–53
Trait ratings, 63–64
Transformation process, 15
Turnover, 48, 66

U
Uncertainty, 187–190, 226
Unit composition, 191–192
Unrealized strategy, 249

V
Valid information exchange. *See* Accurate
    information exchange
Validity
    of appraisal measures, 61
    of selection instruments, 47
Values, 278
Vertical information systems, 206–208
Vertical loading, 84
Vroom-Yetton model, 169–171

W
Western Electric studies, 59
Work design, 88–90, 215
Work flow, 217
Work group effectiveness, 17
Work teams
    design of, 139–145
    leadership of, 171–172
Work team effectiveness
    definition of, 136–137
    and group composition, 142
    and heterogeneity, 142–143
    intermediate criteria of, 137–139
    and interpersonal skills, 143
    and team size, 142